Where do I go

What's the best ar

frommers.travelocity.com

Frommer's, the travel guide leader, has teamed up with **Travelocity.com**, the leader in online travel, to bring you an in-depth, easy-to-use resource designed to help you plan and book your trip online.

At **frommers.travelocity.com**, you'll find free online updates about your destination from the experts at Frommer's plus the outstanding travel planning and purchasing features of Travelocity.com. Travelocity.com provides reservations capabilities for 95 percent of all airline seats sold, more than 47,000 hotels, and over 50 car rental companies. In addition, Travelocity.com offers more than 2,000 exciting vacation and cruise packages. Travelocity.com puts you in complete control of your travel planning with these and other great features:

> **Expert travel guidance from Frommer's** - over 150 writers reporting from around the world!
>
> **Best Fare Finder** - an interactive calendar tells you when to travel to get the best airfare
>
> **Fare Watcher** - we'll track airfare changes to your favorite destinations
>
> **Dream Maps** - a mapping feature that suggests travel opportunities based on your budget
>
> **Shop Safe Guarantee** - 24 hours a day / 7 days a week live customer service, and more!

Whether traveling on a tight budget, looking for a quick weekend getaway, or planning the trip of a lifetime, Frommer's guides and Travelocity.com will make your travel dreams a reality. You've bought the book, now book the trip!

Here's what the critics say about Frommer's:

"Amazingly easy to use. Very portable, very complete."

—Booklist

"The only mainstream guide to list specific prices. The Walter Cronkite of guidebooks—with all that implies."

—Travel & Leisure

"Complete, concise, and filled with useful information."

—New York Daily News

"Hotel information is close to encyclopedic."
—Des Moines Sunday Register

♦

"Detailed, accurate, and easy-to-read information for all price ranges."

—Glamour Magazine

P O R T A B L E

Dublin

3rd Edition

by Robert Emmet Meagher

HUNGRY MINDS, INC.

New York, NY • Cleveland, OH • Indianapolis, IN
Chicago, IL • Foster City, CA • San Francisco, CA

About the Author

Robert Emmet Meagher, a dual citizen of Ireland and the United States, is Professor of Humanities at Hampshire College in Amherst, Massachusetts. The author of more than a dozen books, plays, and translations, he has lived and worked in Ireland, twice holding visiting professorships at Trinity College Dublin.

Published by:

Hungry Minds, Inc.

909 Third Avenue
New York, NY
www.frommers.com

ISBN 0-7645-6344-0
ISSN 1092-1265

Editor: Lisa Renaud/Dog-Eared Pages
Production Editor: Jennifer Connolly
Photo Editor: Richard Fox
Design by Michele Laseau
Cartographer: Roberta Stockwell
Production by Hungry Minds Indianapolis Production Department

Special Sales

For general information on Hungry Minds' products and services please contact our Customer Care department; within the U.S. at 800-762-2974, outside the U.S. at 317-572-3993 or fax 317-572-4002. For sales inquiries and reseller information, including discounts, bulk sales, customized editions, and premium sales, please contact our Customer Care department at 800-434-3422.

Manufactured in the United States of America

5   4   3   2   1

Contents

List of Maps

An Invitation to the Reader

In researching this book, we discovered many wonderful places—hotels, restaurants, shops, and more. We're sure you'll find others. Please tell us about them, so we can share the information with your fellow travelers in upcoming editions. If you were disappointed with a recommendation, we'd love to know that, too. Please write to:

Frommer's Portable Dublin, 3rd Edition
Hungry Minds, Inc.
909 Third Avenue
New York, NY 10022

An Additional Note

Please be advised that travel information is subject to change at any time—and this is especially true of prices. We therefore suggest that you write or call ahead for confirmation when making your travel plans. The authors, editors, and publisher cannot be held responsible for the experiences of readers while traveling. Your safety is important to us, however, so we encourage you to stay alert and be aware of your surroundings. Keep a close eye on cameras, purses, and wallets, all favorite targets of thieves and pickpockets.

What the Symbols Mean

✪ Frommer's Favorites

Our favorite places and experiences—outstanding for quality, value, or both.

The following abbreviations are used for credit cards:

AE	American Express	ER	EnRoute
CB	Carte Blanche	JCB	Japan Credit Bank
DC	Diners Club	MC	MasterCard
DISC	Discover	V	Visa
EC	Eurocard		

Find Frommer's Online

www.frommers.com offers up-to-the-minute listings on almost 200 cities around the globe—including the latest bargains and candid, personal articles updated daily by Arthur Frommer himself. No other Web site offers such comprehensive and timely coverage of the world of travel.

Planning a Trip to Dublin

*I*t may be well to begin with a caution, offered in this case by John Steinbeck in *Travels with Charley:* "A journey is like a marriage. The certain way to be wrong is to think you control it." Fair enough. A trip too tightly packed and planned, with no room for the spontaneous and unexpected, is often not worth the effort. And yet, when you are so poorly prepared that surprise runs riot, you might wish you'd stayed home. In travel, as in Buddhism, the middle ground is recommended. Lay down your plans like pavement, and then romp on the grass at will. Our aim in this chapter is to help you prepare the way.

1 Visitor Information

TOURIST BOARD OFFICES

To get your planning under way, contact the following offices of the Irish Tourist Board and the Northern Ireland Tourist Board. They are eager to answer your questions, and have bags of genuinely helpful information, mostly free of charge.

IN THE UNITED STATES
- **Irish Tourist Board,** 345 Park Ave., New York, NY 10154 (☎ **800/223-6470** from the U.S., or 212/418-0800; fax 212/371-9052).
- **Northern Ireland Tourist Board,** 551 Fifth Ave., Suite 701, New York, NY 10176 (☎ **800/326-0036** from the U.S., or 212/922-0101; fax 212/922-0099).

IN CANADA
- **Irish Tourist Board,** 160 Bloor St. E., Suite 1150, Toronto, ON M4W 1B9 (☎ **416/929-2777;** fax 416/929-6783).
- **Northern Ireland Tourist Board,** 2 Bloor St. W., Suite 1501, Toronto, ON M4W 3E2 (☎ **800/576-8174** or 416/925-6368; fax 416/925-6033).

IN THE UNITED KINGDOM

- **Irish Tourist Board/Bord Fáilte,** 150 New Bond St., London W1Y 0AQ (☎ **020/7493-3201;** fax 020/7493-9065).
- **Northern Ireland Tourist Board,** 11 Berkeley St., London W1X 5AD (☎ **020/7766-9920;** fax 020/7766-9929).

IN AUSTRALIA

- **Irish Tourist Board,** 36 Carrington St., 5th Level, Sydney, NSW 2000 (☎ **02/9299-6177;** fax 02/9299-6323).

IN NEW ZEALAND

- **Irish Tourist Board,** Dingwall Building, 2nd Floor, 87 Queen St., Auckland (☎ **0064-9-379-8720;** fax 0064-9-302-2420).

IN IRELAND

- **Irish Tourist Board/Bord Fáilte,** Baggot Street Bridge, Dublin 2 (☎ **01/602-4000;** fax 01/602-4100; www.ireland.travel.ie).
- **Northern Ireland Tourist Board,** 16 Nassau St., Dublin 2 (☎ **01/679-1977;** fax 01/679-1863).

IN NORTHERN IRELAND

- **Irish Tourist Board,** 53 Castle St., Belfast BT1 1GH (☎ **028/ 9032-7888;** fax 028/9024-0201).
- **Northern Ireland Tourist Board,** St. Anne's Court, 59 North St., Belfast BT1 1NB (☎ **028/9024-6609;** fax 028/9031-2424; www.ni-tourism.com).

SITE SEEING: INFORMATION ON THE WEB

D-Tour: A Visitor's Guide to Ireland for People with Disabilities. http://ireland.iol.ie/infograf/dtour
This site offers various resources for those with disabilities who are traveling in Ireland, including extensive listings of wheelchair-accessible accommodations.

The Event Guide. www.eventguide.ie
The online presence of Dublin's eponymous free weekly, this site chronicles the city's cultural life. You'll find current listings for Dublin's clubs, theaters, cinemas, and concert halls interspersed with interviews, profiles of performers, and some information on events outside Dublin.

Ireland.com. www.ireland.com
Presented by the *Irish Times,* this site includes late-breaking news and perspectives from Dublin's major newspaper.

A section called Dublin Live includes advice on lodging, entertainment, attractions, food and drink, sports, and weather.

✪ **Irish Tourist Board (Bord Fáilte). www.ireland.travel.ie**
The most comprehensive online guide to travel in the Republic of Ireland, the official site of the Irish Tourist Board (Bord Fáilte) provides information for most tourism facilities. You'll find an exhaustive events calendar, the latest tourism news, and access to Gulliver, an online accommodations-booking service.

✪ **Island Ireland. http://islandireland.com/**
This is the best place to begin your search on any topic related to Irish culture, the arts, genealogy, or the outdoors. There aren't many broken links, and each site is screened for the quality of its content.

Ostlan Dublin Restaurant Guide. www.ostlan.com
A searchable database of Dublin restaurant reviews. The site's official reviewers don't offer much in the way of criticism; better are the more candid opinions offered by visitors to the site. There's a concise pub guide, as well as an interesting forum for online discussion.

Temple Bar Properties. www.temple-bar.ie
Here you'll find abundant information on Temple Bar, Dublin's new cultural hub. The heart of the site is a calendar of events, many of them free of charge. Sophisticated graphics and a simple interface make navigating this site a pleasure.

2 Entry Requirements & Customs

ENTRY REQUIREMENTS

For citizens of the United States, Canada, Australia, and New Zealand entering the Republic of Ireland for a stay of up to 3 months, no visa is necessary, but a valid passport is required.

Citizens of the United Kingdom, when traveling on flights originating in Britain, do not need to show documentation to enter Ireland. Nationals of the United Kingdom and colonies who were not born in Great Britain or Northern Ireland must have a valid passport or national identity document.

For entry into Northern Ireland, the same conditions apply.

CUSTOMS
WHAT YOU CAN BRING TO IRELAND

Since the European Union's (EU) introduction of a single market on January 1, 1993, goods brought into Ireland and Northern Ireland fall into two categories: (1) goods bought duty-paid and value-added-tax–paid (VAT–paid) in other EU countries and (2) goods bought under duty-free and VAT-free allowances at duty-free shops.

Regarding the first category, if the goods are for personal use, no further duty or VAT needs to be paid. The limits for goods in this category are 800 cigarettes, 10 liters of spirits, 45 liters of wine, and 55 liters of beer. This category normally applies to Irish citizens, visitors from Britain, and travelers from other EU countries.

The second category pertains primarily to overseas visitors, such as U.S. and Canadian citizens. The following duty-free and VAT-free items may be brought into the country for personal use: 200 cigarettes, 1 liter of liquor, 2 liters of wine, and other goods (including beer) not exceeding the value of £34 ($56.10) per adult. There are no restrictions on bringing currency into Ireland.

The Irish and Northern Irish Customs systems operate on a Green, Red, and Blue Channel format. The first two are for passengers coming from the United States and non-EU countries. The Green Channel is for anyone not exceeding the duty-free allowances, and the Red Channel is for anyone with extra goods to declare. If you are like most visitors, bringing in only your own clothes and personal effects, choose the Green Channel. The Blue Channel is exclusively for use by passengers entering Ireland from another EU country.

In addition to your luggage, you may bring in sports equipment for your own recreational use or electronic equipment for your own business or professional use while in Ireland. Prohibited goods include firearms, ammunition, and explosives; narcotics; meat, poultry, plants, and their byproducts; and domestic animals from outside the United Kingdom.

WHAT YOU CAN BRING HOME

Returning **U.S. citizens** who have been away for 48 hours or more are allowed to bring back, once every 30 days, $400 worth of merchandise duty-free. You'll be charged a flat rate of 10% duty on the next $1,000 worth of purchases. Be sure to have your receipts handy. On gifts, the duty-free limit is $100. You cannot bring fresh foodstuffs into the United States; tinned foods are allowed. For more information, contact the **U.S. Customs Service,** 1301 Constitution Ave. (P.O. Box 7407), Washington, DC 20044 (☎ **202/927-6724**), and request the free pamphlet *Know Before You Go*. It's also available on the Web at **www.customs.ustreas.gov/travel/ kbygo.htm**.

Citizens of the U.K. who are returning from a European Community (EC) country will go through a separate Customs Exit (the Blue Channel) for EC travelers. In essence, there is no limit on what you can bring back from an EC country, as long as the items are for personal use (this includes gifts) and you have already paid the necessary duty and tax. However, Customs law sets out guidance levels. If you bring in more than these levels, you may be asked to prove that the goods are for your own use. Guidance levels on goods bought in the EC for your own use are 800 cigarettes, 200 cigars, 1kg smoking tobacco, 10 liters of spirits, 90 liters of wine (of which not more than 60 liters can be sparkling wine), and 110 liters of beer. For more information, contact **HM Customs & Excise,** Passenger Enquiry Point, 2nd Floor Wayfarer House, Great South West Road, Feltham, Middlesex TW14 8NP (☎ **020/ 8910-3744,** from outside the U.K. 44/181-910-3744; www.hmce.gov.uk).

Canadians should check the booklet *I Declare,* which you can download or order from Revenue Canada (☎ **613/993-0534;**). **Australians** can contact the Australian Customs Service (☎ **1-300/363-263** within Australia, 61-2/6275-6666 from outside Australia; www.customs.gov.au/). **New Zealand** citizens should contact New Zealand Customs (☎ **09/ 359-6655;** www.customs.govt.nz/).

3 Money

CASH/CURRENCY

The Republic of Ireland, unlike the United Kingdom, lies within the new "Eurozone." As of January 1999, Ireland has adopted the single European currency known as the **"euro."** Although the euro will not appear as hard currency until 2002, it is already the medium of exchange in the Republic.

The **punt**, or Irish pound, no longer trades as an independent currency. Its value is permanently fixed at 1.27 euros. Consequently, the fluctuating value of the euro is of concern to you as a visitor, because the punt remains a fixed multiple of that value. In shops and elsewhere, prices already appear in both punts and euros; before we know it, punts will disappear from both signs and pockets. But that day is not yet upon us, so in this guide, prices in the Republic are still given in punts. In converting prices in punts to U.S. dollars, we used the rate IR£1 = $1.40.

Each unit of paper currency is called a "note." The pound notes, which are printed in denominations of £5, £10, £20, £50, and £100, come in different sizes and colors (the larger the size, the greater the value). There are still some £1 notes in circulation, although these are being phased out in favor of the £1 coin. (The old £1 note is a work of art, so try to find one before they disappear altogether.) Since 1971, the Irish monetary system has been on the decimal system. The pound is divided into 100 pence ("p"); coins come in denominations of £1, 50p, 20p, 10p, 5p, and 1p.

Note: The value of the Irish pound fluctuates daily, so it's best to begin checking exchange rates well in advance of your visit to gain a sense of their recent range. Deciding when and where to convert and how much is always a gamble. Shop around and avoid exchanging in airports and train stations. Banks are best, and on any given day one bank will offer a better rate than another. Any purchase on a U.S. credit card offers an exchange rate far more favorable than anything an individual is likely to negotiate, so I make a point of converting as little currency as possible and using my credit card to the max. Whatever you do, don't convert small amounts daily. The fees alone will impoverish you. Rates of exchange are available daily in most newspapers, and on the Net (try **www.xe.net/currency/** or **www.x-rates.com**).

CREDIT CARDS

Leading international credit cards such as American Express, Carte Blanche, Diners Club, MasterCard (also known as Access or Eurocard), and Visa (also known as Visa/Barclay) are readily accepted. MasterCard and Visa are the most widely accepted, with American Express an often-distant third. Note that many banks (including Citibank) are beginning to add a service charge to every transaction made in a foreign currency; check with your card's issuer before you leave to avoid a nasty surprise when you get your bill.

ATMS

Any town large enough to have a bank branch (all but the smallest villages) will have an ATM, most likely linked to a network that includes your home bank. **Cirrus** (☎ **800/ 424-7787**; www.mastercard.com/atm) and **Plus** (☎ **800/ 843-7587**; www.visa.com/atms) are the two most popular networks. Use the toll-free numbers to locate ATMs in your destination.

Check with your bank to make sure the PINs on your bankcards and credit cards will work in Ireland.

TRAVELER'S CHECKS

Traveler's checks are something of an anachronism from the days before the ATM (automated teller machine) made cash accessible at any time, but some travelers still prefer the security they provide. You can get them at almost any bank, for a small service charge. American Express traveler's checks are also available over the phone by calling ☎ **800/221-7282** or 800/721-9768, or you can purchase checks online at **www.americanexpress.com**. AmEx gold or platinum cardholders can avoid paying the fee by ordering over the telephone; platinum cardholders can also purchase checks fee-free in person at AmEx Travel Service locations. American Automobile Association members can obtain checks with no fee at most AAA offices.

4 When to Go

CLIMATE

You have to be part psychic to even begin making bets on Irish weather, but don't bet too heavily. The only thing consistent about Irish weather is its changeability; often, the best of times and the worst of times may be only hours, or minutes, apart.

In Ireland, the thermometers, gratefully, are a lot less busy than the barometers. Temperatures are mild and fluctuate within what any New Englander would call "spring." The generally coldest months, January and February, bring frosts but seldom snow, and the warmest months, July and August, rarely become hot. Remember, in Ireland any temperature over 70°F is "hot," and 32°F is truly "freezing." Both are unusual. For a complete guide to Irish weather on the Net, including year-round averages and daily updates, consult **www.ireland.com/weather**.

When you're packing, *layers* is the word to remember, at any time of year. And don't forget wool—the Irish attraction to it is no accident. *One other tip:* The Irish are becoming more and more casual in their dress, so you can think Oregon rather than Manhattan.

Average Monthly Temperatures in Dublin

	Jan	Feb	Mar	Apr	May	June	July	Aug	Sept	Oct	Nov	Dec
Temp (°F)	36-46	37-48	37-49	38-52	42-57	46-62	51-66	50-65	48-62	44-56	39-49	38-47
Temp (°C)	2–8	3–9	3–9	3–11	6–14	8–17	11–19	10–18	9–17	7–13	4–9	3–8

HIGH & LOW SEASONS

Apart from the mercurial sphere of climatic considerations, there's the matter of cost and crowds. These, too, go up and down in the course of the year.

The precise difference between high and low season, however, varies greatly from one locale to another. These days, Dublin really doesn't have a low season. It's always crowded, and prices there never truly plummet.

A few generalizations, however, might be helpful. Transatlantic airfares often drop significantly in the winter months, which makes a trip to Ireland that much more affordable. And in Dublin, the weather is not likely a defining factor, as so much of Dublin's lure dwells indoors. Elsewhere in Ireland, the more off-season you are, the more negotiable will be your lodging.

It's often the hedge months—April, May, and October—when you can get simultaneously lucky with weather, crowds, and prices.

HOLIDAYS

The Republic observes the following national holidays: New Year's Day (Jan 1), St. Patrick's Day (Mar 17), Easter Monday (lunar/variable), May Day (May 1), first Monday in June and August (Summer Bank Holidays), last Monday in October (Autumn Bank Holiday), Christmas (Dec 25), and

St. Stephen's Day (Dec 26). Good Friday (the Fri before Easter) is mostly observed, but not statutory.

DUBLIN CALENDAR OF EVENTS

Be sure to consult the latest calendar available from the tourist board of Ireland; it's usually released in January of each year. The most up-to-date listings of events can be found at **www.eventguide.ie** and **www.visitdublin.com**.

January
- **Funderland.** Simmonscourt RDS, Dublin 4. An annual indoor Christmas fair. Contact Don Bird (☎ **01/283-8188;** e-mail: bird@iol.ie). The last few days of December to mid-January.
- **Dublin International Theatre Symposium.** An annual event at the Samuel Beckett Centre, Trinity College, Dublin 2. Contact Mary O'Donovan (☎ **01/280-0544;** fax 01/239-0918; e-mail: panpan@iol.ie). Early January.
- **A.I.G. Europe Championship Hurdle Race.** Leopardstown Racetrack. County Dublin. Call (☎ **01/835-1965**). Late January.

February
- **Hennessey Cognac Gold Cup.** Leopardstown Racetrack. County Dublin. Call (☎ **01/835-1965**). Early February.

March
✪ **The National St. Patrick's Day Festival.** Street theater, sports, music, and other festivities culminating in Ireland's grandest parade, with marching bands, drill teams, floats, and delegations from around the world. Contact Festival Office, St. Stephen's Green House, Earlsfort Terrace, Dublin 2 (☎ **01/ 676-3205;** fax 01/676-3208; e-mail: info@paddyfest.ie; www.stpatricksday.ie). March 16 to 19.

April
- **Dublin Film Festival.** The best in Irish and international cinema. More than 100 films are featured, with screenings of the best in Irish and world cinema, plus seminars and lectures on filmmaking. Cinemas throughout Dublin. Contact Aine O'Halloran (☎ **01/679-2937;** fax 01/679-2929; www.iol.ie/dff/). Early to mid-April.

May
- **County Wicklow Gardens Festival.** Heritage properties and gardens, as well as many private grounds, open their gates to

visitors on selected dates throughout County Wicklow, which lies just outside Dublin. Contact Wicklow County Tourism (☎ **0404/20100;** fax 0404/67792). Early May through July.

June

- **AIB Music Festival in Great Irish Houses.** This is a 10-day festival of classical music performed by leading Irish and international artists in some of the Dublin area's great Georgian buildings and mansions. Various venues throughout Dublin and neighboring counties Wicklow and Kildare. Contact Crawford Tipping, Blackrock Post Office, County Dublin (☎ **01/278-1528;** fax 01/278-1529). Early to mid-June.

✪ **Bloomsday.** Dublin's unique day of festivity commemorates 24 hours in the life of Leopold Bloom, the central character of James Joyce's *Ulysses.* Every aspect of the city, including the menus at restaurants and pubs, seeks to duplicate the aromas, sights, sounds, and tastes of Dublin on June 16, 1904. Special ceremonies are held at the James Joyce Tower and Museum, and there are guided walks of Joycean sights. The streets of Dublin and various venues. Contact the James Joyce Centre, 35 N. Great George's St., Dublin 1 (☎ **01/878-8547;** fax 01/878-8488; www.jamesjoyce.ie). June 16.

August

- **Summer Music Festival.** St. Stephen's Green is the setting for this series of free lunchtime band concerts of popular and Irish traditional music, as well as afternoon open-air performances of Shakespearean plays, sponsored by the Office of Public Works. Last 2 weeks of August.

September

✪ **All-Ireland Hurling and Football Final.** Tickets must be obtained months in advance for these two national amateur sporting events, the equivalent of the Super Bowl for Irish national sports. Croke Park, Dublin 3. Contact the Gaelic Athletic Association (☎ **01/836-3222;** fax 01/836-6420). Two weekends in September.

- **Searching for the Elusive Irish Ancestor Family History Conference.** An annual conference focused on family history and on practical research in the country's main genealogical archives. Includes lectures, tours, and entertainment. Contact Shane McAteer (☎ **048/332288;** www.uhf.org.uk). Late September.

- **Irish Antique Dealers' Fair.** Annual show sponsored jointly by the RDS and the Irish Antique Dealers' Association. This is Ireland's premier annual antiques fair. RDS Showgrounds, Ballsbridge, County Dublin. Contact Louis O'Sullivan (☎ **01/ 285-9294**). A week in late September.

October

- ✪ **Dublin Theatre Festival.** A world-class theater festival showcasing new plays by Irish authors and presenting a range of productions from abroad. Theaters throughout Dublin. Call (☎ **01/677-8439;** fax 01/679-7709; www.iftn.ie/dublinfestival). Early to mid-October.

- ✪ **Dublin City Marathon.** More than 3,000 runners from both sides of the Atlantic and the Irish Sea participate in this popular run through the streets of Dublin. For entry forms and information, contact Carol McCabe (☎ **01/626-3746;** www.dublincitymarathon.ie). End of October.

December

- **Dublin Grand Opera.** An operatic fling, with great works presented by the Dublin Grand Opera Society. Gaiety Theatre, South King Street, Dublin 2 (☎ **01/677-1717**). Early December.

- **Christmas Horse Racing Festival.** Three days of winter racing for thoroughbreds. Leopardstown Racetrack. County Dublin. Call (☎ **01/835-1965**). Late December.

5 Tips for Travelers with Special Needs

FOR TRAVELERS WITH DISABILITIES

A disability shouldn't stop anyone from traveling. There are more resources out there than ever before. **The Moss Rehab Hospital** (☎ **215/456-5995;** www.mossresorcenet.org) has been providing friendly and helpful phone advice and referrals for years through its Travel Information Service. You'll find links to a number of travel agents who specialize in planning trips for travelers with disabilities here and through **Access-Able Travel Source** (**www.access-able.com**), another excellent online source.

For the past 30 years, the **National Rehabilitation Board of Ireland,** 24/25 Clyde Rd., Ballsbridge, Dublin 4 (☎ **01/ 608-0400**), has encouraged facilities to accommodate people with disabilities. Consequently, more and more hotels and public buildings now have ramps or graded entrances and rooms specially fitted for wheelchair access. Unfortunately, many of the older hotels, guesthouses, and landmark buildings still have steep steps both outside and within. For a list of the properties that cater to the needs of patrons with disabilities, contact the National Rehabilitation Board in advance.

The **Irish Wheelchair Association,** 24 Blackheath Dr., Clontarf, Dublin 3 (☎ **01/833-8241**), loans free wheelchairs for travelers in Ireland. A donation is appreciated.

If you plan to travel by rail in Ireland, be sure to check out Iarnrod Eireann's Web site (**www.irishrail.ie**), which includes services for travelers with disabilities.

FOR SENIORS

One of the benefits of age is that travel often costs less. Always bring an ID card, especially if you've kept your youthful glow. Also mention the fact that you're a senior when you first make your travel reservations, since many airlines and hotels offer discount programs for senior travelers.

Members of the **American Association of Retired Persons** (**AARP;** ☎ **800/424-3410;** www.aarp.org) get discounts on hotels, airfares, and car rentals. The AARP offers members a wide range of benefits, including *Modern Maturity* magazine and a monthly newsletter.

Seniors, known in Ireland and Northern Ireland as OAPs (old age pensioners), enjoy a variety of discounts and privileges. Native OAPs ride the public transport system free of charge, but the privilege does not extend to tourists. Visiting seniors can avail themselves of other discounts, however, particularly on admission to attractions and theaters. Always ask about a senior discount if special rates are not posted; the discount is usually 10%.

The Irish Tourist Board publishes a list of reduced-rate hotel packages for seniors, *Golden Holidays/For the Over 55s.* These packages are usually available from March to June and September to November.

FOR GAY & LESBIAN TRAVELERS

Gay Ireland has rapidly come out of the closet since homosexuality became legal in the Republic in July 1993. Although the gay and lesbian community has received increasing support over the past several years, much of Ireland continues to discourage its gay population. In Dublin, however, gay and lesbian visitors can find more formal support and an open, if small, gay community.

Two essential publications for the gay or lesbian visitor to Ireland are the *Gay Community News* and *In Dublin* magazine. *Gay Community News* is a free newspaper of comprehensive Irish gay-related information published on the last Friday of each month and widely available in the city center. You can always find a copy at the **National Lesbian and Gay Federation** (see below), where it is published and where you can get advice on gay-related legal issues. The *Gay Community News* is also distributed by Books Upstairs, 36 College Green, across from Trinity College; Waterstone's on Dawson Street, also near Trinity; the Well Fed Cafe on Crow Street in Temple Bar; the George on South Great George's Street off Dame Street; and other progressive haunts.

The most comprehensive Web site for gay organizations, events, issues, and information throughout Ireland can be found on "Ireland's Pink Pages," **http://indigo.ie/~outhouse**.

In Dublin, which comes out twice a month and is for sale at news agents and bookstores throughout the city, has a page that lists gay events, current club information, AIDS and health information resources, accommodations options, and helpful organizations.

The following organizations and help lines are staffed by knowledgeable and friendly people:

- **National Lesbian and Gay Federation (NLGF)**, 6 S. William St., Dublin 2 (☎ **01/670-6377;** fax 01/679-1603; http://homepage.tinet.ie/~nlgf), available Monday to Friday noon to 6pm.
- **Gay Switchboard Dublin,** Carmichael House, North Brunswick Street, Dublin 7 (☎ **01/872-1055;** fax 01/873-5737; gsd@iol.ie), Sunday to Friday 8 to 10pm and Saturday 3:30 to 6pm.
- **Lesbian Line Dublin** (☎ **01/872-9911**), Thursday 7 to 9pm.
- **LOT (Lesbians Organizing Together)**, the umbrella group of the lesbian community, 5 Capel St., Dublin 1 (☎ and fax **01/872-7770**), accommodates drop-ins Fridays 10am to 4pm. LOT also sponsors LEA/Lesbian Education Awareness (☎ and fax **01/872-0460;** e-mail: leanow@indigo.ie).

- **AIDS Helpline Dublin** (☎ **01/872-4277**), run Monday to Friday 7 to 9pm and Saturday 3 to 5pm, offers assistance with HIV/AIDS prevention, testing, and treatment.

Gay and lesbian travelers seeking information and assistance on travel abroad might want to consult the **International Gay and Lesbian Travel Association** (**IGLTA**), 4331 North Federal Hwy., Suite 304, Fort Lauderdale, FL 33308 (☎ **800/448-8550** or 954/776-2626; fax 954-776-3303; www.iglta.org).

General gay and lesbian travel agencies include **Family Abroad** (☎ **800/999-5500** or 212/459-1800) for gays and lesbians, and **Above and Beyond Tours** (☎ **800/397-2681;** www.abovebeyondtours.com), mainly for gays.

6 Getting There

BY PLANE
FROM THE U.S.

The Irish national carrier, **Aer Lingus** (☎ **800/474-7424;** www.aerlingus.ie) is the traditional leader in providing transatlantic flights to Ireland. Aer Lingus offers scheduled flights from Boston, Chicago, Los Angeles, Newark, and New York JFK to Dublin, Shannon, and Belfast International Airports, with connecting flights to Ireland's regional airports.

Note: Aer Lingus offers educational discounts to full-time students, which can be booked through CIEE/Council Travel (☎ **800/226-8624;** www.counciltravel.com). It also sells an attractively priced Eurosaver Green Pass for those who want to combine an Aer Lingus round-trip transatlantic flight to Ireland with a side trip to Britain or the Continent, or a domestic flight within Ireland, including the North.

Excellent transatlantic service is also provided by **Delta Airlines** (☎ **800/241-4141;** www.delta.com). It offers scheduled daily flights from Atlanta and New York JFK to both Dublin and Shannon, with feed-in connections from Delta's network of gateways throughout the United States.

Also offering daily transatlantic service to Ireland is **Continental Airlines** (☎ **800/231-0856;** www.continental.com), with two flights a day from their Newark hub, one to Shannon and one to Dublin.

Backtracking to Ireland

Many travelers opt to fly to Britain and backtrack into Dublin (see "From London to Dublin," below). Carriers serving Britain from the United States include **American Airlines** (☎ 800/433-7300; www.aa.com), **British Airways** (☎ 800/247-9297; www.british-airways.com), **Continental Airlines** (☎ 800/231-0856; www.continental.com), **Delta Airlines** (☎ 800/241-4141; www.delta.com), **Northwest Airlines** (☎ 800/447-4747; www.nwa.com), **TWA** (☎ 800/892-4141; www.twa.com), **United** (☎ 800/241-6522; www.ual.com), and **Virgin Atlantic Airways** (☎ 800/862-8621; www.fly.virgin.com).

From London to Dublin

The following carriers operate air service from London to Dublin: **Aer Lingus** (☎ 800/474-7424 from the U.S. or 020/8899-4747 in Britain); **British Airways** (☎ 0345/222111) offered by **City Flyer Express** (☎ 800/247-9297 from the U.S. or 0345/222111 in Britain); **British Midland** (☎ 800/788-0555 in the U.S. or 0870/607-0555 in Britain; www.iflybritishmidland.com); **CityJet** (☎ 0345/445588 in Britain); and **Ryanair** (☎ 0541/569569 in Britain; www.ryanair.com). In addition, there are flights from more than 20 other British cities to Ireland's airports.

From the Continent

Major direct flights into Dublin from the continent include service from Amsterdam on **KLM** (☎ 800/374-7747 in the U.S.); Barcelona on **Iberia** (☎ 800/772-4642 in the U.S.); Brussels on **Sabena** (☎ 800/952-2000 in the U.S.); Copenhagen on **Aer Lingus** and **SAS** (☎ 800/221-2350 in the U.S.); Frankfurt on **Aer Lingus** and **Lufthansa** (☎ 800/645-3880 in the U.S.); Paris on **Aer Lingus** and **Air France** (☎ 800/237-2747 in the U.S.); Prague on CSA **Czech Airlines** (☎ 212/765-6588 in the U.S.); and Rome on **Aer Lingus**.

Fly for Less: Tips for Getting the Best Airfares

- **Take advantage of APEX fares.** Advance-purchase booking is often the key to getting the lowest fare. You generally must be willing to make your plans and buy your tickets as far ahead as possible. Be sure you understand cancellation and refund policies before you buy.

- **Consolidators,** also known as bucket shops, are a good place to find low fares, often below even the airlines' discounted rates. There's nothing shady about the reliable ones—basically, they're just big travel agents that get discounts for buying in bulk and pass some of the savings on to you. Some of the most reliable consolidators include **Cheap Tickets** (☎ 800/377-1000; www.cheaptickets.com), **Council Travel** (☎ 800/226-8624; www.counciltravel.com), **STA Travel** (☎ 800/781-4040; www.sta.travel.com), **Lowestfare.com** (☎ 888/278-8830; www.lowestfare.com), **Cheap Seats** (☎ 800/451-7200; www.cheapseatstravel.com), and **1-800-FLY-CHEAP** (www. flycheap.com).

- Search the **Internet** for cheap fares—though it's still best to compare your findings with the research of a dedicated travel agent. Two of the better-respected virtual travel agents are **Travelocity** (**www.travelocity.com**) and **Microsoft Expedia** (**www.expedia.com**).

- Consider a **charter flight.** They're often a good value, though they offer fewer frills, and their tickets are ordinarily nonrefundable. From the United States, **Sceptre Charters** (☎ **800/ 221-0924** or 718/738-9400) operates the largest and most reliable charter program to Ireland. It flies to Shannon from Boston, Philadelphia, Chicago, and Los Angeles. Several companies in Canada operate charter flights from Toronto to Ireland, including **Signature Vacations** (☎ **800/268-7063** in Canada or 800/268-1105 from the U.S.), **Air Transat Holidays** (☎ **800/587-2672** in Canada, or 514/987-1550), and **Regent Holidays** (☎ **800/387-4860** in Canada, or 905/673-3343).

BY FERRY

If you're traveling to Ireland from Britain or the Continent, especially if you're behind the wheel of a car, ferries can get you there. The Irish Sea has a reputation, however, so it's always a good idea to consider an over-the-counter pill or patch to guard against seasickness. (Be sure to take any pills *before* you set out; once you're under way, it's generally too late.)

Several car and passenger ferries offer reasonably comfortable furnishings, cabin berths (for longer crossings), restaurants, duty-free shopping, and lounges.

Prices fluctuate seasonally and depend on your route, your time of travel, and whether you are on foot or in a car. It's best to check with your travel agent for up-to-date details, but just to give you an idea, the lowest one-way adult fare in high season on the cruise ferry from Holyhead to Dublin is £20 (that's British pounds, or $33). Add your car, and the grand total will be £149 (again, in pounds sterling, or $245.85). The Web sites given below have regularly updated schedules and prices.

Irish Ferries (**www.irishferries.ie**) operates from Holyhead, Wales to Dublin, and from Pembroke, Wales to Rosslare, County Wexford. For reservations, call Scots-American Travel (☎ **561/563-2856** in the U.S. or 01/638-3333 in Ireland). **Stena Line** (☎ **888/274-8724** in the U.S. or 01233/647022 in Britain; www2.stenaline.com) sails from Holyhead to Dun Laoghaire, 8 miles (13km) south of Dublin; from Fishguard, Wales to Rosslare; and from Stranraer, Scotland to Belfast, Northern Ireland.

2

Getting to Know Dublin

*D*ublin, like most ancient cities, lies sprawled along a river. In fact, three visible and three underground rivers converge and flow into the Irish Sea here, on the shore of Dublin Bay. The greatest of these, or perhaps just the least lazy, is the Liffey, which has divided Dublin into north and south for more than 1,000 years. Neither as romantic as the Seine nor as mighty as the Mississippi, the Liffey is just there, old and polluted, with walls to sit on or lean against when your legs give out. Still, it is and always has been the center of things here, and it does make for a pretty picture on a good day.

While the Liffey may not be a swift and rushing torrent, the city around it is a different story. Motion is always experienced and measured with reference to fixed points, so it may not be apparent to first-time visitors just how fast Dublin is moving. Native "Dubs," however, who leave and return after several years, confess they don't believe their eyes. Greater Dublin—decreed long ago by Henry II to be "within the pale"—is now, by popular consensus, out of sight. This is the lair of the Celtic Tiger, the O'Camelot of the fastest-growing economy in Europe.

The Celts are definitely back. Two millennia ago, no less than Julius Caesar knew that they were the ones to beat, which he more or less did. In 1998, Dublin evened the ancient score when it leapt past Rome to become the fifth-most-visited city in Europe. Already, the year before, it had surpassed Rome, Milan, Amsterdam, and even London in *Fortune* magazine's rankings as the number one European city in which to do business. Then, most recently, in January 2000, an annual survey of world cities conducted by William M. Mercer Ltd. ranked Dublin among the world's top-10 cities in which to live, placing it above New York, Boston, and Washington, D.C. The word is definitely out that, work or play, Dublin is the place to be.

I suppose it all comes down to prosperity and pride, and Dublin currently has plenty of both. Twenty years ago most visitors to Ireland either bypassed Dublin altogether or made a mad dash from the ferry to the train station, determined to spend their first night beyond the pale. Now the opposite is the case. Dublin's centripetal force attracts millions of visitors a year and holds them. Today, the Dublin Renaissance is in full swing. The time has passed when aspiring Irish artists owed it to themselves to emigrate. Today, they dig in. If Joyce and Beckett and Wilde could see Dublin today, they'd be back. Maybe not on Grafton Street, but they'd be here. Dublin is simply contagious, and it's not in the Guinness. (The Irish now have one of the lowest alcohol consumption rates and the highest alcohol prices in Europe.) Neither is it in the water. (The Liffey only gets darker.) It's where it's always been, in the people.

Despite all the changes, the Liffey continues to divide the town as it once divided Viking from Celt and Norman from Norse. So far, the "new Dublin" lies mostly south of the Liffey, though a dramatic transformation of the north bank is well under way. An hour's walk from the top of Grafton Street down O'Connell and into **north Dublin** is a walk through time and, simultaneously, a glimpse of some of the pieces that must eventually fit together.

The tourist precinct of Dublin, as in most cities, is a small, well-defined compound. It comprises a large part of Dublin 2 and a smaller fraction of Dublin 1 (the postal code for each neighborhood is listed in "The Neighborhoods in Brief," later in this chapter). Grafton Street, St. Stephen's Green, and Temple Bar are the operative terms, and they are well worth the effort to see. That said, a visit to Dublin confined to these areas is not a true visit to Dublin, the Dublin that kicked some of the greatest writers in the English language into song. Explore, get a haircut (in a barbershop, not a salon), get lost and ask directions, and you may uncover a time capsule from the Dublin of a century ago—or was it only a generation?

1 Orientation

Just for reference: Dublin is 138 miles (222km) northeast of Shannon Airport, 160 miles (258km) northeast of Cork, 104 miles (167km) south of Belfast, 192 miles (309km) northeast of Killarney, 136 miles (219km) east of Galway, 147 miles (237km) southeast of Derry, and 88 miles (142km) north of Wexford.

ARRIVING

BY PLANE   Aer Lingus, Ireland's national airline, operates regularly scheduled flights into Dublin International Airport from Chicago, Boston, Los Angeles, Newark, and New York. **Delta Airlines** flies to Dublin from Atlanta and New York; and **Continental Airlines** flies to Dublin from Newark. Charters also operate from a number of U.S. and Canadian cities. You can also fly from the United States to London or other European cities and backtrack to Dublin (see "Getting There," in chapter 1).

Dublin International Airport (☎ 01/814-1111) is 7 miles (11km) north of the city center. **Dublin Bus** (☎ 01/873-4222) provides express coach service from the airport into the city's central bus station, **Busaras,** on Store Street. Service runs daily from 7:30am until 7:45pm (8:30pm Sun), with departures every 20 to 30 minutes. One-way fare is £3.50 ($4.90) for adults and £1.25 ($1.75) for children under age 12. These services are expanded during high season, and a **local city bus** (**no. 41**) is also available to the city center for £1.10 ($1.55).

There is also an excellent new private bus service called **AirCoach;** it makes 60 runs a day at 15-minute intervals between 5:30am and 11:30pm. AirCoach runs direct from the airport to Dublin's south side, servicing St. Stephen's Green, Fitzwilliam Square, Merrion Square, Ballsbridge, and Donnybrook—that is, key hotel and business districts. The one-way fare is £4 ($5.60). To confirm AirCoach departures and arrivals, call ☎ **01/844-7118.**

For speed and ease, a **taxi** is the best way to get directly to your hotel or guesthouse. Depending on your destination, fares average between £15 and £20 ($21 to $28). A 10% tip is standard. Taxis are lined up at a first-come, first-served taxi stand outside the arrivals terminal.

Major international and local car-rental companies operate desks at Dublin Airport.

BY FERRY   Passenger and car ferries from Britain arrive at the **Dublin Ferryport** (☎ 01/855-2222), on the eastern end of the North Docks, and at the **Dun Laoghaire Ferryport.**

Call **Irish Ferries** (☎ 01/661-0511) for bookings and information. There is bus and taxi service from both ports.

BY TRAIN   Irish Rail (☎ 01/836-6222) operates daily train service into Dublin from Belfast, Northern Ireland, and all major cities in the Irish Republic, including Cork, Galway, Limerick, Killarney, Sligo, Wexford, and Waterford. Trains from the south, west, and southwest arrive at **Heuston Station,** Kingsbridge, off St. John's Road; from the north and northwest at **Connolly Station,** Amiens Street; and from the southeast at **Pearse Station,** Westland Row, Tara Street.

BY BUS   Bus Eireann (☎ 01/836-6111) operates daily express coach and local bus service from all major cities and towns in Ireland into Dublin's central bus station, **Busaras,** Store Street.

BY CAR   If you are arriving by car from other parts of Ireland or on a car ferry from Britain, all main roads lead into the heart of Dublin and are well signposted to An Lar (City Centre). To bypass the city center, the East Link (toll bridge 60p/84¢) and West Link are signposted, and M50 circuits the city on three sides.

VISITOR INFORMATION

Dublin Tourism operates five year-round walk-in visitor centers in greater Dublin. The principal center is at **St. Andrew's Church,** Suffolk Street, Dublin 2, open from June to August Monday to Saturday from 9am to 8:30pm, Sunday and Bank Holidays 10:30am to 2:30pm, and the rest of the year Monday to Saturday 9am to 5:30pm. The Suffolk Street office includes a currency exchange counter, a car-rental counter, an accommodation reservations service, bus and rail information desks, a gift shop, and a cafe. For accommodation reservations throughout Ireland by credit card, contact Dublin Tourism at ☎ **011 800/668-668-66** (when calling within Ireland, omit the 011), or contact them at **reservations@dublintourism.ie** or **www.visitdublin.com**. For other information, call Bord Fáilte information at ☎ **1850/230330** from within Ireland (a local call from anywhere in the country), or ☎ **066/ 979-2083;** you can also e-mail queries to **information@ dublintourism.ie**.

The other four centers are at the Arrivals Hall of **Dublin Airport;** the new ferry terminal, **Dun Laoghaire;** the **Baggot**

The Bird's-Eye View

To start out with the big picture and to get your bearings once and for all, make your way to the **Old Jameson Distillery** (see chapter 5) and ascend, via glass elevator, to the observation chamber atop "The Chimney." In a city without skyscrapers, this is your best 360° vantage point on Greater (and smaller) Dublin. The trip to the top costs £5 ($7) for adults, £4 ($5.60) for seniors and students, £3.50 ($4.90) for children, and £15 ($21) for a family, which comes down to under 3p (4¢) a foot. Open Monday to Saturday 10am to 6pm and Sunday 11am to 7pm.

Street Bridge, Dublin 2; and **The Square,** Tallaght, Dublin 24 (all telephone inquiries should be directed to the numbers listed above). All centers are open year-round with at least the following hours: Monday to Friday 9am to 5:30pm and Saturday 9am to 1pm.

In addition, an independent center offers details on concerts, exhibits, and other arts events in the **Temple Bar** section at 18 Eustace St., Temple Bar, Dublin 2 (☎ **01/671-5717**), open year-round Monday to Friday 9:30am to 5:30pm, and Saturday 10am to 5:30pm.

At any of these centers you can pick up the free *Tourism News* or the free *Event Guide,* a biweekly entertainment guide, online at **www.eventguide.ie**. *In Dublin,* a biweekly arts-and-entertainment magazine selling for £2.90 ($4.05), is available at most newsstands.

CITY LAYOUT

Compared with other European capitals, Dublin is a relatively small metropolis and easily traversed. The city center—identified in Irish on bus destination signs as AN LAR—is bisected by the River Liffey flowing west to east into Dublin Bay. Canals ring the city center: the Royal Canal encircles the north half, and the Grand Canal the south half.

North of the Royal Canal are the northside suburbs such as Drumcondra, Glasnevin, Howth, Clontarf, and Malahide. South of the Grand Canal are the southside suburbs of Ballsbridge, Blackrock, Dun Laoghaire, Dalkey, Killiney, Rathgar, Rathmines, and other residential areas.

MAIN ARTERIES, STREETS, & SQUARES   The focal point of Dublin is the **River Liffey,** with no fewer than 15 bridges connecting its north and south banks. On the north side of the river, the main thoroughfare is **O'Connell Street,** a wide, two-way avenue that starts at the riverside quays and runs north to **Parnell Square.** Enhanced by statues, trees, and a modern fountain, the O'Connell Street of earlier days was the mainstream of the city. It is still important today, although neither as fashionable nor as safe as it used to be. Work is under way, however, to give the north side of the Liffey a mighty makeover to make it once again a focus of attention.

On the south side of the Liffey, **Grafton Street** is Dublin's main upscale shopping street, and it has clearly bent over backward in recent years to attract and please tourists. Narrow and restricted to pedestrians, Grafton Street sits at the center of Dublin's commercial district, surrounded by smaller and larger streets that boast a variety of shops, restaurants, and hotels. At the south end of Grafton Street is **St. Stephen's Green,** a lovely park and urban oasis ringed by rows of historic Georgian town houses, fine hotels, and restaurants.

Nassau Street starts at the north end of Grafton Street and rims the south side of **Trinity College.** The street is noted not only for its fine shops but because it leads to **Merrion Square,** another fashionable Georgian park surrounded by historic brick-front town houses. Merrion Square is also adjacent to Leinster House, the Irish House of Parliament, the National Gallery, and the National Museum.

In the older section of the city, **High Street** is the gateway to medieval and Viking Dublin, from the city's two medieval cathedrals to the old city walls and nearby Dublin Castle. The other noteworthy street in the older part of the city is **Francis Street,** Dublin's antiques row.

NEIGHBORHOODS IN BRIEF

Trinity College Area   On the south side of the River Liffey, the Trinity College complex is a 42-acre center of academia in the heart of the city, surrounded by fine bookstores and shops. This area lies in the Dublin 2 postal code.

Temple Bar   Wedged between Trinity College and the Old City, this section has recently been spruced up and undergone massive development as the city's cultural and entertainment hub. As Dublin's self-proclaimed Left Bank, Temple Bar is the place to see and be seen. It offers a vibrant array of unique

Dublin Orientation

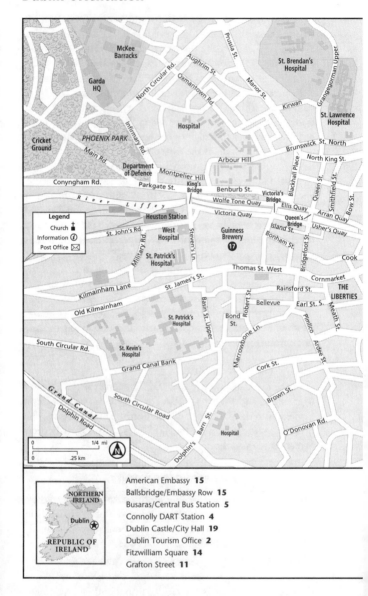

Legend
Church ✝
Information ⓘ
Post Office ✉

McKee Barracks
Garda HQ
Cricket Ground
PHOENIX PARK
Main Rd.
Conyngham Rd.
Department of Defence
Parkgate St.
Aughrim St.
North Circular Rd.
Oxmantown Rd.
Infirmary Rd.
Hospital
Prussia St.
Manor St.
Kirwan
Grangegorman Upper
St. Brendan's Hospital
St. Lawrence Hospital
Brunswick St. North
North King St.
Arbour Hill
Blackhall Place
Queen St.
Smithfield St.
Bow St.
Montpelier Hill
King's Bridge
Benburb St.
Wolfe Tone Quay
Ellis Quay
Arran Quay
Victoria's Bridge
River Liffey
Heuston Station
Victoria Quay
Queen's Bridge
Usher's Quay
Island St.
Bonham St.
Bridgefoot St.
Cook
West Hospital
St. John's Rd.
Steven's Ln.
Guinness Brewery **17**
Cornmarket
St. Patrick's Hospital
Military Rd.
Thomas St. West
THE LIBERTIES
Kilmainham Lane
St. James's St.
Basin St. Upper
Robert St.
Rainsford St.
Bellevue
Earl St. S.
Meath St.
Old Kilmainham
St. Patrick's Hospital
Bond St.
Marrowbone Ln.
Pimlico
Ardee St.
South Circular Rd.
St. Kevin's Hospital
Grand Canal Bank
Cork St.
Grand Canal
Dolphin Road
South Circular Road
Dolphin's Barn St.
Brown St.
Hospital
O'Donovan Rd.

0   1/4 mi
0   .25 km

NORTHERN IRELAND
Dublin ★
REPUBLIC OF IRELAND

American Embassy **15**
Ballsbridge/Embassy Row **15**
Busaras/Central Bus Station **5**
Connolly DART Station **4**
Dublin Castle/City Hall **19**
Dublin Tourism Office **2**
Fitzwilliam Square **14**
Grafton Street **11**

24

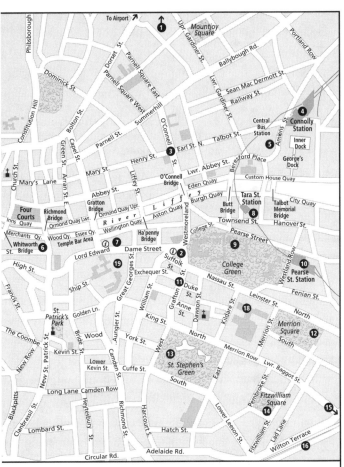

Grand Canal **16**
Guinness Brewery **17**
Leinster House **18**
Merrion Square **12**
O'Connell Street **3**
Old City/Historic Area **6**
Pearse DART Station **10**
Royal Canal **1**

St. Stephen's Green **13**
Tara Street DART Station **8**
Temple Bar **7**
Trinity College **9**
Suburbs—South (Dun Laoghaire, Dalkey, Killiney) **15**
Suburbs—North (Drumcondra, Glasnevin, Howth, Malahide) **1**

shops, art galleries, recording studios, theaters, trendy restaurants, and atmospheric pubs. This is largely the stomping ground of the young, and it's easy to feel over the hill if you're past 25. This area lies in the Dublin 2 and Dublin 8 postal codes.

Old City/Historic Area/Liberties   Dating from Viking and medieval times, the cobblestone enclave of the historic **Old City** includes Dublin Castle, the remnants of the city's original walls, and the city's two main cathedrals, Christ Church and St. Patrick's. The adjacent **Liberties** section, just west of High Street, takes its name from the fact that the people who lived here long ago were exempt from the local jurisdiction within the city walls. Although it prospered in its early days, the Liberties fell on hard times in the 17th and 18th centuries and is only now feeling a touch of urban renewal. Highlights range from the Guinness Brewery and Royal Hospital to the original Cornmarket area. Most of this area lies in the Dublin 8 zone.

St. Stephen's Green/Grafton Street Area   A magnet for visitors, this district is home to some of the city's finest hotels, restaurants, and shops. There are some residential town houses near the Green, but this is primarily a business neighborhood. It is part of the Dublin 2 zone.

Fitzwilliam & Merrion Square   These two little square parks are surrounded by fashionable brick-faced Georgian town houses, each with a distinctive and colorful doorway. Some of Dublin's most famous citizens once resided here; today many of the houses are offices for doctors, lawyers, and other professionals. This area is part of the Dublin 2 zone.

Ballsbridge/Embassy Row   South of the Grand Canal, this is Dublin's most prestigious suburb, yet it is within walking distance of downtown. Although primarily a residential area, it is also the home of some of the city's leading hotels, restaurants, and embassies, including that of the United States. This area is part of the Dublin 4 zone.

O'Connell Street (North of the Liffey)   Once a fashionable and historic focal point, this area has lost much of its charm and importance in recent years. Shops, fast-food restaurants, and movie theaters rim the wide, sweeping thoroughfare, where you'll find a few great landmarks like the

General Post Office and the Gresham Hotel. Within walking distance of O'Connell Street are four theaters, plus the Catholic Pro-Cathedral, the Moore Street open markets, the Henry Street pedestrian shopping area, the new Financial Services Centre, the ILAC Centre, the Jervis Shopping Centre, and the Central Bus Station. Regrettably, it is wise to be cautious after hours, especially after dark, in this section of the city. Most of this area lies in the Dublin 1 postal code.

2 Getting Around

Getting around Dublin is not at all daunting. Public transportation is good and getting better, taxis are plentiful and reasonably priced, and there are always your own two feet. Dublin is quite walkable. In fact, with its current traffic problems, it's a city where the foot is mightier than the wheel. If you can avoid it, don't rent a car while you're in the city. Let me repeat that: Don't rent a car while you're in the city.

BY BUS   Dublin Bus operates a fleet of green double-decker buses, single-deck buses, and minibuses (called "imps") throughout the city and its suburbs. Most buses originate on or near O'Connell Street, Abbey Street, and Eden Quay on the north side; and at Aston Quay, College Street, and Fleet Street on the south side. Bus stops are located every 2 or 3 blocks. Destinations and bus numbers are posted above the front windows; buses destined for the city center are marked with the Irish Gaelic words AN LAR.

Bus service runs daily throughout the city, starting at 6am (10am on Sun), with the last bus at 11:30pm. On Thursday, Friday, and Saturday nights, Nitelink service runs from the city center to the suburbs from midnight to 3am. Buses operate every 10 to 15 minutes for most runs; schedules are posted on revolving notice boards at each bus stop.

Inner-city fares are calculated based on distances traveled. The minimum fare is 55p (77¢); the maximum fare is £1.25 ($1.75). The Nitelink fare is a flat £2.50 ($3.50). Buy your tickets from the driver as you enter the bus; exact change is welcomed but not required. Notes of £5 or higher may not be accepted. Discounted 1-day and 4-day passes are available. A 1-day bus-only pass costs £3.30 ($4.60), and a 4-day bus and city rail pass goes for £10 ($14). With the 4-day pass, bus travel must begin after 9:45am.

For more information, contact **Dublin Bus,** 59 Upper O'Connell St., Dublin 1 (☎ **01/873-4222**).

BY DART   Although Dublin has no subway in the strict sense, there is an electrified-train rapid-transit system, known as the **DART** (Dublin Area Rapid Transit). It travels mostly at ground level or on elevated tracks, linking the city-center stations at **Tara Street, Pearse Street,** and **Amiens Street** with suburbs and seaside communities as far as Howth to the north and Bray to the south. Service operates roughly every 10 to 20 minutes Monday to Saturday from 7am to midnight and Sunday from 9:30am to 11pm. The minimum fare is 80p ($1.10). One-day, 4-day, and weekly passes, as well as family tickets, are available at reduced rates. For further information, contact **DART,** Pearse Station, Dublin 2 (☎ **01/7-3-3054**).

ON FOOT   Small and compact, Dublin is ideal for walking, as long as you remember to look left and right (in the direction opposite your instincts) for oncoming traffic, and to obey traffic signals. Each traffic light has timed "walk–don't walk" signals for pedestrians. Pedestrians have the right of way at specially marked, zebra-striped crossings; as a warning, there are usually two flashing lights at these intersections.

BY TAXI   Dublin taxis do not cruise the streets looking for fares; instead, they line up at ranks. Ranks are located outside all of the leading hotels, at bus and train stations, and on prime thoroughfares such as Upper O'Connell Street, College Green, and the north side of St. Stephen's Green.

You can also phone for a taxi. Some of the companies that operate a 24-hour radio-call service are **Co-Op** (☎ **01/ 677-7777**), **National** (☎ **01/677-2222**), and **VIP Taxis** (☎ **01/478-3333**). If you need a wake-up call, VIP offers that service, along with especially courteous dependability.

Taxi rates are fixed by law and posted in each vehicle. The minimum fare for one passenger within a 10-mile (16km) radius of O'Connell Street is £1.90 ($2.65) for any distance not exceeding 5/9 mile (0.9km) or 3 minutes and 20 seconds; after that, it's 10p (14¢) for each additional 1/9 mile (0.18km) or 40 seconds. At peak times in Dublin traffic, it's the minutes, not the miles, that add up. The per-journey additional charge for each extra passenger and for each suitcase is 40p (56¢). The most costly add-ons are £1.20 ($1.70) for dispatched pickup and £1.30 ($1.80) for service from Dublin

Dublin Area Rapid Transit (DART) Routes

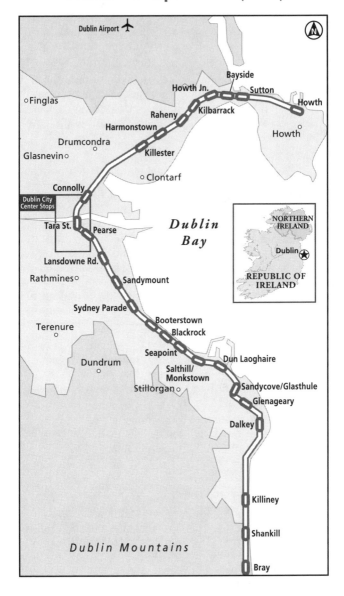

airport. *Be warned:* Some hotel or guesthouse staff members, when asked to arrange for a taxi, will tack on as much as £3 ($4.20) for their services, although this practice violates city taxi regulations.

BY CAR   Unless you plan to do a lot of driving from Dublin to neighboring counties, it's not practical or affordable to rent a car. In fact, getting around the city and its environs is much easier without a car. The city is aggressively discouraging cars for commuters, much less for tourists.

FAST FACTS: Dublin

American Express   American Express International, 41 Nassau St., Dublin 2 (☎ **01/679-9000**), is a full-service travel agency that also offers currency exchange, traveler's checks, and (for members) mail holding. It is opposite Trinity College, just off College Green, and is open Monday to Saturday 9am to 5pm. American Express also has a desk at the **Dublin Tourism Office** on Suffolk Street (☎ **01/605-7709**). In an emergency, report lost or stolen traveler's checks by dialing ☎ **1-44-1-273-571-600,** collect.

Banks   Two convenient banks are the **National Irish Bank,** 66 Upper O'Connell St., open Monday to Friday 10am to 4pm (to 5pm Thurs), and the **Allied Irish Bank,** 100 Grafton St., open Monday to Friday 10am to 4pm (to 5pm Thurs). Both have ATMs that accept Cirrus network cards as well as MasterCard and Visa.

Business Hours   **Banks** are open Monday to Wednesday and on Friday from 10am to 12:30pm and from 1:30 to 3pm, on Thursday from 10am to 12:30pm and from 1:30 to 5pm. Some banks are beginning to stay open through the lunch hour. Most **business offices** are open from 9am to 5pm, Monday to Friday. **Stores and shops** are open from 9am to 5:30pm Monday to Wednesday and Friday to Saturday, and from 9am to 8pm on Thursday. Some bookshops and tourist-oriented stores also are open on Sunday from 11am or noon until 4 or 5pm. During the peak season (May to Sept), many gift and souvenir shops post Sunday hours.

Camera Supplies   For photographic equipment, supplies, and repairs, visit **Dublin Camera Exchange,** 9B Trinity St.,

Dublin 2 (☎ **01/679-3410**); or **City Cameras,** 23A Dawson St., Dublin 2 (☎ **01/676-2891**).

Currency Exchange   Currency-exchange services, signposted as BUREAU DE CHANGE, are in all banks and at many branches of the Irish post office system, known as **An Post.** A bureau de change operates daily during flight arrival and departure times at Dublin airport; a foreign currency note-exchanger machine is also available on a 24-hour basis in the main arrivals hall. Many hotels and travel agencies offer bureau-de-change servic-es, although the best rate of exchange is usually given at banks or, better yet, when you use your credit card for purchases or expenses.

Dentist   For dental emergencies, contact the **Eastern Health Board Headquarters,** Dr. Steevens Hospital, Dublin 8 (☎ **01/679-0700**), or try **Molesworth Clinic,** 2 Molesworth Place, Dublin 2 (☎ **01/661-5544**). See also "Dental Sur-geons" in the Golden Pages (yellow pages) of the telephone book.

Doctor   If you need to see a physician, most hotels and guest-houses will contact a house doctor for you. Otherwise, you can call either the **Eastern Health Board Headquarters,** Dr. Steevens Hospital, Dublin 8 (☎ **01/679-0700**); or the **Irish Medical Organization,** 10 Fitzwilliam Place, Dublin 2 (☎ **01/676-7273**), 9:15am to 5:15pm for a referral.

Electricity   The standard electrical current is 220 volts AC. Most hotels have 110-volt shaver points for use in bathrooms, but other 110-volt equipment (such as hair dryers) will not work without a transformer and a plug adapter. Computers and sensitive electronic equipment may require more than the standard over-the-counter voltage converter. Some laptops have built-in converters. Consult the manufacturer of your computer for specifics. In any event, you will always need a plug adapter.

Embassies/Consulates   **United States Embassy,** 42 Elgin Rd., Ballsbridge, Dublin 4 (☎ **01/668-8777**); **Canadian Embassy,** 65/68 St. Stephen's Green, Dublin 2 (☎ **01/478/1988**); **British Embassy,** 29 Merrion Rd., Dublin 4 (☎ **01/205-3700**); **Australian Embassy,** Fitzwilton House, Wilton Terrace, Dublin 2 (☎ **01/676-1517**).

Emergencies   For police, fire, or other emergencies, dial
☎ **999.**

Eyeglasses   For 1-hour service on glasses or contact lenses, try
Specsavers, Unit 9, GPO Arcade, Henry Street (☎ **01/
872-8155**), or 112 Grafton St., Dublin 2 (☎ **01/677-6980**).

Hairdressers/Barbers   The leading hairstyling names for
women and men are Peter Mark and John Adam. **Peter Mark**
has more than two dozen locations throughout Dublin and its
suburbs, including 74 Grafton St., Dublin 2 (☎ **01/
671-4399**), and 11A Upper O'Connell St., Dublin 1 (☎ **01
/874-5589**). **John Adam** has shops at 13A Merrion Row,
Dublin 2 (☎ **01/661-0354**), and 112A Baggot St., Dublin 2
(☎ **01/661-1952**).

Hospitals   For emergency care, two of the most modern are
St. Vincent's Hospital, Elm Park (☎ **01/269-4533**), on the
south side of the city; and **Beaumont Hospital,** Beaumont
(☎ **01/837-7755**), on the north side.

Hotlines   In Ireland, hotlines are called "helplines." **Aids
Helpline** (☎ **01/872-4277**), Monday to Friday from 7am to
9pm and Saturday from 3 to 5pm; **Alcoholics Anonymous**
(☎ **01/453-8998,** after hours 01/679-5967); **Asthma Line**
(☎ **1850/445464**); **Narcotics Anonymous** (☎ **01/
830-0944**); **Rape Crisis Centre** (☎ **01/661-4911**) and **Free-
Fone** (☎ **1800/778-888,** after 5:30pm and weekends
01/661-4564); and **Samaritans** (☎ **01/872-7700** and
1850/609-090).

Internet Access   In cyber-savvy Dublin, public access terminals are no longer hard to find, appearing in shopping malls,
hotels, and hostels throughout the city center. One of the most
convenient and comfortable of the many cyber cafes in town is
Betacafe, Curve Street, Temple Bar, Dublin 2 (☎ **01/
605-6800;** www.betacafe.com), located above the Arthouse.
Fifteen minutes online will set you back £1.50 ($2.10). It's
open Monday to Saturday 10am to 10:30pm, Sunday noon to
6pm. At the **Planet Cybercafe** (☎ **01/679-0583**), 23 S.
Great Georges St., Dublin 2, 30 minutes online costs £2.75
($3.85). Fast transmission rates are assured at **Cyberia Cafe,**
Eustace Street, Temple Bar, Dublin 2 (☎ **01/679-7607;**
www.cyberiacafe.net), where 15 minutes online costs £1.50
($2.10), or £1.25 ($1.75) for students. It's open Monday to
Saturday 10am to 11pm and Sunday noon to 8pm.

Laundry/Dry Cleaning   Several centrally located do-it-yourself choices are **Suds,** 60 Upper Grand Canal St., Dublin 2 (☎ **01/668-1786**); **Craft Cleaners,** 12 Upper Baggot St., Dublin 4 (☎ **01/668-8198**); and **Grafton Cleaners,** 32 S. William St., Dublin 2 (☎ **01/679-4309**).

Newspapers/Magazines   The three morning Irish dailies are the *Irish Times* (except Sun), *Irish Independent,* and the *Irish Examiner.* In the afternoon, the *Herald,* the *Star,* and the *Evening Echo* hit the stands. The national Sunday editions are the *Sunday Independent, Sunday Press, Sunday Tribune, Sunday World,* and the Irish-language *Anola.* Papers from other European cities can be purchased at **Eason and Son,** 40 Lower O'Connell St., Dublin 1 (☎ **01/873-3811**). The leading magazines for upcoming events and happenings are *In Dublin* (£2.90/$4.05), published every 2 weeks; and the free biweekly *Event Guide* (www.eventguide.ie). The *Event Guide,* which contains up-to-date listings of events throughout Ireland, with a focus on Dublin, is widely available. *Where: Dublin,* published bimonthly, is aimed specifically at tourists and visitors and is a useful one-stop source for shopping, dining, and entertainment. It's free at most hotels.

Pharmacies   Centrally located drugstores, known locally as pharmacies or chemist shops, include **Hamilton Long and Co.,** 5 Lower O'Connell St. (☎ **01/874-8456**), and **Dame Street Pharmacy,** 16 Dame St., Dublin 2 (☎ **01/670-4523**). A late-night chemist shop is **Byrnes Late Night Pharmacy,** 4 Merrion Rd., Dublin 4 (☎ **01/668-3287**). It closes at 9pm on weekdays, 6pm Saturday, 1pm Sunday.

Police   In the Republic of Ireland, a law enforcement officer is called a **Garda,** a member of the *Garda Siochana* (guardian of the peace); in the plural, it's *Gardai* (pronounced *gar*-dee) or simply "the Guards." Dial ☎ **999** to reach the Gardai in an emergency. Except for special detachments, Irish police are unarmed and wear dark blue uniforms. The metropolitan headquarters for the **Dublin Garda Siochana (Police)** is in Phoenix Park, Dublin 8 (☎ **01/677-1156**).

Rest Rooms   Public rest rooms are usually simply called "toilets," or are marked with international symbols. Some of the older ones still carry the Gaelic words *Fir* (Men) and *Mna* (Women). The newest and best-kept rest rooms are found at

---

Telephone Dialing Info at a Glance

- **To place a call from your home country to Ireland,** dial the international access code (011 in the U.S., 0011 in Australia, 0170 in New Zealand, 00 in the U.K.), plus the country code (**353**), and finally the number, remembering to omit the initial 0, which is for use only within Ireland (for example, to call the County Kerry number 066/00000 from the United States, you'd dial 011-353-66/00000).

- **To place a direct international call from Ireland,** dial the international access code (**00**) plus the country code (U.S. and Canada 1, the U.K. 44, Australia 61, New Zealand 64), the area or city code, and the number (for example, to call the U.S. number 212/000-0000 you'd dial 00-1-212/000-0000). Several widely used toll-free international access codes are **AT&T** ☎ 1-800-550-000, **Sprint** ☎ 1-800-552-001, and **MCI** ☎ 1-800-55-1001. *Note:* To dial direct to Northern Ireland from the Republic, simply replace the 028 prefix with 048.

- **To place a collect call to the United States from Ireland,** dial ☎ **1-800/550-000** for USA Direct service.

- **To reach directory assistance,** dial ☎ **1190** within Ireland. From the United States, the (toll) number to call is ☎ **00353-91-770220.**

---

shopping complexes and at multistory car parks. Some cost 10p (14¢) to enter.

Shoe Repairs   Two reliable shops in midcity are **O'Connell's Shoe Repairs,** 3 Upper Baggot St. (☎ **01/667-2020**), and **Mister Minit,** Parnell Mall, ILAC Centre, Henry Street (☎ **01/872-3037**).

Taxes   As in many European countries, sales tax is called VAT (value-added tax) and is often already included in the price quoted to you or shown on price tags. In the Republic, VAT rates vary—for hotels, restaurants, and car rentals, it is 12.5%; for souvenirs and gifts, it is 17.36%. VAT charged on services such as hotel stays, meals, car rentals, and entertainment cannot be refunded to visitors, but the VAT on products such as souvenirs is refundable. For full details on VAT refunds for purchases, see chapter 6.

Telephone   In the Republic, the telephone system is known as Telecom Éireann. Phone numbers in Ireland are currently in flux, as digits are added to accommodate expanded service. Every effort has been made to ensure that the numbers and information in this guide are accurate at the time of writing. If you have difficulty reaching a party, the Irish toll-free number for directory assistance is ☎ **1190.** From the United States, the (toll) number to call is ☎ **00353-91-770220.**

Local calls from a phone booth cost 20p (28¢) within the Republic of Ireland, and 20p (33¢) in the North for the first minute. The most efficient way to make calls from public phones is to use a Callcard, a prepaid computerized card that you insert into the phone instead of coins. They can be purchased in a range of denominations at phone company offices, post offices, and many retail outlets (such as newsstands). There's a local and international phone center at the General Post Office on O'Connell Street.

Overseas calls from Ireland can be quite costly, whether you use a local phone card or your own calling card. If you think you will want to call home regularly while in Ireland, you may want to open an account with **Swiftcall** (toll-free in Ireland ☎ **0800-794-381;** www.swiftcall.com). Its rates represent a considerable savings, not only from Ireland to the United States but vice versa (handy for planning your trip as well as keeping in touch afterward). **Premiere WORLDLINK** (☎ **800/432-6169**) offers an array of additional services for overseas travelers—such as toll-free voice-mail boxes, fax mail, and news services—which can be crucial for keeping in touch when you don't know where or when you can be reached.

Time   Ireland follows Greenwich Mean Time (1 hr. earlier than Central European Time) from November to March, and British Standard Time (the same as Central European Time) from April to October. Ireland is five time zones earlier than the eastern United States (when it's noon in New York, it's 5pm in Ireland).

Ireland's latitude makes for longer days and shorter nights in the summer, and the reverse in the winter. In June, there is bright sun until 11pm, but in December, it is truly dark at 4pm.

Tipping   Most hotels and guesthouses add a service charge to the bill, usually 12.5% to 15%, although some smaller places add only 10% or nothing at all. Always check to see what amount, if any, has been added to your bill. If it is 12.5% to 15%, and you feel this is sufficient, then there is no need for more gratuities. However, if a smaller amount has been added or if staff members have provided exceptional service, it is appropriate to give additional cash gratuities. For porters or bellhops, tip 50p (70¢) to £1 ($1.40) per piece of luggage. For taxi drivers, hairdressers, and other providers of service, tip as you would at home, an average of 10% to 15%.

For restaurants, the policy is usually printed on the menu—either a gratuity of 10% to 15% is added to your bill or no service charge is added, leaving it up to you. Always ask if you are in doubt. As a rule, staff members at bars do not expect a tip, except when table service is provided.

Weather   Phone ☎ **1850/241-222,** or on the Web at **www.ireland.com/weather/.**

3

Accommodations

*F*rom legendary old-world landmarks to sleek high-rises, Dublin offers a great diversity of places to stay. Although prices are rising, even travelers on a moderate budget, with enough advance planning, should be able to find comfortable, attractive accommodations. Dublin is sprouting new hotels at a somewhat-alarming rate—more than 20 in the past handful of years—to meet an ever-accelerating demand. Fortunately, a concerted effort is being made to assure that the new hotels represent the economic diversity of Dublin's visitors, from Midas to Scrooge.

As in the rest of Ireland, Dublin's hotels and guesthouses are now inspected, registered, and graded by Tourism Quality Services. In 1994, the Irish Tourist Board introduced a grading system, consistent with those of other European countries and international standards that ranks them with one to five stars. Six hotels in Dublin currently merit the five-star rating: Berkeley Court, Conrad, Jurys, Merrion, Shelbourne, and Westbury.

In general, rates for Dublin hotels do not vary as greatly with the seasons as they do in the countryside. Some hotels charge slightly higher prices during special events, such as the Dublin Horse Show. For the best deals, try to reserve a room over a weekend, and ask if there is a reduction or a weekend package in effect. Some Dublin hotels cut their rates by as much as 50% on Friday and Saturday nights, when business traffic is low. Just to complicate matters, other hotels, especially in the off-season, offer midweek specials.

Room charges quoted in this guide include 12.5% government tax (VAT) in the Republic of Ireland and 17.5% VAT in Northern Ireland. They do not (unless otherwise noted) include service charges, which are usually between 10% and

Dublin Accommodations

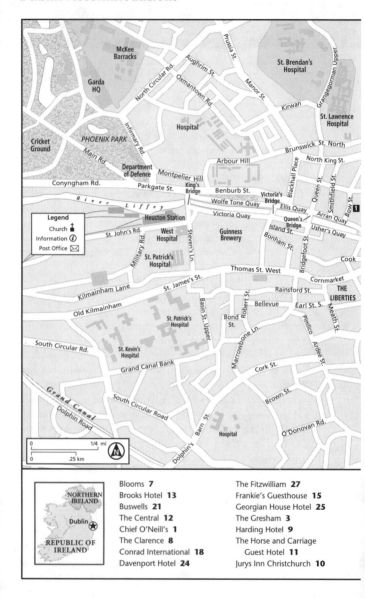

Blooms **7**
Brooks Hotel **13**
Buswells **21**
The Central **12**
Chief O'Neill's **1**
The Clarence **8**
Conrad International **18**
Davenport Hotel **24**

The Fitzwilliam **27**
Frankie's Guesthouse **15**
Georgian House Hotel **25**
The Gresham **3**
Harding Hotel **9**
The Horse and Carriage
  Guest Hotel **11**
Jurys Inn Christchurch **10**

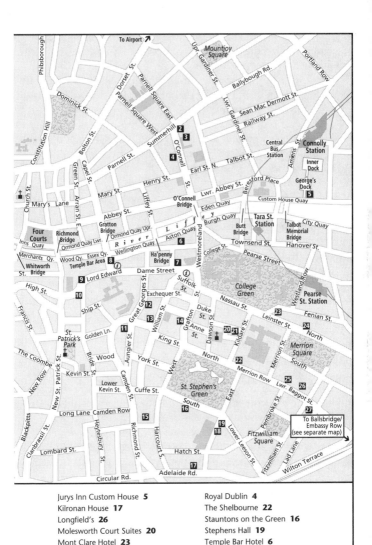

Jurys Inn Custom House **5**	Royal Dublin **4**
Kilronan House **17**	The Shelbourne **22**
Longfield's **26**	Stauntons on the Green **16**
Molesworth Court Suites **20**	Stephens Hall **19**
Mont Clare Hotel **23**	Temple Bar Hotel **6**
Mount Eccles Court Hostel and Self-Catering Apartments **2**	Westbury Hotel **14**

15% (most places add 12.5%). Most hotels and guesthouses automatically add the service charge onto your final bill, although in recent years many family-run or limited-service places have begun the practice of not charging for service, leaving it as an option for the guest. Home-style B&Bs do not ordinarily charge for service.

Ordinarily, the Irish cite the per-person price of a double room—a policy not followed in this guide, which for the sake of uniform comparison assumes double occupancy. Most accommodations make adjustments for children. Children accompanying their parents are often assessed on an ad hoc sliding scale. In other words, a smallish, angelic child may well incur only a nominal fee, if any, but a hellion may pay full price. So it pays to have your children put their best, most silent feet forward when you enter a hotel or guesthouse. If you're traveling on your own, there is most often a supplemental charge for single occupancy of a double room.

The Irish use the phrase "en suite" to indicate a room with private bathroom. A "double" has a double bed, and a "twin" has two single beds. An "orthopedic" bed has an extra-firm mattress. Queen- and king-size beds are not common except in large, deluxe hotels.

Many hotels can be booked through toll-free numbers in the United States; better yet, the prices offered can be appreciably (as much as 40%) lower than those offered at the door. For those properties that do not have a U.S. reservation number, the fastest way to reserve is by telephone, fax, or e-mail. Fax and e-mail are advisable, because they give you a written confirmation. You can then follow up by sending a deposit check (usually the equivalent of one night's room rate) or by giving your credit-card number.

If you arrive in Ireland without a reservation, the staff members at the tourist offices throughout the Republic and Northern Ireland will gladly find you a room using a computerized reservation service known as **Gulliver.** You can also call the Gulliver line directly (☎ **00800/668-668-66**). This is a nationwide and cross-border "freephone" facility for credit-card bookings, operated daily 8am to 11pm. Gulliver is also accessible from the United States (☎ **011800/668-668-66**). You can also e-mail them at **reservations@dublintourism.ie** or find them on the Web at **www.visitdublin.com**.

1 Historic Old City & Temple Bar/ Trinity College Area

VERY EXPENSIVE

The Clarence. 6/8 Wellington Quay, Dublin 2. ☎ **01/670-9000.** Fax 01/670-7800. www.theclarence.ie. 50 units. MINIBAR TV TEL. £195–£210 ($273–$294) double; £450 ($630) 1-bedroom suite; £550 ($770) 2-bedroom suite. Full Irish breakfast £14 ($19.60). Rates include service charge. AE, DC, MC, V. Bus: 51B, 51C, 68, 69, or 79.

Situated between the south bank of the Liffey and Temple Bar, this Regency-style hotel belongs to an investment group that includes the rock band U2. Built in 1852, the Clarence was totally refurbished in 1996 to offer larger rooms and suites upgraded to deluxe standards. In the process, it traded antique charm for bold, contemporary design. Each room or suite is unique but all rooms feature deep colors against light Shaker-style oak furniture that includes orthopedic beds. Suites and deluxe rooms have balconies. Accommodations for nonsmokers and travelers with disabilities are available. All rooms are equipped with VCRs, PC/fax connections, private safes, and hair dryers.

Dining/Diversions: The Clarence's elegant Tea Room restaurant, in what was once the ballroom, is known for its eclectic and excellent contemporary Irish cuisine. For drinks and lighter fare there's the Octagon Bar; and after hours, the Clarence is home to The Kitchen, one of Temple Bar's chic night spots.

Amenities: Room service, concierge, baby-sitter service, laundry service, foreign-currency exchange.

EXPENSIVE

Blooms. 6 Anglesea St., Dublin 2. ☎ **800/44-UTELL** from the U.S., or 01/671-5622. Fax 01/671-5997. www.blooms.ie. 86 units. TV TEL. £138 ($193.20) double. Service charge 12.5%. AE, DC, MC, V. Parking available on street. DART: Tara St. Bus: 21A, 46A, 46B, 51B, 51C, 68, 69, or 86.

Lovers of Irish literature will feel at home at Blooms. Named after Leopold Bloom, a character in James Joyce's *Ulysses,* the hotel is in the heart of Dublin, near Trinity College and on the edge of the Temple Bar district. Guest rooms are modern and functional, with useful extras like garment presses and hair dryers.

Dining/Diversions: For formal dining, reserve a table at the Bia restaurant; for more informal fare, try the Anglesea Bar. Late-night entertainment is available in the basement-level nightclub, known simply as M.

Amenities: Room service, concierge, baby-sitting, valet and laundry/dry-cleaning service, express checkout, foreign-currency exchange.

The Central. 1–5 Exchequer St. (at the corner of Great George's St.), Dublin 2. ☎ **01/679-7302.** Fax 01/679-7303. E-mail: reservations@centralhotel.ie. 70 units. MINIBAR TV TEL. £108–£150 ($151.20–$210) double. Rates include full Irish breakfast and service charge. AE, DC, MC, V. Discounted parking in nearby public lot. Bus: 22A.

Between Trinity College and Dublin Castle, this century-old five-story hotel was renovated in 1991 and totally refurbished in 1997. The public areas retain a Victorian atmosphere, enhanced by an impressive collection of contemporary Irish art. Guest rooms, cheerfully decorated with colorful Irish-made furnishings, offer such extras as a garment press, hair dryer, and tea/coffeemaker.

Dining/Diversions: Lunch and dinner are served in the hotel's Victorian-style dining room. The tucked-away Library Bar is a quiet haven for a drink and a moment's calm.

Amenities: Room service, concierge, baby-sitting, foreign-currency exchange.

Temple Bar Hotel. Fleet St., Temple Bar, Dublin 2. ☎ **800/44-UTELL** from the U.S., or 01/677-3333. Fax 01/677-3088. www.towerhotelgroup.ie. 130 units (4 with shower only). TV TEL. £110–£190 ($154–$266). No service charge. AE, DC, MC, V. Parking available on street. DART: Tara St. Bus: 78A or 78B.

If you want to be in the heart of the action in the Temple Bar district, this is a prime place to stay. Opened in 1993, the five-story hotel was developed from a row of town houses. Great care was taken to preserve the Georgian brick-front facade and Victorian mansard roof. Guest rooms, modern with traditional furnishings and orthopedic beds, include amenities such as a garment press, towel warmer, hair dryer, and tea/coffeemaker. Rooms for nonsmokers are available.

Dining/Diversions: The hotel has a skylit garden-style restaurant, the Terrace Cafe, and an Old Dublin–theme pub, Buskers.

Amenities: Room service, concierge, baby-sitter service, foreign-currency exchange, access to a nearby health club.

INEXPENSIVE

Harding Hotel. Copper Alley, Christchurch, Dublin 2. ☎ **01/679-6500.** Fax 01/679-6504. E-mail: harding@usit.ie. 53 units (all with shower only). TV TEL. £45–£65 ($63–$91) twin, double, or triple. No service charge. MC, V. Bus: 21A, 50, 50A, 78, 78A, or 78B.

The Harding is conveniently tucked away along Dublin's oldest medieval street, with striking views of neighboring Christchurch to the west. The rooms are surprisingly large, and are furnished simply in contemporary style, with lots of pine and bright blue and yellow print fabrics. Each room is equipped with a hair dryer and tea/coffee-making facilities. Single and family rooms are available. The hotel is fully wheelchair accessible and has an open courtyard, bar, and restaurant.

Jurys Inn Christchurch. Christ Church Place, Dublin 8. ☎ **800/44-UTELL** from the U.S., or 01/454-0000. Fax 01/454-0012. www.jurys.com. 183 units. A/C TV TEL. £62–£65 ($86.80–$91) single, double, or family room. No service charge. AE, CB, DC, MC, V. Discounted parking available at adjacent lot. Bus: 21A, 50, 50A, 78, 78A, or 78B.

An ideal location and a winning concept—to offer quality lodging at budget cost—have combined to make this one of Dublin's most sought-after accommodations. Totally refurbished in 1998, the rooms are ample, bright, and inviting, and can accommodate up to three adults or two adults and two children—all for the same price. All have coffeemakers and hair dryers. Facilities include a moderately priced restaurant, a pub lounge, and an adjacent multistory parking area. There are 38 nonsmoking rooms available, and 2 rooms specially adapted for guests with disabilities. Baby-sitting can be arranged. Make your reservations early and request a fifth-floor room facing west for a memorable view of Christchurch. *Tip:* Rooms 501, 507, and 419 are especially spacious.

2 St. Stephen's Green/Grafton Street Area

VERY EXPENSIVE

Brooks Hotel. 59–62 Drury St., Dublin 2. ☎ **01/670-4000.** Fax 01/670-4455. www.iol.ie/_bizpark/s/sinnott. 75 units. A/C MINIBAR TV TEL. £180–£220 ($252–$308) double. No service charge. AE, DC, MC, V. Discounted overnight and weekend parking available at adjacent facility. DART: Tara St. or Pearse. Bus: 10, 11A, 11B, 13, 14, 15, 15A, 15B, 20B, or 46A.

The Brooks Hotel opened in June 1997 and has welcomed many corporate and holiday visitors to its comfortable quarters. The quality furnishings include orthopedic beds, handmade oak furniture from Galway, and tasteful decor. Individual climate control, three phones, powerful showers with bathtubs, hair dryers, trouser presses, and ironing boards are standard issue, as are fax machines, dataports, and current adapters. Three of the six floors are designated for nonsmokers. Superior and executive rooms provide such extras as VCRs, antique radios, and high king-size beds.

Dining/Diversions: Brooks offers Francesca's Restaurant and the more lively and informal Butter Lane Bar. The lounge, paneled in French oak, provides a restful oasis for tea or sherry and the newspaper.

Amenities: 24-hour room service, concierge, laundry/dry-cleaning service, baby-sitting, secretarial services, video rentals, foreign-currency exchange, express checkout.

Conrad International. Earlsfort Terrace, Dublin 2. ☎ **800/HILTONS** from the U.S., or 01/676-5555. Fax 01/676-5424. www.conrad-international.ie. 197 units. A/C MINIBAR TV TEL. £200 ($280) double; £410–£700 ($574–$980) suite. Service charge 15%. DC, MC, V. Free valet parking. DART: Pearse. Bus: 11A, 11B, 13, or 14A.

A member of the international subsidiary of Hilton Hotels and one of the city's newest deluxe hotels, this seven-story red-brick high-rise is opposite the National Concert Hall and across from the southeast corner of St. Stephen's Green. The spacious public areas are rich in marble, brass, contemporary art, and leafy plants. Each guest room is outfitted with contemporary furnishings, with extras such as an electronic safety lock, a writing desk, bathrobes, and three telephone lines. All beds have orthopedic mattresses. Nonsmoking floors are available.

Dining/Diversions: Choices include the Alexandra, a club-by room known for a range of gourmet Continental and Irish fare; Plurabelle, a brasserie-style restaurant; the Lobby Lounge, for traditional afternoon tea or drinks with piano background music; and Alfie Byrne's, a pub named for a former lord mayor of Dublin that serves light lunches.

Amenities: 24-hour room service, concierge, laundry/dry-cleaning, shoeshine, secretarial services, baby-sitting, express checkout, foreign-currency exchange, hairdressing salon.

✪ **The Shelbourne.** 27 St. Stephen's Green, Dublin 2. ☎ **800/225-5843** from the U.S., or 01/676-6471. Fax 01/661-6006. www.shelbourne.ie. 190 units. MINIBAR TV TEL. £390–£490 ($546–$686) double. Service charge 15%. DC, MC, V. Limited free parking. DART: Pearse. Bus: 10, 11A, 11B, 13, or 20B.

With a fanciful red-brick and white-trimmed facade, enhanced by wrought-iron railings and window boxes brimming with flowers, this grand six-story hostelry stands out on the north side of St. Stephen's Green. Built in 1824, it has played a significant role in Irish history—the new nation's constitution was signed in Room 112 in 1921. It has often been host to international leaders, stars of stage and screen, and literary giants. The public areas, replete with glowing fireplaces, Waterford chandeliers, and original art, are popular rendezvous spots for Dubliners. Guest rooms vary in size, but all offer up-to-date comforts and are furnished with antique and period pieces. The front units overlook bucolic St. Stephen's Green. In 1996, nearly $2.5 million went into refurbishing the Shelbourne's guest rooms and meeting space.

Needless to say, you don't stay here just for the beds, which represent the Irish preference for a mattress somewhere beyond soft and short of firm.

Dining/Diversions: The Dining Room offers Irish and Continental cuisine; the Horseshoe Bar and Shelbourne Bar are both ideal for a convivial drink. Locals favor the Lord Mayor's Lounge for a proper afternoon tea.

Amenities: 24-hour room service, concierge, baby-sitting, laundry/dry cleaning, video rental, safe-deposit boxes, foreign-currency exchange, beauty salon, boutiques, access to nearby health club.

Stephens Hall. 14–17 Lower Leeson St., Earlsfort Terrace, Dublin 2. ☎ **800/ 223-6510** from the U.S., or 01/638-1111. Fax 01/638-1122. www.prem-group.ie. 37 units. TV TEL. £160–£250 ($224–$350) double. No service charge. Full breakfast £9 ($12.60). AE, DC, MC, V. Free valet parking. DART: Pearse. Bus: 11, 11A, 11B, 13, 13A, or 13B.

With a gracious Georgian exterior and entranceway, this is Dublin's first all-suite hotel, situated on the southeast corner of St. Stephen's Green. It's ideal for visitors who plan an extended stay or who want to entertain or do their own cooking. All of the suites were redecorated in 1998. Each contains a hallway, sitting room, dining area, kitchen, bathroom, and one or two bedrooms, with orthopedic beds; other extras include fax machines, CD players, and dataports. One full floor is nonsmoking. The luxury penthouse suites, on the upper floors, offer views of the city. Ground-level town-house suites have private entrances.

Dining/Diversions: Although the idea here is for you to do your own cooking, there are a Michelin award–winning restaurant, Morels, and a bar on the premises.

Amenities: Concierge, daily maid service, baby-sitting, safe-deposit boxes, video rentals, valet parking, access to nearby health club.

Westbury Hotel. Grafton St., Dublin 2. ☎ **800/42-DOYLE** from the U.S., or 01/679-1122. Fax 01/679-7078. www.doylehotels.com. 203 units. A/C TV TEL. £230 ($322) double. Service charge 15%. AE, DC, MC, V. Free parking. DART: Tara St. or Pearse. Bus: 10, 11A, 11B, 13, or 20B.

A tasteful hybrid of modern and traditional design, this relatively new midtown hotel blends a sleek contemporary facade with a serene interior. It sits in the heart of the city's fashionable shopping district, and near all the major sights. The guest rooms, many with half-canopy or four-poster beds, are furnished with antiques, dark woods, brass trim, and floral designer fabrics. Many suites have Jacuzzis.

Dining/Diversions: Choices include the Russell Room, a French-Irish restaurant; the Sandbank, a nautical-style pub that serves fresh seafood; Charlie's Coffee Shop; and the Terrace Bar and Lounge, a favorite venue for afternoon tea or a drink, with live piano music.

Amenities: 24-hour room service, concierge, baby-sitting, laundry/dry cleaning, express checkout, hairdressing salon, 20-shop arcade, fitness room, access to Riverview Health and Fitness Club.

EXPENSIVE

Buswells. 25 Molesworth St., Dublin 2. ☎ **800/473-9527** from the U.S., or 01/614-6500. Fax 01/676-2090. E-mail: buswells@quinn-group.com. 69 units. TV TEL. £165 ($231) double. No service charge. Rates include full breakfast. AE, DC, MC, V. DART: Pearse. Bus: 10, 11A, 11B, 13, or 20B.

On a street that's oddly quiet—considering it's only 2 blocks from Trinity College and opposite the National Museum—this vintage four-story hotel has long been a meeting place for artists, poets, scholars, and politicians. Originally two 1736 Georgian town houses, it became a hotel in 1928. The public rooms contain period furniture, intricate plasterwork, Wedgwood flourishes, old prints, and memorabilia. Recent refurbishment has preserved the Georgian decor and character throughout. With a few exceptions, guest rooms are quite spacious, with bright wallpaper, mahogany beds, desks, and

wardrobes, and white tiled bathrooms. All include tea/
coffeemakers, hair dryers, and trouser presses.

Dining/Diversions: The hotel has an à la carte restaurant,
a carvery, and two bars.

Amenities: 24-hour room service, concierge, baby-sitting,
laundry, ISDN/modem facilities, foreign-currency exchange.

Georgian House Hotel. 18 Lower Baggot St., Dublin 2. ☎ **01/661-8832.**
Fax 01/661-8834. E-mail: hotel@georgianhouse.ie. 70 units. TV TEL.
£100–£150 ($140–$210) double. AE, CB, MC, V. Free parking. DART: Pearse.
Bus: 10.

Less than 2 blocks from St. Stephen's Green, this four-story,
200-year-old brick town house sits in the heart of Georgian
Dublin, within walking distance of most major attractions. Its
original guest rooms were smallish, though they offered all the
essentials and a colorful decor with pine furniture. The hotel
has recently undergone a dramatic expansion; it now offers
larger rooms and new facilities.

Dining/Diversions: The hotel has a new restaurant, spe-
cializing in shellfish and seafood, and a bar.

Amenities: Room service, concierge, baby-sitting, laun-
dry/dry cleaning, secretarial services, leisure center with
indoor pool, foreign-currency exchange.

MODERATE

Stauntons on the Green. 83 St. Stephen's Green, Dublin 2. ☎ **01/
478-2300.** Fax 01/ 478-2263. E-mail: hotels@indigo.ie. 36 units. TV TEL. £120
($168) double. No service charge. Rates include full breakfast. AE, DC, MC, V.
Valet parking £5 ($7) per day. DART: Pearse. Bus: 14A or 62.

Opened in 1993, this beautifully restored guesthouse occupies
a four-story Georgian town house on the south side of St.
Stephen's Green, next door to the Irish Department of Foreign
Affairs. There is no elevator, but there are rooms on the
ground level. Guest rooms are decorated in traditional style,
enhanced by tall windows and high ceilings; front rooms overlook the Green, and rooms at the back have views of the adjacent Iveagh Gardens. Beds are firm. Public areas include a
breakfast room and a parlor with an open fireplace.

INEXPENSIVE

Frankie's Guesthouse. 8 Camden Place (off Camden St./Harcourt St.),
Dublin 2. ☎ and fax **01/478-3087.** www.frankiesguesthouse.com. 12 units,
9 with private bathroom (shower only). TV. £68 ($95.20) double with private

bathroom; £57 ($79.80) double with shared bathroom. Rates include break-
fast. AE, MC, V. Parking available on street. Bus: 16, 16A, 16C, 19A, 22, or 22A.

Frankie has run this pleasant guest hotel for over 10 years,
maintaining the small but fresh, simple white rooms to a high
standard. Set on a quiet back street, the house has a Mediterranean feel, with a lovely walkway and roof garden. It welcomes mature gay, lesbian, and straight visitors alike. The
double room downstairs can accommodate a traveler with disabilities. It is an easy walk to St. Stephen's Green and Grafton
Street, and you can make coffee or tea in your room. I recommend that you book this place well in advance, especially
for a weekend stay.

The Horse and Carriage Guest Hotel. 15 Aungier St. (at S. Great George's
St.), Dublin 2. ☎ **01/478-3537.** Fax 01/478-4010. E-mail: liamtony@indigo.ie.
9 units, 3 with private bathroom. TV. £55–£70 ($77–$98) double. Rates include
breakfast and unlimited use of Incognito Sauna Club facilities. AE, MC, V. Parking
available at nearby lot. Bus: 14, 14A, 47, or 47A.

Set in the heart of busy Dublin center, this 3-year-old hotel
warmly welcomes people of all ages and orientations, and has
predominantly gay male visitors. The Incognito Sauna Club is
part of the hotel complex, and the atmosphere is casual and
bustling. Most rooms have soft king-size beds, and the shared
bathrooms are clean and private. The three highest-priced
units, the "carriage rooms," are more spacious and quieter
than the others, which face a busy street. Heavily flowered
wallpaper makes the rooms feel small and a bit dark, but all
the accommodations are comfortable. The hotel has won
awards for its remodeled turn-of-the-century facade. Hosts
Liam Ledwidge and Tony Keogan are helpful and well
informed on Dublin life. Aungier Street is a continuation of
South Great George's Street.

SELF-CATERING

Molesworth Court Suites. Schoolhouse Lane (off Molesworth St.), Dublin 2.
☎ **01/676-4799.** Fax 01/676-4982. 12 units. TV TEL. £105–£220
($147–$308) per night. £75 ($105) deposit required with booking and balance
payable 4 weeks prior to arrival. AE, MC, V. DART: Pearse. Bus: 10, 11A, 11B,
13, or 20B.

In Dublin, location may not be everything, but it's close—and
you can't ask for a better location than this. Tucked away
behind Mansion House, Molesworth Courts is no more than
5 minutes on foot to Stephens Green and yet is country quiet.

These stylish, comfortable units (one- or two-bedroom apartments, or two- or three-bedroom penthouses) offer everything you need to set up your own base in Dublin, whether for a night or a month. They're full of light and good taste and come fully furnished and equipped. They all have small balconies; and the bilevel penthouses have quite spacious verandas. The staff here goes the extra mile to be helpful. The internal phone system provides you with a private extension and your own voice mail. If, despite the fact that you have your own kitchen, you want to let others do your cooking, you can order out from any of the roughly 25 local restaurants listed in the *Restaurant Express* menu booklet lying only an arm's reach from the couch.

3 Fitzwilliam Square/Merrion Square Area

VERY EXPENSIVE

Davenport Hotel. Merrion Sq., Dublin 2. ☎ **800/569-9983** from the U.S., or 01/607-3500. Fax 01/661-5663. www.ocallaghanhotels.ie. 120 units. A/C TV TEL. £145–£225 ($203–$315) double. Service charge 12.5%. AE, DC, MC, V. Free valet parking. DART: Pearse. Bus: 6, 7A, or 8.

Opened as a hotel in 1993, this building incorporates the neoclassical facade of Merrion Hall, an 1863 church. Classic Georgian windows and pillars encircle the impressive domed entranceway, with a six-story atrium lobby, marble flooring, and plaster moldings. The guest rooms, in a newly built section, have traditional furnishings, orthopedic beds, textured wall coverings, quilted floral bedspreads and matching drapes, and brass accoutrements. Each room has three telephone lines plus a computer data line, work desk, personal safe, garment press, tea and coffee welcome tray, and hair dryer. Two floors are nonsmoking. The hotel shares valet parking arrangements with its sister hotel, the Mont Clare, across the street.

Dining/Diversions: The Georgian-theme restaurant, Lanyon's, is named after a leading 19th-century Irish architect. The clubby President's Bar, decorated with framed pictures of world leaders past and present, serves drinks as well as morning coffee and afternoon tea.

Amenities: 24-hour room service, concierge, health club, laundry/dry cleaning, baby-sitting, secretarial services, express checkout.

EXPENSIVE

✪ **Longfield's.** 10 Lower Fitzwilliam St., Dublin 2. ☎ **01/676-1367.** Fax 01/676-1542. E-mail: lfields@indigo.ie. 26 units. TV TEL. £110–£160 ($154–$224) double. No service charge. Rates include full breakfast. AE, DC, MC, V. No parking available. DART: Pearse. Bus: 10.

Created from two 18th-century Georgian town houses, this small, classy hotel is named after Richard Longfield (also known as Viscount Longueville), who originally owned this site and was a member of the Irish Parliament 2 centuries ago. Totally restored and recently refurbished, it combines Georgian decor and reproduction period furnishings of dark woods and brass trim. Guest rooms offer extras such as clock radios and hair dryers. Like the eye of a storm, Longfield's is centrally located yet remarkably quiet, an elegant yet unpretentious getaway 5 minutes' walk from St. Stephen's Green.

Dining: Longfield's offers award-winning cuisine in its "No. 10" Restaurant.

Amenities: 24-hour room service, concierge, laundry/dry cleaning, baby-sitting, secretarial services, foreign-currency exchange.

Mont Clare Hotel. Merrion Sq., Dublin 2. ☎ **800/569-9983** from the U.S., or 01/607-3800. Fax 01/661-5663. www.ocallaghanhotels.ie. 74 units. A/C MINIBAR TV TEL. £110–£160 ($154–$224) double. Service charge 12.5%. AE, DC, MC, V. Free valet parking. DART: Pearse. Bus: 5, 7A, or 8.

Overlooking the northwest corner of Merrion Square, this vintage six-story brick-faced hotel recently underwent a thorough restoration. It has a typically Georgian facade, matched inside by period furnishings of dark woods and polished brass. Guest rooms were completely refurbished in 1998 and given a brighter, more contemporary feel. Each has a hair dryer, tea/coffeemaker, and garment press. Beds are orthopedic, and nonsmoking floors are available.

Dining/Diversions: The main restaurant, Goldsmith's (named for Oliver Goldsmith, one of Ireland's great writers), has a literary theme. There is also a traditional lounge bar.

Amenities: 24-hour room service, concierge, complimentary access to nearby fitness center, laundry/dry cleaning, baby-sitting, secretarial services, express checkout.

MODERATE

The Fitzwilliam. 41 Upper Fitzwilliam St., Dublin 2. ☎ **01/662-5155.** Fax 01/676-7488. 12 units. TV TEL. £70–£85 ($98–$119) double. Service charge

10%. Rates include full breakfast. AE, DC, MC, V. Limited free overnight parking. DART: Pearse. Bus: 10.

This guesthouse occupies a meticulously restored 18th-century town house on the best-preserved Georgian thoroughfare in Dublin. It's a convenient location for exploring the city. The entrance parlor has a homey atmosphere, with a carved marble fireplace and antique furnishings. The bright guest rooms have high ceilings, orthopedic beds, hair dryers, and clock radios; bathrooms are somewhat small, but impeccably clean. Tea/coffeemakers are available just outside each room. Facilities include a French restaurant in the vaulted basement.

Kilronan House. 70 Adelaide Rd., Dublin 2. ☎ **01/475-5266.** Fax 01/478-2841. www.dublinn.com. 15 units, 13 with private bathroom (shower only). TV TEL. £70–£90 ($98–$126) double. Children under 7 stay free in parents' room. Rates include full breakfast. AE, MC, V. Free private parking. Bus: 14, 15, 19, 20, or 46A.

Noel Comer is the outgoing proprietor at this comfortable guesthouse, located within 5 minutes' walk of St. Stephen's Green, just north of the Royal Canal. The sitting room on the ground floor is small and intimate, with a fire glowing through the cold months of the year. The rooms are very well kept, and those facing the front have commodious bay windows; each comes equipped with tea and coffee facilities and hair dryers. If you don't like stairs, request a room on the second floor, because there isn't an elevator. The front rooms, facing Adelaide Street, are also preferable to those in back, which face onto office buildings and a parking lot. When you book, ask about a reduction for Frommer's readers.

4 Ballsbridge/Embassy Row Area

VERY EXPENSIVE

Berkeley Court. Lansdowne Rd., Ballsbridge, Dublin 4. ☎ **800/42-DOYLE** from the U.S., or 01/660-1711. Fax 01/661-7238. www.doyle-hotels.com. 188 units. TV TEL. £175–£220 ($245–$308) double; from £250 ($350) suite. AE, DC, MC, V. Free valet parking. DART: Lansdowne Rd. Bus: 7, 8, or 45.

The flagship of the Irish-owned Doyle Hotel group, and the first Irish member of Leading Hotels of the World, the Berkeley Court (pronounced *Bark*-lay) is nestled in a residential area near the American Embassy. The well-tended grounds were once part of the Botanic Gardens of University College. A favorite haunt of diplomats and international business leaders, the hotel is known for its posh lobby decorated with fine antiques, original paintings, mirrored columns, and Irish-made carpets and furnishings. The guest rooms, which aim to convey an air of elegance, have designer fabrics, firm half-canopy beds, dark woods, and bathrooms fitted with marble accoutrements. Suites have Jacuzzis. There are only 20 rooms for nonsmokers, so be specific when making reservations.

Dining/Diversions: Choices include the formal Berkeley Room for gourmet dining; the skylit Conservatory for casual meals; the Royal Court, a gothic-style bar; and the Court Lounge, a proper setting for afternoon tea or a relaxing drink.

Amenities: 24-hour room service, concierge, laundry service, express checkout, foreign-currency exchange, boutiques, health club.

The Burlington. Upper Leeson St., Dublin 4. ☎ **800/42-DOYLE** from the U.S., or 01/660-5222. Fax 01/660-8496. www.doylehotels.ie. 504 units. TV TEL. £164–£268 ($229.60–$375.20) double. Children under 7 stay free in parents' room. Rates include full breakfast. AE, DC, MC, V. Free parking. Bus: 10 or 18.

A favorite headquarters for conventions, meetings, conferences, and group tours, this is the largest hotel in Ireland. It's a block south of the Grand Canal, in a fashionable residential section within walking distance of St. Stephen's Green. The modern, crisply furnished seven-story property is constantly being refurbished. Guest rooms are outfitted with brass-bound oak furniture and designer fabrics. The connecting units are ideal for families.

Dining/Diversions: Choices include the Sussex, a large formal dining room; a buffet restaurant; and a coffee shop. For a real Old Dublin pub atmosphere, try Buck Mulligans, which serves a carvery-style lunch (read: lots of meat) and light evening meals as well as drinks. Annabel's is the basement-level nightclub. From May to early October, the main ballroom stages Doyle's Irish Cabaret, a 3-hour dinner show.

Amenities: 24-hour room service, concierge, valet and laundry service, foreign-currency exchange, underground and outdoor parking, gift shops, newsstand, hairdressing salons.

Jurys Hotel and Towers. Pembroke Rd., Ballsbridge, Dublin 4. ☎ **800/843-3311** from the U.S., or 01/660-5000/667-0033. Fax 01/660-5540. www.jurys.com. 394 units. AC MINIBAR TV TEL. Main hotel £195 ($273) double; Towers wing £220 ($308) double. Towers wing rates include continental breakfast. Service charge 12.5%. AE, DC, MC, V. Limited free parking. DART: Lansdowne Rd. Bus: 5, 7, 7A, or 8.

Ballsbridge/Embassy Row Area Accommodations

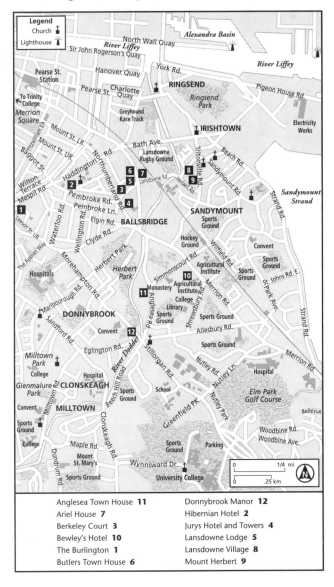

Legend
Church ✝
Lighthouse ⚓

Anglesea Town House **11**
Ariel House **7**
Berkeley Court **3**
Bewley's Hotel **10**
The Burlington **1**
Butlers Town House **6**
Donnybrook Manor **12**
Hibernian Hotel **2**
Jurys Hotel and Towers **4**
Lansdowne Lodge **5**
Lansdowne Village **8**
Mount Herbert **9**

Setting a progressive tone in a city steeped in tradition, this massive hotel, which enjoyed a major refurbishment in 1999, welcomes guests to a skylit, three-story atrium lobby with a marble and teak decor. Situated opposite the American Embassy, this sprawling property is actually two interconnected hotels in one: a modern, eight-story high-rise and a 100-unit tower with its own check-in desk, separate elevators, and private entrance, as well as full access to all the main hotel's amenities. The guest rooms in the main wing have dark wood furnishings, brass trim, and designer fabrics. The Towers section is an exclusive wing of oversized concierge-style rooms with bay windows. Each unit has computer-card key access, stocked minibar, three telephone lines, well-lit work area with desk, reclining chair, tile and marble bathroom, walk-in closet, and either a king- or queen-size bed. Decor varies, from contemporary light woods with floral fabrics to dark tones with Far Eastern motifs. Towers guests also enjoy exclusive use of a private hospitality lounge with library, boardroom, and access to complimentary continental breakfast, daily newspapers, and coffee/tea service throughout the day.

Dining/Diversions: Choices include the Embassy Garden for Irish and Continental cuisine; the Kish for seafood; and the Coffee Dock, an around-the-clock coffee shop. This is also the home of Jurys Irish Cabaret show, Ireland's longest-running evening entertainment; the Dubliner Bar, a pub with a turn-of-the century theme; and the skylit Pavilion Lounge, overlooking the indoor/outdoor pool.

Amenities: 24-hour room service, concierge, foreign-currency exchange, valet and laundry service, safe-deposit boxes, express checkout, heated indoor/outdoor pool, therapeutic hot whirlpool, hairdressing salons, craft and clothes shops, Aer Lingus ticket office.

EXPENSIVE

✪ **Ariel House.** 50/52 Lansdowne Rd., Ballsbridge, Dublin 4. ☎ **01/ 668-5512.** Fax 01/668-5845. 28 units. TV TEL. £136–£158 ($190.40–$221.20) double. MC, V. Closed Dec 23–Jan 9. Free parking. DART: Lansdowne Rd. Bus: 7, 7A, 8, or 45.

Ariel House, a bastion of distinction and quality, sets the standard for Dublin guesthouses. Michael and Maurice O'Brien are warm and consummate hosts. Opened over 25 years ago by Dublin-born and San Francisco–trained hotelier Michael

O'Brien, Ariel House has been expanded and enhanced over the years. At its core is a historic mid–19th-century mansion. The Victorian-style drawing room has Waterford glass chandeliers, an open fireplace, and delicately carved cornices. Guest rooms are individually decorated with period furniture, fine paintings and watercolors, and crisp Irish linens, as well as modern extras such as a hair dryer, garment press, tea/coffeemaker, and iron and ironing board. Ariel House is 1 block from the DART station.

Dining/Diversions: The conservatory-style dining room serves breakfast, morning coffee, and afternoon tea, and there's a wine bar.

Butlers Town House. 44 Lansdowne Rd., Ballsbridge, Dublin 4. ☎ **800/ 44-UTELL** from the U.S., or 01/667-4022. Fax 01/667-3960. www.butlers-hotel.com. 19 units. A/C TV TEL. £90–£180 ($126–$252) double. Rates include full breakfast. AE, DC, MC, V. Closed Dec 24–27. DART: Lansdowne Rd. Bus: 7, 7A, 8, or 45.

This beautifully restored and expanded Victorian town house opened its doors to guests in 1997. The aim is formal yet welcoming elegance, class without the starched collar. Rooms are richly furnished with four-poster or half-tester beds, and equipped with computer modems and individual climate control activated from a handheld remote. It's hard to elude comfort here, and the staff is especially solicitous. One room is equipped for travelers with disabilities. The gem here, in our opinion, is the Glendalough Room, which can be requested if you book early. The hotel offers free tea and coffee all day.

Dining: Breakfast, afternoon tea, and high tea are served in the atrium dining room.

Amenities: Room service (offering a limited dinner menu), baby-sitting, laundry/dry cleaning, secretarial services.

Hibernian Hotel. Eastmoreland Place, Ballsbridge, Dublin 4. ☎ **800/ 525-4800** from the U.S., or 01/668-7666. Fax 01/660-2655. www.hibernian-hotel.com. 40 units. TV TEL. £150–£170 ($210–$238) double; £185 ($259) junior suite. No service charge. AE, CB, DC, MC, V. Free valet parking. Bus: 10.

Although the name is similar, this is not a reincarnation of the legendary Royal Hibernian Hotel that stood on Dawson Street until the early 1980s. This handsome four-story Victorian building was originally part of Baggot Street Hospital. After a complete restoration, it opened as a hotel in 1993, and offers up-to-date comforts with the charm of a country inn. In 1995, it became a member of Small Luxury Hotels of the

World, and in 1997, it was named its Hotel of the Year. Antiques, graceful pillars, and floral arrangements fill the public areas. The top floor sports a beautifully restored dome-shaped skylight. The guest rooms, of varying size and layout, are outfitted with orthopedic beds and individually decorated with dark woods, floral fabrics, and specially commissioned paintings of Dublin and wildlife scenes. There's one floor for nonsmokers. In-room conveniences include a full-length mirror, garment press, hair dryer, and tea/coffeemaker. Unlike some converted 19th-century buildings, it has an elevator.

Dining/Diversions: On the lobby level are a cozy, parlor-like bar and a conservatory-style restaurant.

Amenities: 24-hour room service, concierge, access to nearby health club (extra fee), laundry/dry cleaning, 24-hour butler, turndown service, baby-sitting, secretarial services, express checkout.

MODERATE

Anglesea Town House. 63 Anglesea Rd., Ballsbridge, Dublin 4. ☎ 01/668-3877. Fax 01/668-3461. 7 units. TV TEL. £90–£100 ($126–$140) double. No service charge. Rates include full breakfast. AE, MC, V. DART: Lansdowne Rd. Bus: 10, 46A, 46B, 63, or 84.

A true bed-and-breakfast experience is the best way to describe this 1903 Edwardian-style guesthouse. Close to the Royal Dublin Showgrounds and the American Embassy, it is furnished with comfort in mind—rocking chairs, settees, a sundeck, and lots of flowering plants, as well as modern conveniences in the guest rooms. You can count on a warm welcome from hostess Helen Kirrane, and the homemade breakfast is worth getting up for.

Lansdowne Lodge. 6 Lansdowne Terrace, Shelbourne Rd., Ballsbridge, Dublin 4. ☎ 01/660-5755. Fax 01/660-5662. www.dublinhotels.com. 12 units. TV TEL. £50–£140 ($70–$196) double. Service charge 10%. Rates include full breakfast. MC, V. Free parking. DART: Lansdowne Rd. Bus: 5, 7, or 8.

With a lovely two-story brick facade, this guesthouse enjoys a convenient location, between Lansdowne and Haddington Roads, and within a block of the DART station and major bus routes. Owner Finbarr Smyth offers a variety of individually styled rooms with armchairs and homey furnishings, including decorative bed coverings and framed paintings. All the recently renovated guest rooms have firm beds; nonsmoking rooms are available. There's a garden on the grounds.

Mount Herbert. 7 Herbert Rd., Ballsbridge, Dublin 4. ☎ **01/668-4321.** Fax 01/660-7077. www.mountherberthotel.ie. 185 units. TV TEL. £69–£99 ($96.60–$138.60) double. No service charge. AE, DC, MC, V. Free parking available only to 100 cars. DART: Lansdowne Rd. Bus: 2, 3, 5, 7, 7A, 8, 18, or 45.

Over 40 years ago, the Loughran family welcomed their first guests to what had once been the family home of Lord Robinson. The gracious residence, with its own mature floodlit gardens, now forms the core of a somewhat-sprawling complex. The Mount Herbert has expanded from 4 guest rooms to 185, and the result is a curious mix of family hospitality and large-scale uniformity. The guest rooms are bright, comfortable, and convenient to the city center, though without remarkable charm. Tea/coffee-making facilities and garment presses are standard. The property has a restaurant, a wine bar, a sauna, an indoor solarium, and a gift shop.

INEXPENSIVE

Bewley's Hotel. Merrion Rd., Ballsbridge, Dublin 4. ☎ **01/668-1111.** Fax: 01/668-1999. www.bewleyshotels.com. TV TEL. 220 units. £69 ($96.60) per room (sleeps up to 3 adults); £138 ($193.20) deluxe suite. AE, DC, MC, V. DART: Sandymount (5-min. walk). Bus: 7, 7A, 7X, 8, or 45.

The new Bewley's Hotel, located in a fashionable suburb 2 miles (3.2km) south of the city center, occupies an elegant 19th-century brick Masonic school building adjacent to the R.D.S. showgrounds and next to the British Embassy. A new wing harmonizes well with the old structure, and is indistinguishable on the interior. The hotel is an excellent value for families and groups; the only downside is its location outside the city center, a small obstacle given the frequent bus and DART service.

Public lounges and reception areas are spacious and thoughtfully restored, with mahogany wainscoting, marble paneling, and polished bronze creating a formal ambience. Rooms, too, are spacious and generously furnished—each has a writing desk, an armchair, a trouser press, tea/coffee facilities, and either a king bed or a double and a twin bed. Bathrooms are medium in size. The suites include an additional room with foldout couch, table (seats six), a tiny kitchen/bar cleverly hidden in a cabinet, and an additional bathroom (shower only). A basement restaurant (O'Connell's) is run by the Allen family of Ballymaloe fame, and offers very good food at reasonable prices; there's also an informal Bewley's tearoom.

SELF-CATERING

Donnybrook Manor. Donnybrook Manor, Donnybrook, Dublin 4. ☎ **01/ 676-6784.** Fax 01/676-6868. www.dubchamber.ie/brookman. 20 units. TV TEL. £650–£1,750 ($910–$2,450) per week. AE, DC, MC, V. Bus: 10, 46A, or 46B.

Donnybrook Manor, a community of tasteful red-brick town houses with stained-glass doors, is strategically situated in Donnybrook, a 25-minute walk from Grafton Street and College Green. Set well back from Donnybrook Road (N11) in its own parklands, the town houses are all but oblivious of the surrounding city. Each two-, three-, or four-bedroom unit comes complete with virtually every appliance and convenience you could want in a home-away-from-home. This is an attractive, cost-efficient alternative to a hotel or guesthouse for couples, families, or groups who will be in Dublin for 4 or more days. Rates vary depending on the size of the apartment and the season. The immediate environs are thick with exceptional gourmet shops. You can also order out or walk to a range of fine restaurants. Each town house has its own enclosed garden, complete with table and chairs. Cots, cribs, and high chairs are available.

Lansdowne Village. Newbridge Ave. (off Lansdowne Rd.), Ballsbridge, Dublin 4. ☎ **01/ 668-3534.** Fax 01/660-6465. 19 units. TV TEL. £400–£595 ($560–$833) per week, depending on size of apt and season. Shorter periods available at reduced rates Oct–Mar. MC, V. DART to Lansdowne Rd. Station. Bus: 2, 3, 5, 7, 7A, 8, 18, or 45.

Lansdowne Village is a modest and appealing residential development on the banks of the River Dodder, directly across from Lansdowne Stadium. Within this community, Trident Holiday Homes offers fully equipped two- and three-bedroom rental units, each with a pull-out double-bed sofa in the living room. They are bright and comfortable, well maintained so that everything really works. The location is ideal—a 5-minute walk from the DART and less than a half-hour's walk from St. Stephen's Green, but only 10 minutes from the Sandymount Strand, a favorite walking spot for Dubliners that's perfect for an after-dinner stroll. There are several shops and supermarkets nearby, so you can manage quite well without a car. The smaller units are perfect for couples, perhaps with one child; the considerably more spacious three-bedroom units are recommended for larger families or for more than one couple.

5   O'Connell Street Area/North of the Liffey
VERY EXPENSIVE
The Gresham. 23 Upper O'Connell St., Dublin 1. ☎ **01/874-6881.** Fax 01/878-7175. E-mail: ryan@indigo.ie. 288 units. AC TV TEL. £180–£280 ($252–$392) double. Rates include service charge and full breakfast. AE, DC, MC, V. Parking £5 ($7). DART: Connolly. Bus: 40A, 40B, 40C, or 51A.

Centrally located on the city's main business thoroughfare, this Regency-style hotel is one of Ireland's oldest (established in 1817) and best-known lodgings. Although much of the tourist trade in Dublin has shifted south of the River Liffey in recent years, the Gresham is still synonymous with stylish Irish hospitality. It provides easy access to the Abbey and Gate theaters and other northside attractions. The lobby and public areas are a panorama of marble floors, molded plasterwork, and crystal chandeliers. With high ceilings and individual decor, the older guest rooms vary in size and style; all have soft lighting, tile bathrooms, and period furniture, including padded headboards and armoires. Quite recently, 100 new air-conditioned superior rooms were added in the Lavery Wing. Nonsmoking rooms are available. One-of-a-kind luxury terrace suites grace the upper front floors.

Dining/Diversions: The Aberdeen Restaurant serves formal meals; Toddy's, a trendy pub and lounge, offers light meals all day. Another bar, Magnums, attracts a late-night crowd.

Amenities: 24-hour room service, concierge, fitness center, conference rooms, well-equipped business center, ISDN/modem facilities, valet/laundry, baby-sitting, foreign-currency exchange.

EXPENSIVE
Royal Dublin. 40 Upper O'Connell St., Dublin 1. ☎ **800/528-1234** from the U.S., or 01/873-3666. Fax 01/873-3120. www.royaldublin.com. 117 units. TV TEL. £105–£154 ($147–$215.60) double. Rates include full Irish breakfast and service charge. AE, DC, MC, V. Free parking; secure car park available nearby. DART: Connolly. Bus: 36A, 40A, 40B, 40C, or 51A.

Romantically floodlit at night, this modern five-story hotel is near Parnell Square at the north end of Dublin's main thoroughfare, within walking distance of all the main theaters and northside attractions. The contemporary skylit lobby lies adjacent to lounge areas that were part of the original 1752 building. These Georgian-themed rooms are rich in high molded ceilings, ornate cornices, crystal chandeliers, gilt-edged mirrors, and open fireplaces. Guest rooms are strictly modern, with light woods, pastel fabrics, and three-sided full-length windows that extend over the busy street below. Corridors are extremely well lit, with lights at each doorway.

Dining/Diversions: The Cafe Royale Brasserie, for full meals; Raffles Bar, a clubby room with portraits of Irish literary greats, for snacks or drinks; the Georgian Lounge, for morning coffee or afternoon tea beside the open fireplace.

Amenities: 24-hour room service, concierge, laundry, foreign-currency exchange, car-rental desk, baby-sitting.

MODERATE

✪ **Chief O'Neill's.** Smithfield Village, Dublin 1. ☎ **01/817-3838.** Fax 01/817-3839. www.chiefoneills.com. 73 units. TV TEL. £125 ($175) twin or double room; £295 ($413) penthouse suites. Rates include service charge. AE, MC, V. Free parking. Bus: 25, 25A, 67, 67A, 68, 69, 79, or 90.

Chief O'Neill's is the centerpiece of Smithfield Village, a 2.5-acre "cultural urban village" newly created north of the Liffey just in from the Four Courts. The operative word throughout the village is music, traditional Irish music. This is home as well to Ceol, the Old Jameson Distillery, and The Chimney (see chapter 5). There's plenty to do here; and, when you've done it all, you're only 15 minutes on foot from Temple Bar.

The rooms here quite defy description. Think primary colors, glass, light wood, chrome, Zen, and the Starship *Enterprise,* and you're part way there. Nothing scary, just a bit bold and very comfortable. There's nothing else quite like Chief O'Neill's in Dublin, and it's sure to intrigue anyone able to spend a night without a trace of anything Georgian or Victorian. Firm beds with duvets are the solid norm; coffeemakers, hair dryers, CD players, and high-speed ISDN connections are all standard. The penthouses have raised lounge areas, Jacuzzis, and rooftop balconies. One entire floor (19 rooms) is nonsmoking, and 4 rooms are specially adapted for guests with disabilities. Chief O'Neill's Bar (featuring live Irish music most summer nights) and the Kelly and Ping Bar and Restaurant are popular destinations in themselves, as is the adjacent upscale Duck Lane shopping complex.

INEXPENSIVE

Jurys Inn Custom House. Custom House Quay, Dublin 1. ☎ **800/44-UTELL** from the U.S., or 01/607-5000. Fax 01/829-0400. www.jurys.com.

239 units. A/C TV TEL. £69 ($96.60) single, double, or family room. Rates include service charge. Full Irish breakfast £6.50 ($9.10). AE, CB, DC, MC, V. Discounted parking available at adjacent lot (£6.40/$8.96 for 24 hr.). DART: Tara Street. Bus: 27A, 27B, or 53A.

Ensconced in the grandiose new financial services district and facing the quays on which generations of Irish émigrés tore themselves from their mother soil, this the newest of the Jurys Inns looks out on both the old and the new Ireland. Following the successful Jurys formula of affordable convenience and comfort without frills, Jurys Inn Custom House provides rooms to meet most needs at one unprovocative price. Single rooms have a double bed and a pull-out sofa, while double rooms offer both a double and a twin bed. Twenty-two especially spacious rooms, if available, cost nothing extra. An ample number of nonsmoking rooms and handicapped-adapted rooms are also available. Rooms facing the quays also enjoy vistas of the Dublin hills, while those facing the financial district tend to be more quiet. All have coffeemakers, hair dryers, and modem connections. Facilities include a moderately priced restaurant, a pub lounge, and an adjacent multistory parking area. As occupancy runs at 100% from May to September and at roughly 95% for the rest of the year, be sure to book well in advance. The hotel lies a 5-minute walk from the Custom House east along Custom House Quay. Be sure to notice the painfully poignant Famine Memorial along the same quay.

Mount Eccles Court Hostel and Self-Catering Apartments. 42 N. Great George's St., Dublin 1. ☎ **01/873-0826.** Fax 01/878-3554. E-mail: info@eccleshostel.com. 10 units, 8 with private bathroom; 16 dorm units, 4 with private bathroom. £36 ($50.40) double without bathroom, £40 ($56) double with bathroom; £12.50–£15 ($17.50–$21) per person in 4-bed dorm; £10–£11 ($14–$15.40) per person in 6- to 16-bed dorm. Self-catering units £340–£440 ($476–$616) per week. MC, V. Hostel rates include continental breakfast. Bus: 1, 40A, 40B, 40C, or 41 (from the airport). 1 block east of Parnell Sq. E., at the top of O'Connell St.

If you're intrigued by the architecture of Georgian Dublin, you'll love this place. North Great George's Street comprises a short row of beautiful Georgian town houses—the splendid house that's now the James Joyce Centre is adjacent to the hostel. The massive building, constructed as a convent, has been renovated into accommodations over the past few years. The rooms in front have somewhat more appealing views than those in back, which look out on a parking lot. The first floor has a large sitting room with high ceilings, intricate plaster-work, and massive windows. Breakfast is served in a dark but atmospheric basement room with stone walls. The owners recently renovated four magnificent rooms in an adjacent town house as luxury self-catering apartments. Each has a loft sleeping area, small but well-stocked kitchen, bathroom, and hide-a-bed couch.

4

Dining

*Y*ou're here. You're famished. Where do you go? A formal, old-world hotel dining room? Perhaps a casual bistro or wine bar? Ethnic cuisine, maybe? Dublin has the goods, across a wide range of price categories. Expect generally higher prices than you'd pay for comparable fare in a comparable U.S. city. (Hey, Dublin's hip—you always pay for hip.) As befits a European capital, there's plenty of Continental cuisine, with a particular leaning toward French and Italian influences. The city has a fine selection of international restaurants, with menus from Scandinavia, Russia, the Mediterranean, and China, and even exotic fare from someplace called California.

Meal prices at restaurants include a 12.5% VAT, but the service charge is extra. In perhaps half of all restaurants, a set service charge is added automatically; it can range from 10% to 15%. In the remaining restaurants, it is now the custom not to add any service charge, leaving the amount of the tip up to you. This can be confusing for a visitor, but each restaurant normally prints its policy on the menu. If it is not clear, ask.

When no service charge is added, tip as you normally would in the United States, up to 15% depending on the quality of the service. If 10% to 12.5% has already been added to your bill, leave an appropriate amount that will total 15% if service has been satisfactory.

Some restaurants offer a fixed-price three-course tourist menu during certain hours and days. These menus offer limited choices, but are usually lower in price than the restaurant's regular table d'hôte menu. Look for a tourist menu with a green Irish chef symbol in the window, listing the choices and the hours when the prices are in effect.

1 Historic Old City/Liberties Area

MODERATE

Lord Edward. 23 Christ Church Place, Dublin 8. ☎ **01/454-2420.** Reservations required. Main courses £9.95–£15.95 ($13.95–$22.35); fixed-price

Dublin Dining

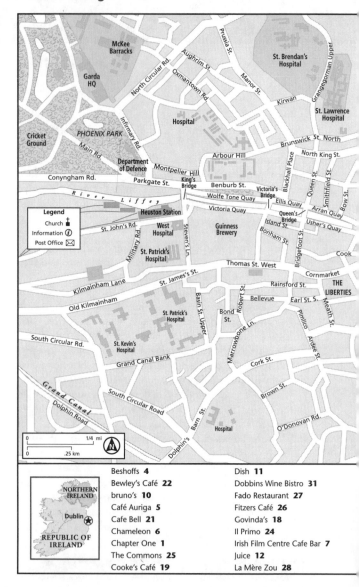

Legend
- Church ✝
- Information ⓘ
- Post Office ✉

McKee Barracks
Garda HQ
Prussia St.
St. Brendan's Hospital
Aughrim St.
North Circular Rd.
Oxmantown Rd.
Manor St.
Kirwan
Grangegorman Upper
St. Lawrence Hospital
Infirmary Rd.
Hospital
Brunswick St. North
North King St.
Arbour Hill
Blackhall Place
Queen St.
Smithfield St.
Bow St.
Cricket Ground
PHOENIX PARK
Main Rd.
Department of Defence
Montpelier Hill
King's Bridge
Benburb St.
Victoria's Bridge
Ellis Quay
Arran Quay
Conyngham Rd.
Parkgate St.
Wolfe Tone Quay
Queen's Bridge
Usher's Quay
River Liffey
Victoria Quay
Island St.
Bridgefoot St.
Cook
Heuston Station
St. John's Rd.
West Hospital
Steven's Ln.
Guinness Brewery
Bonham St.
Cornmarket
THE LIBERTIES
Military Rd.
St. Patrick's Hospital
Thomas St. West
Rainsford St.
Robert St.
Earl St. S.
Meath St.
Kilmainham Lane
St. James's St.
Bellevue
Pimlico
Ardee St.
Old Kilmainham
St. Patrick's Hospital
Basin St. Upper
Bond St.
South Circular Rd.
St. Kevin's Hospital
Cork St.
Grand Canal Bank
Marrowbone Ln.
Brown St.
Grand Canal
South Circular Road
Barn St.
Dolphin Road
Hospital
Dolphin's
O'Donovan Rd.

0 — 1/4 mi
0 — .25 km

NORTHERN IRELAND
Dublin ★
REPUBLIC OF IRELAND

Beshoffs **4**
Bewley's Café **22**
bruno's **10**
Café Auriga **5**
Cafe Bell **21**
Chameleon **6**
Chapter One **1**
The Commons **25**
Cooke's Café **19**

Dish **11**
Dobbins Wine Bistro **31**
Fado Restaurant **27**
Fitzers Café **26**
Govinda's **18**
Il Primo **24**
Irish Film Centre Cafe Bar **7**
Juice **12**
La Mère Zou **28**

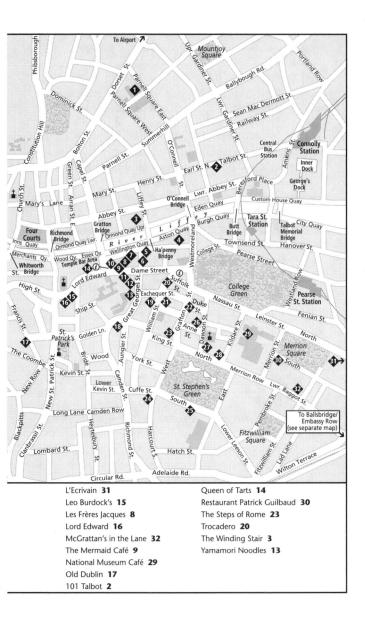

L'Ecrivain **31**	Queen of Tarts **14**
Leo Burdock's **15**	Restaurant Patrick Guilbaud **30**
Les Frères Jacques **8**	The Steps of Rome **23**
Lord Edward **16**	Trocadero **20**
McGrattan's in the Lane **32**	The Winding Stair **3**
The Mermaid Café **9**	Yamamori Noodles **13**
National Museum Café **29**	
Old Dublin **17**	
101 Talbot **2**	

dinner £20 ($28). AE, CB, DC, MC, V. Mon–Fri noon–10:45pm; Sat 6–10:45pm. Closed Dec 24–Jan 3. Bus: 50, 54A, 56A, 65, 65A, 77, 77A, 123, or 150. SEAFOOD.

Established in 1890 and situated in the heart of the Old City opposite Christ Church Cathedral, this cozy upstairs dining room claims to be Dublin's oldest seafood restaurant. A dozen preparations of sole, including au gratin and Veronique, are served; there are many variations of prawns, from thermidor to Provençal; and fresh lobster is prepared au naturel or in sauces. Fresh fish—from salmon and sea trout to plaice and turbot—is served grilled, fried, meunière, or poached. Vegetarian dishes are also available. At lunch, light snacks and simpler fare are served in the bar.

The Mermaid Cafe. 69/70 Dame St., Dublin 2. ☎ **01/670-8236.** Reservations recommended. Dinner main courses £13.95–£18.95 ($19.55–$26.55). MC, V. Mon–Sat 12:30–2:30pm and 6–10:30pm; Sun noon–2:30pm and 6–9pm. Bus: 50, 50A, 54, 56A, 77, 77A, or 77B. IRISH/CONTINENTAL.

The Mermaid Cafe is a small place with a big reputation. Like the mild-mannered reporter for the *Daily Planet,* this could be something very ordinary. But it's not. The food here is consistently remarkable. The combination of ingredients and the blending of spices are, on paper, rather boldly inventive; and yet the resulting dishes are subtle and harmonious. As a starter, the beetroot, quail egg, and baby spinach salad offers a good launch without threatening your appetite, though the paprika smoked chicken with avocado and cilantro (especially when combined with the dangerously appealing assortment of freshly baked breads) may leave you with the will but not the room for the generous entrees soon to emerge from the kitchen. The grilled swordfish with mango relish, the roast duck breast on curried noodles, the wild salmon, and the chargrilled monkfish are all flawlessly prepared and quite memorable. After all that, we won't admit to having had dessert, but you won't be disappointed if you succumb. Complimentary caramelized pecans prove a tasty final touch. The Mermaid continues to live up to her reputation.

Old Dublin. 90/91 Francis St., Dublin 8. ☎ **01/454-2028.** Reservations recommended. Fixed-price lunch £13.50 ($18.90); fixed-price dinner £21 ($29.40). Main courses £11.50–£15.50 ($16.10–$21.70). AE, DC, MC, V. Mon–Fri 12:30–2:15pm; Mon–Sat 6–11pm. Bus: 21A, 78A, or 78B. SCANDINAVIAN/ RUSSIAN.

In the heart of Dublin's antiques row, this restaurant is also on the edge of the city's medieval quarter, once settled by Vikings. It's not surprising, therefore, that many recipes reflect this background, with a long list of imaginative Scandinavian and Russian dishes. Among the best entrees are fillet of beef *Novgorod,* rare beef thinly sliced and served on sauerkraut with fried barley, mushrooms, garlic butter, sour cream, and caviar; salmon *Kulebjaka,* a pastry filled with salmon, dill herbs, rice, egg, mushrooms, and onion; and black sole *Metsa,* filled with mussels and served with prawn butter and white wine. There's a varied selection of vegetarian dishes.

INEXPENSIVE

Govinda's. 4 Aungier St., Dublin 2. ☎ **01/475-0309.** Main courses £4.95 ($6.95); soup and freshly baked bread £1.75 ($2.45). MC, V. Mon–Sat noon–9pm. Closed Dec 24–Jan 2. Bus: 16, 16A, 19, or 22. VEGETARIAN.

Govinda's serves healthy square meals on square plates for very good prices. The meals are generous, belly-warming concoctions of vegetables, cheese, rice, and pasta. Two main courses are offered cafeteria-style. One is East Indian, and the other a simple, plainly flavored staple like lasagna or macaroni and cheese. Veggie burgers are also prepared to order. All are accompanied by a choice of two salads and can be enjoyed unaccompanied by smoke—the restaurant is nonsmoking throughout. Desserts are healthy and huge, like the rich wedge of carob cake with a dollop of cream or homemade ice cream (£1.50/$2.10).

✪ **Leo Burdock's.** 2 Werburgh St., Dublin 8. ☎ **01/454-0306.** Main courses £2.50–£4.50 ($3.50–$6.30). No credit cards. Mon–Sat noon–midnight; Sun 4–midnight. Bus: 21A, 50, 50A, 78, 78A, or 78B. FISH-AND-CHIPS/FAST FOOD

Established in 1913, this quintessential fish-and-chips take-out shop remains a cherished Dublin institution, despite a devastating fire in 1998. Rebuilt from the ground up, Burdock's is back. For three generations, Brian Burdock's family has served the country's best fish-and-chips. Cabinet ministers, university students, poets, Americans tipped off by locals, and almost every other type in Ireland can be found in the queue. They're waiting for fish bought fresh that morning and those good Irish potatoes, both cooked in "drippings" (none of that modern cooking oil!). Service is takeout only—there's no seating, but you can sit on a nearby bench or stroll down to the park at

---

Tea for Two

As in Britain, afternoon tea is a revered tradition in Ireland, especially in Dublin's grand hotels. Afternoon tea in its fullest form is a sit-down event and a relaxing experience, not just a quick hot beverage taken on the run.

Properly presented, afternoon tea is almost a complete meal. It includes a pot of freshly brewed tea accompanied by finger sandwiches, pastries, hot scones, cream-filled cakes, and other sweets arrayed on a silver tray. To enhance the ambience, there is often live piano or harp music. This sumptuous midafternoon pick-me-up averages £10 to £15 ($14 to $21) per person, even in the lounges of the city's best hotels.

Afternoon tea hours are usually 3 to 4:30pm. Among the hotels offering this repast are the Berkeley Court, Conrad, Davenport, Gresham, Royal Dublin, Shelbourne, and Westbury (see chapter 3 for addresses and phone numbers).

St. Patrick's Cathedral. It's across from Christchurch, around the corner from Jurys Christchurch Inn.

✪ **Queen of Tarts.** 4 Corkhill, Dublin 2. ☎ **01/670-7499.** Soup and fresh bread £2.25 ($3.15), sandwiches and savory tarts £3–£4 ($4.20–$5.60), baked goods and cakes 50p–£3 (70¢–$4.20). No credit cards. Mon–Fri 7:30am–7pm, Sat 9am–6pm, Sun 10am–6pm. Bus: Any city-center bus. TEA SHOP.

This tearoom is David to the Goliath of Irish tearooms (Bewley's, see below), but its small physical size packs a solid pie-filled punch. Tarts of ham and spinach or cheddar cheese and chives can be followed up with the flaky sweetness of warm almond cranberry or blackberry pie. The scones here are tender and light, dusted with powdered sugar and accompanied by a little pot of fruit jam. The restaurant is small, smoke-free, and delicious.

2 Temple Bar/Trinity College Area
EXPENSIVE

Les Frères Jacques. 74 Dame St., Dublin 2. ☎ **01/679-4555.** Reservations recommended. Fixed-price lunch £13.50 ($18.90); fixed-price dinner £21 ($29.40). AE, DC, MC, V. Mon–Fri 12:30–2:30pm; Mon–Thurs 7:15–10:30pm; Fri–Sat 7:15–11pm. Closed Dec 24–Jan 4. Bus: 50, 50A, 54, 56, or 77. FRENCH.

Well situated between Crampton Court and Sycamore Street opposite Dublin Castle, this restaurant brings a touch of haute cuisine to the lower edge of the trendy Temple Bar district. The menu offers such entrees as Daube of beef with root vegetables, rabbit lasagne with medeira sauce, and rosette of spring lamb in meat juice sabayon and tomato coulis with crispy potato straws. You might also try veal on rainbow pasta with garlic and basil sauce, and grilled lobster (from the tank) flamed in whiskey. À la carte dishes are also available.

MODERATE

bruno's. 30 E. Essex St., Dublin 2. ☎ **01/670-6767.** Reservations recommended. Dinner main courses £10.95–£13.95 ($15.35–$19.55). Service charge 10% on tables over 4. AE, CB, DC, MC, V. Mon–Fri 12:30–10:30pm; Sat 5–10:30pm. DART to Tara St. Station. Bus: 21A, 46A, 46B, 51B, 51C, 68, 69, or 86. FRENCH/MEDITERRANEAN.

This is a sure-fire spot for a flawlessly prepared, interesting lunch or dinner without serious damage to the budget. The atmosphere is light and modern, with the focus on food that is consistently excellent without flourish or pretense. The spinach and goat cheese tart; the salad of prawns with honey, lime, sesame seeds, and jalapeño peppers; and the bruscetta of chicken are all worthy of mention. The new Millennium Bridge makes bruno's all the more convenient as it crosses the Liffey at Eustace Street, which is directly opposite the restaurant.

You can now also find a bruno's at 21 Kildare St., Dublin 2 (☎ **01/662-4724**).

Café Auriga. Temple Bar Sq., Dublin 2. ☎ **01/671-8228.** Main courses £8.95–£14.95 ($12.55–$20.95); early-bird menu (5:30–7:30pm) with 3 courses for the price of the main course £8.95–£10.50 ($12.55–$14.70). AE, MC, V. Tues–Sat 5:30–11pm. Bus: Any city-center bus. CONTEMPORARY IRISH.

Café Auriga is a stylish second-floor cafe whose main dining room overlooks Temple Bar Square. Dinner is served under a ceiling of twinkling stars and is accompanied not by the sweet serenade of a lone violinist, but by the louder melodies of Dublin's top 40. The decor is stylish and simple and the crowd young, sleek, and professional. The food demonstrates the chef's facility in combining simple ingredients to create a piquant surprise for the palate. Subtly spiced, imaginative sauces accompany well-prepared fish and meat dishes, such as salmon in ginger soy sauce or breast of chicken stuffed with basil mousse. Vegetarian offerings include a succulent tagliatelle of goat cheese, cherry tomatoes, spinach, fresh herbs, and cream.

Chameleon. 1 Fownes St. Lower, Temple Bar, Dublin 2. ☎ **01/671-0362.**
Set dinner menus £13.50–£21.50 ($18.90–$30.10); early-bird main courses
£6.50–£7 ($9.10–$9.80). MC, V. Tues–Sat 6–11:30pm; Sun 6–10pm. Bus: Any
city-center bus. INDONESIAN.

Only a dim candlelit window and an orange sign signal
Chameleon, well camouflaged on a small side street off Temple
Bar Square. Incense tinges the air, and rich Indonesian batiks
form sumptuous backdrops for the traditional puppets and
dark wood carvings that lurk in the corners. The Chameleon
offers a variety of menus that feature samplings of seven different dishes and an assortment of condiments. The staff is quick
to explain how to best complement chicken sate with roasted
peanuts. Sambal-badjak, a red curry paste, gives rice a robust,
pleasantly spicy flavor. Finally, a small morsel of pickled vegetable is also suggested as a "palate cleanser"—good advice to
swallow if you want to take advantage of the abundance of delicately flavored dishes that Chameleon has to offer.

✪ **Dish.** 2 Crow St., Dublin 2. ☎ **01/671-1248.** Reservations recommended. Lunch £10.95 ($15.35); dinner main courses £7.95–£16.95 ($11.15–
$23.75). Service charge 10% on tables of 6 or more. AE, DC, MC, V. Daily
noon–11:30pm. DART: Tara St. Bus: 21A, 46A, 46B, 51B, 51C, 68, 69, or 86.
NOUVEAU INTERNATIONAL.

With floor-to-ceiling windows, wide-beamed pine floors, light
walls, and dark blue linens, Dish presents a relaxed, tasteful
atmosphere. The menu is eclectic and enticing, with an
emphasis on fresh grilled seafood and Mediterranean flavors,
complex without being confusing. Grilled salmon with avocado, papaya, and tequila-lime dressing, baked hake, and char-
grilled tiger prawns were outstanding. The desserts we
tried—caramelized lemon tart with cassis sauce and amaretti
chocolate cheesecake—were superb. Only organic meats and
the finest fresh ingredients find their way into your dish. This
promises to be one of Temple Bar's finest venues, and at a
modest price.

Juice. Castle House, 73 S. Great George's St., Dublin 2. ☎ **01/475-7856.**
Reservations recommended Fri–Sat. Main courses £4.95–£7.25 ($6.95–
$10.15); early-bird set-price dinner (Mon–Fri 5:30–7pm) £8.95 ($12.55).
MC, V. Sun–Wed 9am–10:30pm; Thurs–Sat 5:30pm–4am. Bus: 50, 50A, 54,
56, or 77. VEGETARIAN.

Juice tempts carnivorous, vegan, macrobiotic, celiac, and yeast-
free diners alike, using organic produce to create delicious

dressings and entrees among its largely conventional but well-prepared offerings. The avocado fillet of blue cheese and broccoli wrapped in filo was superb, and I also highly recommend the spinach-and-ricotta cannelloni. The latter is included in the early-bird dinner—a great deal. Coffees, fresh-squeezed juices, organic wines, and late weekend hours add to the lure of this casual modern place, which is usually frequented by mature diners who know their food. The one anomaly here is that a restaurant so focused on health is often rather clouded in smoke.

✪ **Yamamori Noodles.** 71–2 S. Great George's St., Dublin 2. ☎ **01/ 475-5001.** Reservations only for parties of 4 or more persons. £3.50–£22 ($4.90–$30.80). MC, V. Sun–Wed 12:30–11pm; Thurs–Sat 12:30–11:30pm. Bus: 50, 50A, 54, 56, or 77. JAPANESE.

If you're still skeptical about Japanese cuisine, Yamamori will make you an instant believer. In a pop, casual, and exuberant atmosphere in which conversation becomes an unwarranted distraction from the fare, you may just be startled by how good the food is here. The splendid menu is a who's who of Japanese cuisine, and the prices range from budget to the big splurge. Regardless of the bottom line, however, everyone goes away feeling full and feted. It's difficult not to rave. On a raw, drizzly Dublin day, the chili chicken ramen is best summed up as a pot of bliss, while the Yamamori Yaki Soba offers, in a mound of wok-fried noodles, a well-rewarded treasure hunt for prawns, squid, chicken, and roast pork. And vegetarians will feel far from overlooked. The keywords here are freshness and perfection. The selective international wine list is well-suited to the cuisine. At 9:30pm on a Monday night, this place was jammed, not by tourists but by local Dubs, which among other things, tells you that the secret is out.

INEXPENSIVE

Irish Film Centre Cafe Bar. 6 Eustace St., Temple Bar, Dublin 2. ☎ **01/ 677-8788.** Lunch and dinner £5–£8 ($7–$11.20). MC, V. Mon–Fri 12:30–3pm; Sat–Sun 1–3pm; daily 6–9pm. Bus: 21A, 78A, or 78B. IRISH/INTERNATIONAL.

One of the most popular drinking spots in Temple Bar, the Cafe Bar features an excellent menu that changes daily. A vegetarian and Middle-Eastern menu is available for both lunch and dinner. The weekend entertainment usually includes music or comedy.

3   St. Stephen's Green/Grafton Street Area

EXPENSIVE

The Commons. 86 St. Stephen's Green, Dublin 2. ☎ **01/475-2597** or
01/478-0530. Reservations required. Fixed-price lunch £22 ($30.80); main-
courses £20–£23 ($28–$32.20). AE, DC, MC, V. Mon–Fri 12:30–3pm; Mon–Sat
7:30–10:30pm. Closed 2 weeks after Christmas and first 2 weeks in Aug. DART:
Pearse. Bus: 10, 11, 13, or 46A. MODERN EUROPEAN.

Nestled on the south side of St. Stephen's Green, this Miche-
lin-starred restaurant occupies the basement level of Newman
House, the historic seat of Ireland's major university. The din-
ing-room decor blends Georgian architecture, cloister-style
arches, and original contemporary artwork with Joycean influences. For a cocktail in fine weather, a "secret garden" of lush
plants and trees surrounds the lovely stone courtyard terrace.
The inventive menu changes daily, but you'll often see dishes
such as magret of duck flavored with honey and spices, grilled
shark with peppered carrot, and loin of rabbit with a stuffing
of marinated prune.

EXPENSIVE/MODERATE

Cookes Café. 14 S. William St., Dublin 2. ☎ **01/679-0536.** Reservations
required. Fixed-price lunch menu £14.95 ($20.95); early-bird menu 6–7:30pm
£14.95 ($20.95); dinner main courses £10–£18 ($14–$25.20). Service charge
12.5%. AE, DC, MC, V. Daily 12:30–3pm; Mon–Sat 6–11pm; Sun 6–10pm.
DART: Tara St. Bus: 16A, 19A, 22A, 55, or 83. CALIFORNIAN/MEDITERRANEAN.

Named for owner and chef Johnny Cooke, this shop-front
restaurant is a longtime Dublin favorite. The open kitchen
and murals dominate the room; there is also an outdoor seating area with antique tables and chairs. House specialties
include grilled duck with pancetta, marsala balsamic sauce,
and wilted endive; sautéed brill and Dover sole with capers
and croutons; and baked grouper with a ragoût of mussels,
clams, artichokes, and tomatoes.

Fado Restaurant. Mansion House, Dawson St., Dublin 2. ☎ **01/676-7200.**
Reservations required. Fixed-price 2-course lunch £11 ($15.40); fixed-price 3-
course dinner £25 ($35); dinner main courses £11–£19.50 ($15.40–$27.30).
No service charge except for larger parties. AE, MC, V. Daily 11am–10pm.
DART: Pearse St. Bus: 10, 11A, 11B, 13, or 20B. CONTINENTAL.

On a bright sunny day or a balmy summer evening (they do
happen in Ireland!), the spacious veranda of this eccentric Ital-
ianate venue is simply the place to be. In the nastiest of weather, too, Fado's whimsically painted vaulted Victorian dining

room puts the damp far out of mind. Everything about this place suggests "occasion," so you may want to save it for such, or just conjure one on the spot. The menu is enticingly diverse. Neither rich sauces nor bistro austerities prevail. Portion sizes vary greatly in scale from one entree to another, so ask directions, as the service is excellent. We found the terrine of chicken and pistachios, the oven-baked seafood, the braised shank of Irish lamb, and the panfried fusilli with tarragon cream all to be flawless. Finishing with the fudge terrine garnished with double cream and fresh red currants proved deliciously daunting. The international wine list is judicious and contains some bright surprises, like the Stonleigh sauvignon blanc, an inspired choice from New Zealand.

La Mère Zou. 22 St. Steven's Green, Dublin 2. ☎ **01/661-6669.** Reservations recommended. Fixed-price lunch £11.50 ($16.10); early-bird dinner menu £13.50 ($18.90); dinner main courses £9.50–£17.50 ($13.30–$24.50). AE, CB, DC, MC, V. Mon–Fri 12:30–2:30pm; Mon–Thurs 6–10:30pm; Fri–Sat 6–11pm; Sun 6–9:30pm. DART: Pearse. Bus: 10, 11A, 11B, 13, or 20B. FRENCH COUNTRY.

Chef-proprietor Eric Tydgadt has created a warm, comfortable Mediterranean ambience in which to savor his fresh French country specialties. They evoke memories of superb Gallic cooking *en famille.* The emphasis is on perfectly cooked food accompanied by persuasive but "unarmed" sauces served in an unpretentious manner. Mussels are a house specialty, with an array of poultry, seafood, lamb, and game offerings. The quality of ingredients and attention to enhancing the flavor of all dishes is consistent from appetizers to dessert. The excellent wine list favors the French, but also includes several £10 ($14) house wines.

MODERATE

✪ **Fitzers Café.** 51a Dawson St., Dublin 2. ☎ **01/677-1155.** Reservations recommended. Dinner main courses £9.95–£15.95 ($13.95–$22.35). AE, DC, MC, V. Daily noon–11pm. Closed Dec 24–27 and Good Friday. DART: Pearse. Bus: 10, 11A, 11B, 13, or 20B. INTERNATIONAL.

Wedged in the middle of a busy shopping street, this bright, airy Irish-style bistro has a multiwindowed facade and modern decor. The excellent, reasonably priced food is contemporary and quickly served. Choices range from chicken breast with hot chili cream sauce or brochette of lamb tandoori with mild curry sauce to gratin of smoked cod. There are also tempting vegetarian dishes made from organic produce.

Picnic, Anyone?

The parks of Dublin offer plenty of sylvan settings for a picnic lunch; so feel free to park it on a bench, or pick a grassy patch and spread a blanket. In particular, try **St. Stephen's Green** at lunchtime (in the summer there are open-air band concerts), the **Phoenix Park,** and **Merrion Square.** You can also take a ride on the DART to the suburbs of **Dun Laoghaire, Dalkey, Killiney,** and **Bray** (to the south) or **Howth** (to the north) and picnic along a bayfront pier or promenade.

In recent years, some fine delicatessens and gourmet food shops ideal for picnic fare have sprung up. For the best selection of fixings, we recommend the following: **Gallic Kitchen,** 49 Francis St., Dublin 8 (☎ **01/454-4912**), has gourmet prepared food to go, from salmon en croûte to pastries filled with meats or vegetables, pâtés, quiches, sausage rolls, and homemade pies, breads, and cakes. **Magills Delicatessen,** 14 Clarendon St., Dublin 2 (☎ **01/671-3830**), offers Asian and Continental delicacies, meats, cheeses, spices, and salads. For a fine selection of Irish cheeses, luncheon meat, and other delicacies, seek out **Sheridan's Cheesemongers,** 11 S. Anne St., Dublin 2 (☎ **01/ 679-3143**), perhaps the best of Dublin's cheese emporiums, or the **Big Cheese Company,** 14/15 Trinity St. (☎ **01/671 1399**).

Fitzers has several other Dublin locations, including one just a few blocks away at the National Gallery, Merrion Square West (☎ **01/661-4496**); another in Ballsbridge, at 51 Dawson St. (☎ **01/677-1155**); and Fitzers Café at Temple Bar Square (☎ **01/679-0440**). Consistency is the operative word—count on Fitzers not to disappoint.

✪ **Il Primo.** 16 Montague St. (off Harcourt St.), Dublin 2. ☎ **01/ 478-3373.** Reservations required on weekends. Dinner main courses £8.90– £15.90 ($12.45–$22.25). AE, CB, DC, MC, V. Mon–Fri noon–3pm and Mon– Sat 6–11pm. MODERN ITALIAN.

Word of mouth is what brought me to Il Primo, and it's a good thing, because I doubt I would have found it myself. It's tucked away off Harcourt Street, 50 yards down from St. Stephen's Green. Once inside, you'll find some of the most distinguished, innovative Italian cuisine this side of Rome and Tuscany. Awaken your palate with a glass of sparkling Venetian prosecco; begin with a plate of Parma ham, avocado, and balsamic vinaigrette; and then go for broke with ravioli *Il Primo*—an open handkerchief of pasta over chicken, Parma ham, and mushrooms in a light tarragon cream sauce. The proprietor, Dieter Bergmann, will assist you in selecting appropriate wines, all of which he personally chooses and imports from Tuscany. Wines are available by the milliliter, not the bottle. Open any bottle and you pay for only what you drink. Il Primo is full of surprises. And if you head north, there's no need to leave Il Primo behind—Bergmann has two branches in Belfast with the same menu as the Dublin original.

Trocadero. 3 St. Andrew St., Dublin 2. ☎ **01/677-5545.** Reservations recommended. Early-bird menu (6–7:30pm) £12.50 ($17.50). Main courses £11–£18 ($15.40–$25.20). AE, DC, MC, V. Mon–Sat 6pm–midnight; Sun 6–11:15pm. DART: Tara St. Bus: 16A, 19A, 22A, 55, or 83. INTERNATIONAL.

Close to the Andrews Lane and other theaters, Trocadero is a favorite gathering spot for theatergoers, performers, and press. As might be expected, the decor is theatrical, with subdued lighting, banquette seating, close-set tables, and photos of entertainers on the walls. Steaks are the specialty, but the menu also offers rack of lamb, daily fish specials, pastas, and traditional dishes such as Irish stew and corned beef and cabbage with parsley sauce. The food is not memorable, but that fails to matter here at one of Dublin's more revered auld haunts.

INEXPENSIVE

✪ **Bewley's Café.** 78/79 Grafton St., Dublin 2. ☎ **01/677-6761.** Homemade soup £2.25 ($3.15); main courses £3–£6.50 ($4.20–$9.10); lunch specials from £5 ($7). Dinner main courses from £12 ($16.80). AE, DC, MC, V. Sun–Thurs 7:30am–11pm; Fri–Sat 7:30am–1am (continuous service for breakfast, hot food, and snacks). Bus: Any city-center bus. TRADITIONAL/PASTRIES.

Bewley's, a three-story landmark founded in 1840 by a Quaker named Joshua Bewley, is a quintessential part of the Dublin experience. The interior is a subdued, mellow mix of dark wood, amber glass, and deep red velvet. Bewley's bustles with the clink of teapots and the satisfied hum of customers sated on scones, almond buns, and baked goods. Less appealing but equally filling are warm suppers of lasagne, sausages and chips, or a variety of casseroles.

Most Bewley's establishments are self-service cafeterias, but Bewley's of Grafton Street also has several full-service tearooms. Other locations are at 11 Westmoreland St., Dublin 2; 13 S. Great George's St., Dublin 2; 40 Mary St., Dublin 1 (near the ILAC shopping center north of the Liffey); shopping centers in Dundrum, Stillorgan, and Tallaght; and Dublin Airport.

Cafe Bell. St. Teresa's Courtyard, Clarendon St., Dublin 2. ☎ **01/677-7645.** All items £2–£5 ($2.80–$7). No credit cards. Mon–Sat 9am–5:30pm. Bus: 16, 16A, 19, 19A, 22A, 55, or 83. IRISH/SELF-SERVICE.

In the cobbled courtyard of early 19th-century St. Teresa's Church, this serene little place is one of a handful of dining options springing up in historic or ecclesiastical surroundings. With high ceilings and an old-world decor, Cafe Bell is a welcome contrast to the bustle of Grafton Street a block away and Powerscourt Town House Centre across the street. The menu changes daily but usually includes homemade soups, sandwiches, salads, quiches, lasagna, sausage rolls, hot scones, and other baked goods.

✪ **The Steps of Rome.** Chatham St., Dublin 2. ☎ **01/670-5630.** Main courses £4.50–£9 ($6.30–$12.60); pizza slices £1.60–£2 ($2.25–$2.80). No credit cards. Daily 10am–2pm and 7–11pm. ITALIAN/PIZZA.

Word is out that this restaurant just off the busy shopping thoroughfare of Grafton Street offers some of the best simple Italian fare in Dublin. Large succulent pizza slices available for takeout are one way to enjoy the wonders of this authentic Italian kitchen when the dining room is full—the seven tables huddled within this tiny restaurant seem to be perennially occupied. The potato, mozzarella, and rosemary pizza, with a thick crust resembling focaccia, is unusual and exceptionally delicious. Although the pasta dishes are also quite good, it's that pizza that remains unforgettable.

4 Fitzwilliam Square/Merrion Square Area

VERY EXPENSIVE

✪ **Restaurant Patrick Guilbaud.** 21 Upper Merrion St., Dublin 2. ☎ **01/676-4192.** Reservations required. Fixed-price lunch £22 ($30.80); main courses £17–£56 ($23.80–$78.40). AE, DC, MC, V. Tues–Sat 12:30–2pm and 7:30–10:15pm. DART: Westland Row. Bus: 10, 11A, 11B, 13, or 20B. NOUVELLE FRENCH.

After being tucked away for many years on James Place, this distinguished restaurant has been transferred to elegant new quarters, and taken with it the same glowing Michelin-star reputation for fine food and artful service. The menu features such dishes as roasted West Cork turbot, veal sweetbreads with black truffles, wild sea bass with ragout of mussels, and a casserole of winter vegetables with wild mushrooms. Just to say you did, start with the open ravioli of lobster with coconut cream, and finish with the *assiette gourmande au chocolat* (five small hot and cold chocolate desserts). A private dining room is available for parties of 2 to 25.

EXPENSIVE

Dobbins Wine Bistro. 15 Stephen's Lane (off Upper Mount St.), Dublin 2. ☎ **01/676-4670.** Reservations recommended. Dinner main courses £13.50–£23 ($18.90–$32.20). AE, DC, MC, V. Mon–Fri 12:30–2:30pm; Tues–Sat 7:30–10:30pm. DART: Pearse. Bus: 5, 7A, 8, 46, or 84. IRISH/CONTINENTAL.

Almost hidden in a lane between Upper and Lower Mount Streets a block east of Merrion Square, this friendly enclave is a haven for inventive cuisine. The menu changes often, but usually includes such items as duckling with orange and port sauce; steamed paupiette of black sole with salmon, crab, and prawn filling; panfried veal kidneys in pastry; and fillet of beef topped with crispy herb bread crumbs with shallot and Madeira sauce. You'll have a choice of sitting in the bistro, with checkered tablecloths and sawdust on the floor, or on the tropical patio, with an all-weather sliding-glass roof.

✪ **L'Ecrivain.** 109 Lower Baggot St., Dublin 2. ☎ **01/661-1919.** Reservations recommended. Fixed-price 3-course lunch £16.50 ($23.10). Fixed-price 4-course dinner £33 ($46.20). Vegetarian dinner £27.50 ($38.50). Main courses £19.50–£21.50 ($27.30–$30.10). Service charge 10% on food only. AE, DC, MC, V. Mon–Fri 12:30–2pm; Mon–Sat 7–11pm. Bus: 10. FRENCH/IRISH.

This is one of Dublin's truly fine restaurants, from start to finish. The atmosphere is relaxed, welcoming, and unpretentious. You can dine on the garden terrace, weather permitting, or in the newly renovated and expanded dining rooms. Each course seems to receive the same devoted attention, and most consist of traditional "best of Irish" ingredients, prepared without dense sauces. The seared sea trout with sweet potato purée and the entrecôte with caramelized onion were perfectly prepared for me, and the presentation more than competes with anything in the Museum of Modern Art. The desserts are not an afterthought, but the creations of a talented pastry chef. The crème brûlée here is the best I've tasted north of the Chunnel. The restaurant is a 5-minute walk from St. Stephen's Green. If you drive, there's ample street parking on nearby Merrion Square.

MODERATE

McGrattan's in the Lane. 76 Fitzwilliam Lane, Dublin 2. ☎ **01/661-8808.**
Reservations recommended. Dinner main courses £11–£18 ($15.40–$25.20).
AE, MC, V. Sun–Thurs 6pm–midnight; Fri–Sat 6pm–1am. IRISH/FRENCH.

Out of view from the general flow of traffic, this restaurant is
in a lane between Baggot Street and Merrion Square. The
decor ranges from a homey fireside lounge with oldies background music to a skylit, plant-filled dining room. The creative menu includes main dishes such as breast of chicken
Fitzwilliam (stuffed with cheddar cheese in pastry), roast
pheasant with wild mushrooms and red wine sauce, and
paupiette of salmon stuffed with scallop mousse and wrapped
in a pancake of puff pastry.

INEXPENSIVE

National Museum Cafe. National Museum of Ireland, Kildare St., Dublin 2.
☎ **01/662-1269.** Soup £2 ($2.80), lunch main courses under £6 ($8.40).
MC, V. Tues–Sat 10am–5pm; Sun 2–5pm. Bus: 7, 7A, 8, 10, 11, or 13.
CAFETERIA/TEA SHOP.

The tall windows of the National Museum Cafe look out
toward the National Library across a cobbled yard; inside the
cafe, an elaborate mosaic floor, enameled fireplace, marble
tabletops, and chandelier lend an element of elegance to this
otherwise-informal eatery. Everything is made from scratch:
beef salad, chicken salad, quiche, an abundance of pastries.
The soup of the day is often vegetarian, and quite good. This
is a great place to step out of the rain, warm yourself, and then
wander among the nation's treasures. Admission to the museum is free, so you can visit at your own pace, as often as your
curiosity (and appetite) demand.

5 Ballsbridge/Embassy Row Area

VERY EXPENSIVE

Le Coq Hardi. 35 Pembroke Rd., Ballsbridge, Dublin 4. ☎ **01/668-9070.**
Reservations required. Fixed-price lunch £24.50 ($34.30); fixed-price dinner
£35 ($49). Service charge 12½%. AE, CB, MC, V. Mon–Fri 12:30–2:30pm; Mon–
Sat 7–10:45pm. DART: Lansdowne Rd. Bus: 18, 46, 63, or 84. FRENCH.

Decorated in radiant autumn colors, this plush 50-seat
restaurant (with a new cocktail bar) draws a well-heeled local
and international business clientele. Award-winning chef
John Howard offers such specialties as Dover sole stuffed
with prawns, *darne* (steak) of Irish wild salmon on fresh
spinach leaves, fillet of hake roasted on green cabbage and

Ballsbridge/Embassy Row Area Dining

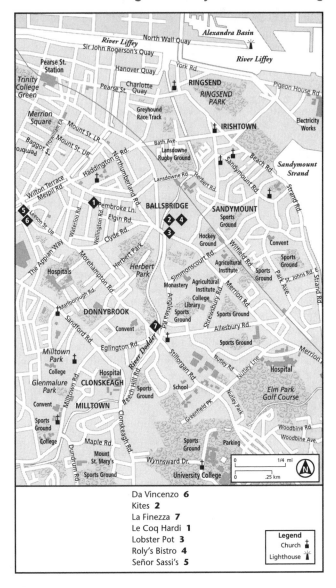

Da Vincenzo **6**
Kites **2**
La Finezza **7**
Le Coq Hardi **1**
Lobster Pot **3**
Roly's Bistro **4**
Señor Sassi's **5**

Legend
🕇 Church
☀ Lighthouse

bacon with Pernod butter sauce, and fillet of prime beef flamed in Irish whiskey. The 700-bin wine cellar boasts a complete collection of Château Mouton Rothschild, dating from 1945 to the present.

EXPENSIVE

Kites. 15/17 Ballsbridge Terrace, Ballsbridge, Dublin 4. ☎ **01/660-7415.** Reservations recommended. Dinner main courses £11–£20 ($15.40–$28). AE, DC, MC, V. Mon–Fri 12:30–2pm; daily 6:30–11pm. DART: Lansdowne Rd. Bus: 5, 7, 7A, 8, 46, 63, or 84. CANTONESE.

Kites is renowned in Dublin for its excellent Cantonese cuisine, a reputation focused on its seafood and hot-and-spicy dishes. The menu features the usual chow mein, curries, and sweet-and-sour dishes, as well as a host of creative entrees, such as king prawns with Chinese leaves in oyster sauce, stuffed crab claws, Singapore fried noodles, and birds' nests of fried potatoes.

Lobster Pot. 9 Ballsbridge Terrace, Ballsbridge, Dublin 4. ☎ **01/668-0025.** Reservations required. Dinner main courses £14–£19.50 ($19.60–$27.30). Lobster dinner roughly £30 ($42). AE, DC, MC, V. Mon–Fri 12:30–2:30pm; Mon–Sat 6:30–10:30pm. DART: Lansdowne Rd. Bus: 5, 7, 7A, 8, 46, 63, or 84. SEAFOOD.

This upstairs restaurant is known for its lobster dishes, as you might guess from its name. The menu also regularly includes salmon, black sole, monkfish, halibut, plaice, hake, turbot, sea trout, and Dublin Bay prawns, all variously rendered. And an array of steak, lamb, and chicken dishes will tempt the landlubber's palate.

MODERATE

La Finezza. Over Kiely's, Donnybrook Rd. (N11), Donnybrook, Dublin 4. ☎ **01/283-7166.** Reservations recommended. Early-bird menu (5:30–7pm) £12.95 ($18.15). Main courses £8.95–£17.50 ($12.55–$24.50). AE, MC, V. Mon–Sat 5–11pm; Sun 4–9:30pm. Bus: 10, 46A, or 46B. ITALIAN/ MEDITERRANEAN.

Since its opening in the mid-1990s, La Finezza has garnered a number of awards, including restaurant of the year. Its candlelit mirrored-gallery decor is quite tasteful. The menu is imaginative and ambitious—perhaps overly so for a purist's palate. Panfried lamb cutlets and fresh pepper and black-bean mousse are simply exquisite. The presentation is delightful, and the service superb. La Finezza deserves its accolades.

⭐ **Roly's Bistro.** 7 Ballsbridge Terrace, Dublin 4. ☎ **01/668-2611.** Reservations required. Main courses £9.50–£14.95 ($13.30–$20.95); set-price lunch £12.50 ($17.50). AE, DC, MC, V. Daily noon–3pm and 6–10pm. DART to Lansdowne Rd. Station. Bus: 5, 6, 7, 8, 18, or 45. IRISH/INTERNATIONAL.

Opened in 1992, this two-story shop-front restaurant quickly skyrocketed to success, thanks to its genial and astute host Roly Saul and its master chef Colin O'Daly. What you get is excellent and imaginatively prepared food at mostly moderate prices. The main dining rooms, with a bright and airy decor and lots of windows, can be noisy when the house is full, but the nonsmoking section has a quiet enclave of booths laid out in an Orient Express style for those who prefer a quiet tête-à-tête. Main courses include roasted venison, panfried Dublin Bay prawns, game pie with chestnuts, and wild mushroom risotto. An excellent array of international wines is offered, starting at £10.95 ($15.35) a bottle.

Señor Sassi's. 146 Upper Leeson St., Dublin 4. ☎ **01/668-4544.** Reservations recommended. Dinner main courses £8.50–£14.95 ($11.90–$20.95). AE, DC, MC, V. Mon–Thurs 12–2:30pm and 6–10:45pm; Fri 12–2:30pm and 6–11pm; Sat 7–11pm; Sun 12–4pm. Bus: 11, 11A, 11B, 13, 46A, or 46B. MEDITERRANEAN.

This innovative restaurant blends the simple and spicy flavors of Spain, Italy, southern France, and the Middle East. In a busy location, the contemporary and casual space has slate floors, marble-topped tables, and walls painted a sunny shade of yellow; seating is also available in a conservatory extension overlooking a courtyard garden. The menu includes items such as Moroccan-style couscous, tagliatelle, prawns sautéed in rum with Creole sauce, charcoal steaks, tortilla *español* (traditional omelet with potato and onions), vegetarian dishes, and warm salads. Be sure to try the unusual olive bread.

INEXPENSIVE

Da Vincenzo. 133 Upper Leeson St., Dublin 4. ☎ **01/660-9906.** Reservations recommended. Fixed-price lunch £7.95 ($11.15); dinner main courses £6.50–£12.50 ($9.10–$17.50). AE, DC, MC, V. Daily 12:30–11pm; Sun 1–10pm. Bus: 10, 11A, 11B, 46A, or 46B. ITALIAN.

Located within a block of the Burlington hotel, this informal, friendly bistro offers ground-level and upstairs seating. Glowing brick fireplaces illuminate pine walls, vases and wreaths of dried flowers, modern art posters, blue and white pottery, and a busy open kitchen. Pizza on light pita-style dough, cooked in a wood-burning oven, is the specialty. Other entrees range from pastas—such as tagliatelle, lasagna, cannelloni, spaghetti, and fettuccine—to veal and beef dishes, including an organically produced fillet steak.

6 O'Connell Street Area/North of the Liffey

EXPENSIVE

Chapter One. 18 Parnell Sq. N., Dublin 1. ☎ **01/873-2266.** Reservations recommended. Fixed-price 4-course lunch £15.50 ($21.70); fixed-price pretheater dinner £16.50 ($23.10); dinner main courses £14.95–£18.95 ($20.95–$26.55). Service charge 10%. AE, MC, V. Tues–Fri 12:30–2:30pm; Tues–Sat 6–11pm. DART: Connolly. Bus: 10, 11, 11A, 11B, 12, 13, 14, 16, 16A, 19, 19A, 22, 22A, or 36. IRISH.

A literary theme prevails at this restaurant, in the basement of the Dublin Writers Museum, just north of Parnell Square and the Garden of Remembrance. It spreads over three rooms and alcoves, all accentuated by stained-glass windows, paintings, sculptures, and literary memorabilia. The staff, affiliated with the Old Dublin restaurant (see the review under "Historic Old City/Liberties Area," above), has added a few Scandinavian influences. Main courses include fillet of salmon on a bed of avocado with smoked tomato vinaigrette, black sole with citrus fruit and dill cucumber cream sauce, and roast half-duck with apricot sauce.

MODERATE

101 Talbot. 101 Talbot St. (at Talbot Lane near Marlborough St.), Dublin 1. ☎ **01/874-5011.** Reservations recommended. Main courses £8.75–£12.50 ($12.25–$17.50). AE, MC, V. Tues–Sat 5–11pm. DART: Connolly. Bus: 27A, 31A, 31B, 32A, 32B, 42B, 42C, 43, or 44A. INTERNATIONAL/VEGETARIAN.

Open since 1991, this second-floor restaurant features light, healthy foods, with a strong emphasis on vegetarian and vegan dishes. The setting is bright and casual, with contemporary Irish art on display, big windows, yellow rag-rolled walls, ash-topped tables, and newspapers to read. Entrees include seared fillet of tuna with mango cardamom salsa, roast duck breast with plum and ginger sauce, Halloumi cheese and mushroom brochette served with couscous and raita, and a blue cheese, pistachio cream sauce on pasta. The dinner menu changes weekly. Espresso and cappuccino are always available, and there is a full bar. The restaurant is convenient to the Abbey

Theatre. In the works are an early-bird menu and specials for theatergoers.

INEXPENSIVE

Beshoffs. 6 Upper O'Connell St., Dublin 1. ☎ **01/872-4400.** All items £2–£5 ($2.80–$7). No credit cards. Mon–Sat 10am–9pm; Sun noon–9pm. DART: Tara St. Bus: Any city-center bus. SEAFOOD/FISH-AND-CHIPS.

The Beshoff name is synonymous with fresh fish in Dublin, and it's no wonder. Ivan Beshoff emigrated here from Odessa, Russia, in 1913 and started a fish business that developed into this top-notch fish-and-chips eatery. Recently renovated in Victorian style, it has an informal atmosphere and a simple self-service menu. Crisp chips (french fries) are served with a choice of fresh fish, from the original recipe of cod to classier variations using salmon, shark, prawns, and other local sea fare—some days as many as 20 varieties. The potatoes are grown on a 300-acre farm in Tipperary and freshly cut each day.

A second shop is just south of the Liffey at 14 Westmoreland St., Dublin 2 (☎ **01/677-8026**).

The Winding Stair. 40 Lower Ormond Quay, Dublin 1. ☎ **01/873-3292.** All items £1.50–£4 ($2.10–$5.60). AE, MC, V. Mon–Sat 10am–6pm; Sun 1–6pm. Bus: 70 or 80. IRISH.

Retreat from the bustle of the north side's busy quays at this self-service cafe and bookshop, and indulge in a light meal while browsing through some books. There are three floors— one smoke-free, and each chock-full of used books (from novels, plays, and poetry to history, art, music, and sports). A winding 18th-century staircase connects them. (A cage-style elevator serves, on request, those who are unable or prefer not to climb the stairs.) Tall, wide windows provide expansive views of the Halfpenny Bridge and River Liffey. The food is simple and healthy—sandwiches made with additive-free meats or fruits (such as banana and honey), organic salads, homemade soups, and natural juices. Evening events include poetry readings and recitals.

5

Exploring Dublin

*D*ublin is a city of many moods and landscapes. There are medieval churches and imposing castles, graceful Georgian squares and lantern-lit lanes, broad boulevards and crowded bridges, picturesque parks and pedestrian walkways, intriguing museums and markets, gardens and galleries, and—if you have any energy left after all that—electric nightlife. Enjoy!

1 The Top Attractions

Áras an Uachtaráin (The Irish White House). In Phoenix Park, Dublin 7. ☎ 01/670-9155. Free admission. Sat 9:40am–4:20pm. Closed Dec 24–26. Same-day tickets issued at Phoenix Park Visitors Centre (see below). Bus: 10, 37, or 39.

Áras an Uachtaráin (Irish for "House of the President") was once the Viceregal Lodge, the summer retreat of the British viceroy, whose ordinary digs were in Dublin Castle. From what were never humble beginnings, the original 1751 country house was expanded several times, gradually accumulating splendor. President Mary McAleese recently opened her home to visitors; guided tours originate at the Phoenix Park Visitors Centre every Saturday. After an introductory historical film, a bus brings visitors to and from Áras an Uachtaráin. The focus of the tour is the state reception rooms. The entire tour lasts 1 hour. Only 525 tickets are given out, first-come, first-served; arrive before 1:30pm, especially in summer.

Note: For security reasons, no backpacks, travel bags, strollers, buggies, cameras, or mobile phones are allowed on the tour. No smoking, eating, or drinking are permitted, and no visitor toilets are available once the tour begins.

✪ **Ceol—The Irish Traditional Music Centre.** Smithfield Village, Dublin 7. ☎ 01/817-3820. www.ceol.ie. £5 ($7) adults, £4 ($5.60) seniors and students, £3.50 ($4.90) children, £15 ($21) family. Mon–Sat 10am–6pm; Sun 11am–6pm (last film 45 min. before closing). Bus: 25, 25A, 67, 67A, 68, 69, 79, or 90.

Ceol means "music" in Irish, and here is the place to appreciate the mighty meaning of that word. This is a must for any lover of Irish traditional music and dance, or for anyone else wondering just what all the fuss is about. No matter how much you think you know, you'll learn something more here that will deepen your appreciation of one of Ireland's most profound legacies. The beautifully designed ultra–high-tech center offers a plethora of interactive audiovisual displays and videos presenting the basic ingredients of Irish traditional music—song, dance, story, and instruments. A dazzling diversity of riches is packed into a relatively small space here. The climax of Ceol is the extraordinary film, shown in the 180° wide-screen main auditorium, titled *The Music of the People,* which is reason enough for going well out of your way to pay Ceol a visit. Plan on at least a couple of hours here. Some visitors, intending to spend an hour, make it a day without realizing it.

Christ Church Cathedral. Christ Church Place, Dublin 8. ☎ **01/ 677-8099.** cccdub@indigo.ie. Suggested donation £2 ($2.80) adults, £1 ($1.40) students and children under 15, £5 ($7) family. Daily 10am–5:30pm. Closed Dec 26. Bus: 21A, 50, 50A, 78, 78A, or 78B.

Standing on high ground in the oldest part of the city, this cathedral is one of Dublin's finest historic buildings. It dates from 1038, when Sitric, Danish king of Dublin, built the first wooden Christ Church here. In 1171, the original simple foundation was extended into a cruciform and rebuilt in stone by Strongbow. The present structure dates mainly from 1871 to 1878, when a huge restoration took place. Highlights of the interior include magnificent stonework and graceful pointed arches, with delicately chiseled supporting columns. This is the mother church for the diocese of Dublin and Glendalough of the Church of Ireland. The new Treasury in the crypt is now open to the public, and you can hear new bells pealing in the belfry.

Collins Barracks. Benburb St., Dublin 7. ☎ **01/677-7444.** Free admission. Tours (hours vary) £1 ($1.40) adults, free for seniors and children. Tues–Sat 10am–5pm; Sun 2–5pm. Bus: 34, 70, or 80.

Officially part of the National Museum, Collins Barracks is the oldest military barracks in Europe. Even if it were empty, it would be well worth a visit for the structure itself, a splendidly restored early-18th-century masterwork by Colonel

Thomas Burgh, Ireland's Chief Engineer and Surveyor General under Queen Anne.

The collection housed here focuses on the decorative arts. Most notable is the extraordinary display of Irish silver and furniture. Until the acquisition of this vast space, only a fraction of the National Museum's collection could be displayed, but that is changing, as more and more treasures find their way here. It is a prime site for touring exhibitions, so consult *The Event Guide* for details. There is also a cafe and gift shop on the premises.

Dublin Castle. Palace St. (off Dame St.), Dublin 2. ☎ **01/677-7129.** Admission £3 ($4.20) adults, £2 ($2.80) seniors and students, £1 ($1.40) children under 12. Mon–Fri 10am–5pm; Sat–Sun and holidays 2–5pm. Guided tours every 20–25 min. Bus: 50, 50A, 54, 56A, 77, 77A, or 77B.

Built between 1208 and 1220, this complex represents some of the oldest surviving architecture in the city. It was the center of British power in Ireland for more than 7 centuries, until the new Irish government took it over in 1922. Highlights include the 13th-century Record Tower; the State Apartments, once the residence of English viceroys; and the Chapel Royal, a 19th-century Gothic building with particularly fine plaster decoration and carved oak gallery fronts and fittings. The newest developments are the Undercroft, an excavated site on the grounds where an early Viking fortress stood, and the Treasury, built between 1712 and 1715 and believed to be the oldest surviving office building in Ireland. Also here are a craft shop, heritage center, and restaurant.

Dublin Writers Museum. 18–19 Parnell Sq. N., Dublin 1. ☎ **01/ 475-0854.** Admission £3.15 ($4.40) adults, £2.65 ($3.70) seniors/students, £1.50 ($2.10) ages 3–11, £8.50 ($11.90) families (2 adults and up to 4 children). AE, DC, MC, V. Mon–Sat 10am–5pm (6pm June–Aug); Sun and holidays 11am–5pm. DART to Connolly Station. Bus: 11, 13, 16, 16A, 22, or 22A.

Housed in a stunning 18th-century Georgian mansion with splendid plasterwork and stained glass, the museum is itself an impressive reminder of the grandeur of the Irish literary tradition. Yeats, Joyce, Beckett, Shaw, Wilde, Swift, and Sheridan are among those whose lives and works are celebrated here. One of the museum's rooms is devoted to children's literature.

Dvblinia. St. Michael's Hill, Christ Church, Dublin 8. ☎ **01/679-4611.** Admission £3.95 ($5.55) adults; £2.90 ($4.05) seniors, students, and children, £10 ($14) family. AE, MC, V. Apr–Sept daily 10am–5pm; Oct–Mar Mon–Sat 11am–4pm, Sun 10am–4:30pm. Bus: 50, 78A, or 123.

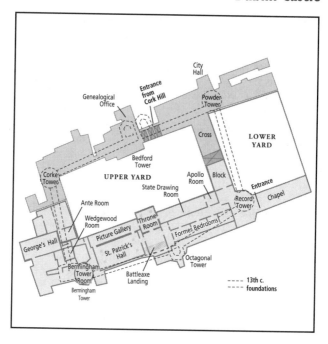

What was Dublin like in medieval times? To find out, visit this historically accurate presentation of the Old City from 1170 to 1540, re-created through a series of theme exhibits, spectacles, and experiences. Highlights include an illuminated Medieval Maze, complete with visual effects, background sounds, and aromas that lead you on a journey through time from the arrival of the Anglo-Normans in 1170 to the closure of the monasteries in the 1530s. Another segment depicts everyday life in medieval Dublin with a diorama, as well as a prototype of a 13th-century quay along the banks of the Liffey. A new addition is the medieval Fayre, displaying the wares of merchants from all over Europe. You can try on a flattering new robe or, if you're feeling vulnerable, stop in at the armorer's and be fitted for chain mail and a proper helm.

Irish Film Centre. 6 Eustace St., Dublin 2. ☎ **01/679-5744,** or 01/679-3477 for cinema box office. Free admission; cinema admission £3–£4.50 ($4.20–$6.30). Centre open daily 10am–11pm; cinemas daily 2–11pm; cinema box office daily 1:30–9pm. Bus: 21A, 78A, or 78B.

Since it opened in 1991, this institute has fast become a focal point in Dublin's artsy Temple Bar district. The Irish Film Centre houses two cinemas, the Irish Film Archive, a library, a bookshop and bar, and eight film-related organizations. Free screenings of *Flashback*, a history of Irish film since 1896, start at noon Wednesday to Sunday from June to mid-September. Follow with lunch in the bar for a perfect midday outing.

Kilmainham Gaol Historical Museum. Kilmainham, Dublin 8. ☎ **01/ 453-5984.** Guided tour £3.50 ($4.90) adults, £2.50 ($3.50) seniors, £1.50 ($2.10) children, £8 ($11.20) family. Apr–Sept daily 9:30am–4:45pm; Oct–Mar Mon–Fri 9:30am–4pm, Sun 10am–4:45pm. Bus: 51, 51B, 78, 78A, 78B, or 79 at O'Connell Bridge.

Within these walls political prisoners were incarcerated, tortured, and killed from 1796 until 1924, when President Eamon de Valera left as its final prisoner. To walk along these corridors, through the exercise yard, or into the main compound is a moving experience that lingers hauntingly in the memory.

Note: The **War Memorial Gardens** (☎ **01/677-0236**), along the banks of the Liffey, are a 5-minute walk from Kilmainham Gaol. The gardens were designed by the famous British architect Sir Edwin Lutyens (1869–1944), who completed a number of commissions for Irish houses and gardens. The gardens are fairly well maintained, and continue to present a moving testimony to Ireland's war dead. This is one of the finest small gardens in Ireland. It's open weekdays 8am to dark, Saturday 10am to dark.

✪ **National Gallery.** Merrion Sq. W., Dublin 2. ☎ **01/661-5133.** Free admission. Mon–Wed and Fri–Sat 10am–5:30pm; Thurs 10am–8:30pm; Sun 2–5pm. Guided tours Sat 3pm, Sun 2:15, 3, and 4pm. DART: Pearse. Bus: 5, 6, 7, 7A, 8, 10, 44, 47, 47B, 48A, or 62.

Established by an act of Parliament in 1854, this gallery opened in 1864, with just over 100 paintings. Today the collection of paintings, drawings, watercolors, miniatures, prints, sculpture, and objets d'art is one of Europe's finest. Every major European school of painting is represented, including an extensive assemblage of Irish work. A $14 million refurbishment of the museum was completed in 1996, and the new 44,000-square-foot Millennium Wing is scheduled to open by 2001. All public areas are wheelchair accessible. The museum has a fine gallery shop and an excellent self-service restaurant operated by Fitzers, a name synonymous with excellent, interesting cuisine at near-budget prices.

✪ **National Museum.** Kildare St. and Merrion St., Dublin 2. ☎ **01/677-7444.** Free admission. Tours (hours vary) £1 ($1.40) adults, free for seniors and children. Tues–Sat 10am–5pm; Sun 2–5pm. DART: Pearse. Bus: 7, 7A, 8, 10, 11, or 13.

Established in 1890, this museum is a reflection of Ireland's heritage from 2000 B.C. to the present. It is the home of many of the country's greatest historical finds, including the Treasury exhibit, which toured the United States and Europe in the 1970s with the Ardagh Chalice, Tara Brooch, and Cross of Cong. Other highlights range from the artifacts from the Wood Quay excavations of the Old Dublin Settlements to "Or," an extensive exhibition of Irish Bronze Age gold ornaments dating from 2200 to 700 B.C. The museum has a shop and a cafe. *Note:* The National Museum encompasses two other attractions, Collins Barracks and the Natural History Museum; see their separate listings.

The Phoenix Park. Parkgate St., Dublin 7. ☎ **01/677-0095.** Free admission. Daily 24 hr. Visitor center admission £2 ($2.80) adults, £1.50 ($2.10) seniors, £1 ($1.40) students and children, £5 ($7) family. Late Mar and Oct daily 9:30am–5pm; Apr–May daily 9:30am–5:30pm; June–Sept daily 10am–6pm; Nov to mid-Mar Sat–Sun 9:30am–4:30pm. Bus: 10, 37, or 39.

Two miles (3.2km) west of the city center, the Phoenix Park, the largest urban park in Europe, is the playground of Dublin. A network of roads and quiet pedestrian walkways traverses its 1,760 acres, which are informally landscaped with ornamental gardens and nature trails. Avenues of trees, including oak, beech, pine, chestnut, and lime, separate broad expanses of grassland. The homes of the Irish president (see below) and the U.S. ambassador are on the grounds, as is the Dublin Zoo (see section 4 of this chapter, "Especially for Kids"). Livestock graze peacefully on pasturelands, deer roam the forested areas, and horses romp on polo fields. The new Phoenix Park Visitor Centre, adjacent to Ashtown Castle, offers exhibitions and an audiovisual presentation on the park's history. The cafe/restaurant is open 10am to 5pm weekdays, 10am to 6pm weekends. Free car parking is adjacent to the center. A shuttle bus runs on Saturday only from the visitor center, with stops throughout the park. One-day hop-on, hop-off service is £1 ($1.40) per person.

✪ **St. Patrick's Cathedral.** 21–50 Patrick's Close, Patrick St., Dublin 8.
☎ **01/475-4817.** www.stpatrickscathedral.ie. Admission £2.30 ($3.20)
adults, £1.60 ($2.25) students and seniors, £5.50 ($7.70) family. MC, V.
Mon–Fri 9am–6pm year-round; Mar–Oct Sat 9am–6pm and Sun 9–11am,
12:45–3pm, 4:15–6pm; Nov–Feb Sat 9am–5pm and Sun 10–11am,
12:45–3pm. Closed except for services Dec 24–26 and Jan 1. Bus: 65, 65B, 50,
50A, 54, 54A, 56A, or 77.

It is said that St. Patrick baptized converts on this site, and
consequently a church has stood here since A.D. 450, making
it the oldest Christian site in Dublin. The present cathedral
dates from 1190, but because of a fire and 14th-century
rebuilding, not much of the original foundation remains. It is
mainly early English in style, with a square medieval tower
that houses the largest ringing peal bells in Ireland, and an
18th-century spire. The 300-foot-long interior makes it the
longest church in the country. St. Patrick's is closely associated with Jonathan Swift, who was dean from 1713 to 1745
and whose tomb lies in the south aisle. Others memorialized
within the cathedral include Turlough O'Carolan, a blind
harpist and composer and the last of the great Irish bards;
Michael William Balfe, the composer; and Douglas Hyde, the
first president of Ireland. St. Patrick's is the national cathedral
of the Church of Ireland.

✪ **Trinity College and The Book of Kells.** College Green, Dublin 2.
☎ **01/608-2320.** www.tcd.ie/library. Free admission to college grounds.
Old Library/Book of Kells £4.50 ($6.30) adults, £4 ($5.60) seniors/students, £9
($12.60) families, free for children under 12. Dublin Experience £3 ($4.20)
adults, £2.50 ($3.50) seniors/students, £1.50 ($2.10) children, £6 ($8.40) fam-
ily. Combination tickets also available. Library Mon–Sat 9:30am–5pm, Sun
noon–4:30pm (opens at 9:30am June–Sept). Dublin Experience May–Sept daily
10am–5pm; closed Oct–Apr. Bus: All city center buses.

The oldest university in Ireland, Trinity was founded in 1592
by Queen Elizabeth I. It sits in the heart of the city on a beautiful 40-acre site just south of the River Liffey, with cobbled
squares, gardens, a picturesque quadrangle, and buildings
dating from the 17th to the 20th centuries. The college is
home to the **Book of Kells,** an 8th-century version of the four
Gospels with elaborate scripting and illumination. This
famous treasure and other early Christian manuscripts are on
permanent public view in the Colonnades, an exhibition area
on the ground floor of the Old Library. Also housed in the
Old Library is the **Dublin Experience** (see separate listing

Arts Building/	Graduate Memorial Building **2**
Douglas Hyde Gallery/	New Library **11**
Davis Theatre **10**	Old Library (Book of Kells) **13**
Campanile **5**	Provost's Garden **9**
Chapel **3**	Provost's House **8**
Dining Hall/Buttery **1**	Reading Room **7**
Exam Hall **6**	Regent House **4**
Forecourt **12**	Samuel Beckett Centre **14**

below; ☎ **01/608-1177**), an excellent multimedia introduction to the history and people of Dublin.

2 More Attractions

ART GALLERIES & ART MUSEUMS

Boulevard Gallery. Merrion Sq. W., Dublin 2. Free admission. May–Sept Sat–Sun 10:30am–6pm. DART: Pearse. Bus: 5, 7A, 8, 46, or 62.

The fence around Merrion Square doubles as a display railing on summer weekends for an outdoor display of local art similar to those you'll find in Greenwich Village or Montmartre. Permits are given to local artists only to sell their own work, so this is a chance to meet an artist as well as to browse or buy.

Hugh Lane Municipal Gallery of Modern Art. Parnell Sq. N., Dublin 1. ☎ **01/874-1903.** Free admission but donations accepted. Tues–Thurs 9:30am–6pm; Fri–Sat 9:30am–5pm; Sun 11am–5pm. DART to Connolly or Tara stations. Bus: 10, 11, 11A, 11B, 13, 16, 16A, 19, 19A, 22, 22A, or 36.

Dublin Attractions

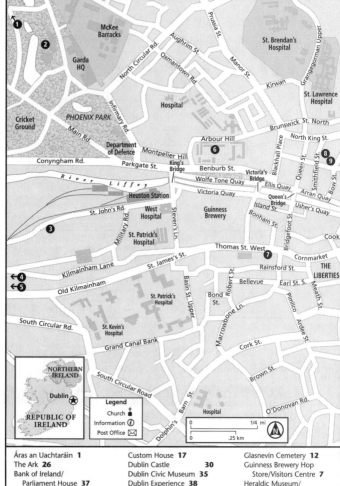

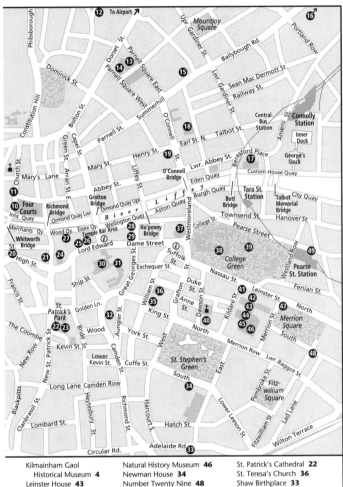

Kilmainham Gaol	
Historical Museum **4**	
Leinster House **43**	
Mansion House **40**	
Marsh's Library **23**	
National Gallery **42**	
National Library	
of Ireland **44**	
National Museum **45**	
National Photographic	
Archive **25**	

Natural History Museum **46**	
Newman House **34**	
Number Twenty Nine **48**	
Old Jameson Distillery	
and The Chimney **9**	
Our Lady of Mount Carmel/	
Whitefriar Street	
Carmelite Church **32**	
St. Audoen's Church **20**	
St. Mary's Pro-Cathedral **18**	
St. Michan's Church **11**	

St. Patrick's Cathedral **22**	
St. Teresa's Church **36**	
Shaw Birthplace **33**	
Temple Bar Gallery	
and Studios **29**	
Trinity College/	
The Book of Kells **39**	
War Memorial Gardens **4**	
Waterways Visitor	
Centre **49**	

The Book of Kells

The Book of Kells is a large-format illuminated manuscript of the four Gospels in Latin, dated on comparative grounds to about A.D. 800. It's impossible to be more precise about its date because some leaves from the end of the book, where such information was normally recorded, are missing. It is the most majestic work of art to survive from the early centuries of Celtic Christianity, and has often been described as "the most beautiful book in the world." A team of talented scribes and artists working in a monastic scriptorium produced the book.

Its fascination derives from the dignified but elusive character of its main motifs, and the astonishing variety and complexity of the linear ornamentation that adorns every one of its 680 pages. Its creators managed to combine new artistic influences from Eastern Christendom with the traditional interlace patterning of Celtic metalwork to produce what Gerald of Wales, a 13th-century chronicler, called "the work not of men, but of angels." The message sometimes may not be easy to read, but everyone can admire the elegant precision of the standard script, the subtlety of the color harmonies, and the exuberant vitality of the human and animal ornamentation.

In the medieval period, the book was (wrongly) regarded as the work of St. Columba himself, and was known as the "great Gospel book of Colum Cille" (Colum of the Churches). The designation "Book of Kells" seems to have originated with the famous biblical scholar James Ussher, who made a study of its original Latin text in the 1620s. The gift shop in the Colonnades of the Old Library in Trinity College stocks a large selection of illustrative materials relating to the Book of Kells.

—J. V. Luce, Trinity College and the Royal Irish Academy

Housed in a finely restored 18th-century building known as Charlemont House, this gallery is situated next to the Dublin Writers Museum. It is named after Hugh Lane, an Irish art connoisseur, who was killed in the sinking of the *Lusitania* in 1915 and who willed his collection (including works by Courbet, Manet, Monet, and Corot) to be shared between the government of Ireland and the National Gallery of London. With the Lane collection as its nucleus, this gallery also contains paintings from the Impressionist and post-Impressionist traditions, sculptures by Rodin, stained glass, and works by modern Irish artists. In 1998, the museum received its most important donation since its establishment in 1908: the studio of Irish painter Francis Bacon, which will open in 2001. Bookshop open during museum hours.

Irish Museum of Modern Art (IMMA). Military Rd., Kilmainham. ☎ 01/612-9900. www.modernart.ie. Free admission. Tues–Sat 10am–5:30pm; Sun noon–5:30pm. Bus: 79 or 90.

Housed in the splendidly restored 17th-century edifice known as the Royal Hospital, IMMA is a showcase of Irish and international art from the latter half of the 20th century. The buildings and grounds also provide a venue for theatrical and musical events, overlapping the visual and performing arts. The galleries contain the work of Irish and international artists from the small but impressive permanent collection, with numerous temporary exhibitions. There's even a drawing room, where kids and parents can record their impressions of the museum with the crayons provided. The formal gardens, an important early feature of this magnificent structure, have been restored and are open to the public during museum hours. In 2000, a series of new galleries will be housed in the restored Deputy Master's House, in the northeast corner of the Royal Hospital site.

Temple Bar Gallery and Studios. 5–9 Temple Bar, Dublin 2. ☎ 01/671-0073. Fax 01/677-7527. Free admission. Tues–Wed 11am–6pm; Thurs 11am–7pm; Sun 2–6pm. Bus: 21A, 46A, 46B, 51B, 51C, 68, 69, or 86.

Founded in 1983 in the heart of Dublin's "Left Bank," this is one of the largest studio and gallery complexes in Europe. More than 30 Irish artists work here at a variety of contemporary visual arts, including sculpture, painting, printing, and photography. Only the gallery section is open to the public; with advance notice, you can make an appointment to view individual artists at work.

BREWERIES/DISTILLERIES

Guinness Brewery Hop Store/Visitor Centre. St. James's Gate, Dublin 8. ☎ 01/408-4800. www.guinness.ie. Admission £5 ($7) adults, £4 ($5.60) seniors and students, £1 ($1.40) children under 12. AE, MC, V. Apr–Sept Mon–Sat 9:30am–5pm, Sun 10:30am–4:30pm; Oct–Mar Mon–Sat 9:30am–4pm, Sun 12–4pm. Guided tours every ½ hour. Bus: 51B, 78A, or 123.

Founded in 1759, the Guinness Brewery is one of the world's largest breweries, producing the distinctive dark beer called stout, famous for its thick, creamy head. Although tours of the brewery itself are no longer allowed, visitors are welcome to explore the adjacent Guinness Hopstore, a converted 19th-century four-story building. It houses the World of Guinness Exhibition, an audiovisual presentation showing how the stout is made; the Cooperage Gallery, displaying one of the finest collections of tools in Europe; the Gilroy Gallery, dedicated to the graphic design work of John Gilroy; and last but not least, a bar where visitors can sample a glass of the famous brew. By 2001, this will also be home to the largest glass of stout in the world, roughly 200 feet tall, whose head will in fact be an observatory restaurant offering spectacular views of the city.

The Old Jameson Distillery. Bow St., Smithfield Village, Dublin 7. ☎ **01/ 807-2355.** Admission £3.95 ($5.53) adults, £3 ($4.20) students and seniors, £1.50 ($2.10) children, £9.50 ($13.30) family. Daily 9:30am–6pm (last tour at 5pm). Chimney ascent £5 ($7) adults, £4 ($5.60) seniors and students, £3.50 ($4.90) children, £15 ($21) family. Mon–Sat 10am–6pm; Sun 11am–7pm. Bus: 67, 67A, 68, 69, 79, or 90.

This museum illustrates the history of Irish whiskey, known as *uisce beatha* (the water of life) in Irish. Housed in a former distillery warehouse, it consists of a short introductory audiovisual presentation, an exhibition area, and a whiskey-making demonstration. At the end of the tour, visitors can sample whiskey at an in-house pub, where an array of fixed-price menus (for lunch, tea, or dinner) is available. A new added attraction here at Smithfield Village is **"The Chimney,"** a ride to the top of a 185-foot brick chimney built in 1895 and converted to support an observation chamber from which you'll enjoy unparalleled views of the city.

CATHEDRALS & CHURCHES

St. Patrick's Cathedral and Christ Church Cathedral are listed in section 1 of this chapter, "The Top Attractions."

Our Lady of Mount Carmel/Whitefriar Street Carmelite Church. 56 Aungier St., Dublin 2. ☎ **01/475-8821.** Free admission. Mon and Wed–Fri 8am–6:30pm; Sat 8am–7pm; Sun 8am–7:30pm; Tues 8am–9:30pm. Bus: 16, 16A, 19, 19A, 122, 155, or 83.

One of the city's largest churches, this edifice was built between 1825 and 1827 on the site of a pre-Reformation Carmelite priory (1539) and an earlier Carmelite abbey (13th c.). It has since been extended, with a new entrance from Aungier Street. This is a favorite place of pilgrimage, especially on February 14, because the body of St. Valentine is enshrined here (Pope Gregory XVI presented it to the church in 1836). The other highlight is the 15th-century black oak Madonna, Our Lady of Dublin.

St. Audeon's Church. Cornmarket (off High St.), Dublin 8. ☎ **01/ 677-0088.** Admission and tour £1.50 ($2.10) adults, £1 ($1.40) seniors, 60p (84¢) children or students, £4 ($5.60) families. June–Sept daily 9:30am– 5:30pm. Last admission 45 min. prior to closing. Bus: 21A, 78A, or 78B.

Situated next to the only remaining gate of the Old City walls (1214), this church is said to be the only surviving medieval parish in Dublin. Although it is partly in ruins, significant parts have survived, including the west doorway, which dates from 1190, and the 13th-century nave. In addition, the 17th-century bell tower houses three bells cast in 1423, making them the oldest in Ireland. It's a Church of Ireland property, but nearby is another St. Audeon's Church, this one Catholic and dating from 1846. It was in the latter church that Father Flash Kavanagh used to say the world's fastest mass so that his congregation was out in time for the football matches. Since 1999, entrance to the ancient church is through the new visitors' center. The center's exhibition, relating the history of St. Audeons, is self-guided, while visits to the church itself are by guided tour only.

St. Mary's Pro-Cathedral. Cathedral and Marlborough sts., Dublin 1. ☎ **01/874-5441.** Free admission. Mon–Fri 8am–6pm; Sat and Sun 8am– 7pm. DART: Connolly. Bus: 28, 29A, 30, 31A, 31B, 32A, 32B, or 44A.

Because Dublin's two main cathedrals (Christ Church and St. Patrick's) belong to the Protestant Church of Ireland, St. Mary's is the closest the Catholics get to having their own. Tucked into a corner of a rather-unimpressive back street, it is in the heart of the city's north side and is considered the main Catholic parish church of the city center. Built between 1815 and 1825, it is of the Greek Revival Doric style, providing a distinct contrast to the Gothic Revival look of most other churches of the period. The exterior portico is modeled on the Temple of Theseus in Athens, with six Doric columns, while the Renaissance-style interior is patterned after the Church of St. Philip de Reule of Paris. The church is noted for its Palestrina Choir, which sings a Latin Mass every Sunday at 11am.

St. Michan's Church. Church St., Dublin 7. ☎ **01/872-4154.** Free admission. Guided tour of church and vaults £2 ($2.80) adults, £1.50 ($2.10) seniors and students, 50p (70¢) children under 12. Nov–Feb Mon–Fri 12:30–2:30pm, Sat 10am–1pm; Mar–Oct Mon–Fri 10am–12:45pm and 2–4:45pm, Sat 10am–1pm. Bus: 134 (from Abbey St.).

Built on the site of an early Danish chapel (1095), this 17th-century edifice claims to be the only parish church on the north side of the Liffey surviving from a Viking foundation. Now under the Church of Ireland banner, it has some fine interior woodwork and an organ (dated 1724) on which Handel is said to have played his *Messiah*. The church was completely and beautifully restored in 1998. A unique (and, let it be noted, most macabre) feature of this church is the underground burial vault. Because of the dry atmosphere, bodies have lain for centuries without showing signs of decomposition. The church is wheelchair accessible, but the vaults are not.

St. Teresa's Church. Clarendon St., Dublin 2. ☎ **01/671-8466.** Free admission; donations welcome. Daily 8am–8pm or longer. Bus: 16, 16A, 19, 19A, 22, 22A, 55, or 83.

The foundation stone was laid in 1793, and the church was opened in 1810 by the Discalced Carmelite Fathers. After continuous enlargement, it reached its present form in 1876. This was the first post–Penal Law church to be legally and openly erected in Dublin, following the Catholic Relief Act of 1793. Among the artistic highlights are John Hogan's *Dead Christ*, a sculpture displayed beneath the altar, and Phyllis Burke's seven beautiful stained-glass windows.

WHERE THE BODIES ARE BURIED

✪ **Glasnevin Cemetery.** Finglas Rd., Dublin 11. ☎ **01/830-1133.** Free admission. Daily 8am–4pm. Free guided tours Wed and Fri 3pm from Roger Casement's grave, at the foot of the O'Connell Round Tower. Bus: 19, 19A, 40, 40A, 40B, or 40C.

Situated north of the city center, the Irish National Cemetery was founded in 1832 and covers more than 124 acres. Most people buried here were ordinary citizens, but there are also many famous names on the headstones. They range from former Irish presidents such as Eamon de Valera and Sean T. O'Kelly to other political heroes such as Michael Collins, Daniel O'Connell, Roger Casement, and Charles Stewart Parnell. Literary figures also have their place here, including poet Gerard Manley Hopkins and writers Christy Brown and Brendan Behan. Though open to all, this is primarily a Catholic burial ground, with more than the usual share of Celtic crosses. A heritage map, on sale in most bookshops, serves as a guide to who's buried where, or you can take a free 1-hour guided tour. Call the main number to book in advance.

MORE HISTORIC BUILDINGS

Although it's not open to the public, one building whose exterior is worth a look is **Mansion House,** Dawson Street, Dublin 2 (☎ **01/676-1845**). Built by Joshua Dawson, the Queen Anne–style building has been the official residence of Dublin's lord mayors since 1715. Here the first Dáil Éireann (House of Representatives) assembled, in 1919, to adopt Ireland's Declaration of Independence and ratify the Proclamation of the Irish Republic by the insurgents of 1916. Ride the DART to Pearse, or take bus no. 10, 11A, 11B, 13, or 20B.

✪ **Bank of Ireland Centre/Parliament House.** 2 College Green, Dublin 2. ☎ **01/661-5933,** ext. 2265. Free admission. Mon–Wed and Fri 10am–4pm; Thurs 10am–5pm. Guided 45-min. tours of House of Lords chamber Tues 10:30am, 11:30am, and 1:45pm (except holidays). DART: Tara St. Bus: Any city-center bus.

Although it's now a busy bank, this building was erected in 1729 to house the Irish Parliament. It became superfluous when the British and Irish Parliaments were merged in London. In fact, the Irish Parliament voted itself out of existence, becoming the only recorded parliament in history to do so. Highlights include the windowless front portico, built to avoid distractions from the outside when Parliament was in session, and the unique House of Lords chamber. The room is famed for its Irish oak woodwork, 18th-century tapestries, golden mace, and a sparkling Irish crystal chandelier of 1,233 pieces, dating from 1765.

This is also the home of the **Bank of Ireland Arts Centre,** which plays host to an impressive program of art exhibitions, concerts, and poetry readings. Entry to readings, lunchtime recitals, and exhibitions is free. Another attraction in the bank center is the **Story of Banking,** an interactive museum offering a glimpse of the history of banking and of Ireland more generally over the past 2 centuries. It's open Tuesday to Friday 10am to 4pm; admission is £1.50 ($2.10) for adults, £1 ($1.40) students.

Custom House. Custom House Quay, Dublin 1. ☎ **01/878-7760.** Admission £1 ($1.40), £3 ($4.20) family. Mid-Mar to Oct Mon–Fri 10am–12:30pm, Sat–Sun 2–5pm; Nov to mid-Mar Wed–Fri 10am–12:30pm, Sun 2–5pm. DART: Tara St.

The Custom House, which sits prominently on the Liffey's north bank, is one of Dublin's finest Georgian buildings. Designed by James Gandon and completed in 1791, it is beautifully proportioned, with a long classical facade of graceful pavilions, arcades, and columns, and a central dome topped by a 16-foot statue of Commerce. The 14 keystones over the doors and windows are known as the Riverine Heads, because they represent the Atlantic Ocean and the 13 principal rivers of Ireland. Although burned to a shell in 1921, the building has been masterfully restored and its bright Portland stone recently cleaned. The new visitor center's exhibitions and audio-visual presentation unfold the remarkable history of the structure from its creation by James Gandon to its reconstruction after the War of Independence.

✪ **Four Courts.** Inns Quay, Dublin 8. ☎ **01/872-5555.** Free admission. Mon–Fri 11am–1pm and 2–4pm. Bus: 34, 70, or 80.

Home to the Irish law courts since 1796, this fine 18th-century building overlooks the north bank of the Liffey on Dublin's west side. With a sprawling 440-foot facade, it was designed by James Gandon and is distinguished by its graceful Corinthian columns, massive dome (64 ft. in diameter), and exterior statues of Justice, Mercy, Wisdom, and Moses (sculpted by Edward Smyth). The building was severely burned during the Irish Civil War of 1922, but has been artfully restored. The public is admitted only when court is in session, so phone in advance.

✪ **General Post Office (GPO).** O'Connell St., Dublin 1. ☎ **01/705-8833.** www.anpost.ie. Free admission. Mon–Sat 8am–8pm; Sun 10:30am–6:30pm. DART: Connolly. Bus: 25, 26, 34, 37, 38A, 39A, 39B, 66A, or 67A.

With a 200-foot-long, 56-foot-high facade of Ionic columns and Greco-Roman pilasters, this is more than a post office; it is the symbol of Irish freedom. Built between 1815 and 1818, it was the main stronghold of the Irish Volunteers in 1916. Set afire, the building was gutted and abandoned after the surrender and execution of many of the Irish rebel leaders. It reopened as a post office in 1929 after the formation of the Irish Free State. In memory of the building's dramatic role in

Monumental Humor

Dublin boasts countless public monuments, some modest, others boldly evident. The Irish make a sport of naming them, giving their irrepressible wit and ridicule yet another outlet. A sampler:

Anna Livia, Joyce's mythical personification of the River Liffey, may be found cast in bronze on O'Connell Street across from the General Post Office. Reclining in a pool of streaming water, Anna has been renamed by locals "the floozie in the Jacuzzi."

Sweet **Molly Malone,** another figment of Irish imagintion—inspiring poetry, song, and most recently sculpture—appears complete with her flower cart, all larger than life, at the intersection of Nassau and Grafton Streets, across from the Trinity College Provost's house. Ms. Malone's plunging neckline has to be a part of why she is known as "the tart with the cart."

Just around the corner from Molly on Dame Street stands another sculpture, a silent frenzy of **trumpeters** and streaming columns of water, proclaiming "You're a nation again"—popularly transliterated as "urination again."

Then there's Dublin's testimonial to arguably Ireland's greatest patriot and Dublin's most eminent native son, **Theobald Wolfe Tone.** Born at 44 Stafford St. in 1763 and graduated from Trinity College, Tone went on to spark a revolutionary fervor among the Irish. His timeless contribution to Ireland and the world is commemorated in a semicircular assemblage of rough-hewn columns on the north side of Stephen's Green—better known as "Tonehenge."

Irish history, an impressive bronze statue of Cuchulainn, the legendary Irish hero, is on display. Look closely at the pillars outside—you can still see bullet holes from the siege.

Leinster House. Kildare St. and Merrion Sq., Dublin 2. ☎ **01/618-3000.** Free admission. By appointment only, Oct–May Mon and Fri 10am–4:30pm. DART: Pearse. Bus: 5, 7A, or 8.

Dating from 1745 and originally known as Kildare House, this building is said to have been the model for Irish-born architect James Hoban's design for the White House in Washington, D.C. It was sold in 1815 to the Royal Dublin Society, which developed it as a cultural center. The National Museum, Library, and Gallery all surround it. In 1924, however, it took on a new role when the Irish Free State government acquired it as a parliament house. Since then, it has been the meeting place for the Dáil Éireann (Irish House of Representatives) and Seanad Éireann (Irish Senate), which together constitute the Oireachtas (National Parliament). Tickets for a guided tour when the Dáil is in session (Oct to May, Tues to Thurs) must be arranged in advance from the **Public Relations Office** (☎ **01/618-3066**).

✪ **Newman House.** 85–86 St. Stephen's Green, Dublin 2. ☎ **01/ 706-7422.** Fax 01/706-7211. Guided tours £3 ($4.20) adults, £2 ($2.80) seniors, students, and children under 12. June–Aug Tues–Fri noon–5pm, Sat 2–5pm, Sun 11am–2pm. Oct–May by appointment only. Bus: 10, 11, 13, 14, 14A, 15A, or 15B.

In the heart of Dublin on the south side of St. Stephen's Green, this is the historic seat of the Catholic University of Ireland. Named for Cardinal John Henry Newman, the 19th-century writer and theologian and first rector of the university, it consists of two of the finest Georgian town houses in Dublin. They date from 1740 and are decorated with out-standing Palladian and rococo plasterwork, marble tiled floors, and wainscot paneling. No. 85 has been magnificently restored to its original splendor.

Note: Every other Sunday, Newman House hosts an antiques and collectibles fair, where dealers from throughout Ireland sell a wide range of items, including silver, rare books, paintings and prints, coins, stamps, and so forth.

LIBRARIES
✪ **Chester Beatty Library and Gallery of Oriental Art.** Clock Tower Building. Dublin Castle, Dublin 2. ☎ **01/407-0750.** E-mail: info@cbl.ie. Free admission. Tues–Fri 10am–5pm; Sat 11am–5pm; Sun 1–5pm. Free guided tours Wed and Sat 2:30pm. DART: Sandymount. Bus: 5, 6, 6A, 7A, 8, 10, 46, 46A, 46B, or 64.

Bequeathed to the Irish nation in 1956 by Sir Alfred Chester Beatty, this extraordinary collection contains approximately 22,000 manuscripts, rare books, miniature paintings, and objects from Western, Middle Eastern, and Far Eastern cultures. There are more than 270 copies of the Koran to be found here, and the library has especially impressive biblical and early Christian manuscripts. There's a new gift shop on the premises.

Marsh's Library. St. Patrick's Close, Upper Kevin St., Dublin 8. ☎ **01/454-3511.** www.kst.dit.ie/marsh. Donation of £1 ($1.40) expected, free for children. Mon 10am–12:45pm and 2–5pm; Wed–Fri 10am–12:45pm and 2–5pm; Sat 10:30am–12:45pm. Bus: 50, 54A, or 56A.

This is Ireland's oldest public library, founded in 1701 by Narcissus Marsh, Archbishop of Dublin. It is a repository of more than 25,000 scholarly volumes, chiefly on theology, medicine, ancient history, maps, Hebrew, Syriac, Greek, Latin, and French literature. In his capacity as dean of St. Patrick's Cathedral, Jonathan Swift was a governor of Marsh's Library. The interior—a magnificent example of a 17th-century scholar's library—has remained very much the same for 3 centuries. Special exhibits are designed and mounted annually.

National Library of Ireland. Kildare St., Dublin 2. ☎ **01/603-0200.** Fax 01/676-6690. Free admission. Mon–Wed 10am–9pm; Thurs–Fri 10am–5pm; Sat 10am–1pm. DART: Pearse. Bus: 10, 11A, 11B, 13, or 20B.

If you're coming to Ireland to research your roots, this library should be one of your first stops (along with the Heraldic Museum; see below). It has thousands of volumes and records that yield ancestral information. Opened at this location in 1890, this is the principal library of Irish studies. It's particularly noted for its collection of first editions and the papers of Irish writers and political figures, such as W. B. Yeats, Daniel O'Connell, and Patrick Pearse. It also has an unrivaled collection of maps of Ireland.

National Photographic Archive. Meeting House Sq., Temple Bar, Dublin 2. ☎ **01/603-0200.** E-mail: photoarchive@nli.ie. Free admission. Mon–Fri 10am–5pm. DART: Tara St. Bus: 21A, 46A, 46B, 51B, 51C, 68, 69, or 86.

The newest member of the Temple Bar cultural complex, the National Photographic Archive houses the extensive (more than 300,000 items) photo collection of the National Library, and serves as its photo exhibition space. In addition to the exhibition area, there are a library and a small gift shop. Admission to the reading room is by appointment.

LITERARY LANDMARKS

See also "Libraries," above, and the listing for the Dublin Writers Museum in section 1 of this chapter, "The Top Attractions." You might also be interested in the James Joyce Museum, in nearby Sandycove; it's described in chapter 8, "Side Trips from Dublin."

James Joyce Centre. 35 N. Great George's St., Dublin 1. ☎ **01/878-8547.** www.jamesjoyce.ie. Admission £2.75 ($3.85) adults, £2 ($2.80) seniors and students, 75p ($1.05) children, £6 ($8.40) family. Separate fees for walking tours and events. AE, MC, V. Mon–Sat 9:30am–5pm; Sun 12:30–5pm. Closed Dec 24–26. DART: Connolly. Bus: 3, 10, 11, 11A, 13, 16, 16A, 19, 19A, 22, or 22A.

Near Parnell Square and the Dublin Writers Museum, the Joyce center is in a restored 1784 Georgian town house, once the home of Denis J. Maginni, a dancing instructor who appears briefly in *Ulysses.* The Ulysses Portrait Gallery on the second floor has a fascinating collection of photographs and drawings of characters from *Ulysses* who had a life outside the novel. The recently opened Paul Leon Exhibition Room holds the table and writing table used by Joyce in Paris when he was working on *Finnegan's Wake.* The room is named after Paul Leon, an academic who aided Joyce in literary, business, and domestic affairs and salvaged many of the author's papers after Joyce and his family left Paris. There are talks and audiovisual presentations daily. Guided walking tours through the neighborhood streets of "Joyce Country" in Dublin's north inner city are offered daily.

Shaw Birthplace. 33 Synge St., Dublin 2. ☎ **01/475-0854.** Admission £2.70 ($3.80) adults, £2.20 ($3.10) seniors and students, £1.40 ($1.95) children, £7.95 ($11.15) family. Discounted combination ticket with Dublin Writers Museum and James Joyce Museum available. May–Oct Mon–Sat 10am–5pm, Sun 11am–5pm. Closed Nov–Apr. Bus: 16, 16, 19, or 22.

This simple two-story terraced house, built in 1838, was the birthplace in 1856 of George Bernard Shaw, one of Dublin's three winners of the Nobel Prize for Literature. Recently restored, it has been furnished in Victorian style to re-create the atmosphere of Shaw's early days. Rooms on view are the kitchen, the maid's room, the nursery, the drawing room, and a couple of bedrooms, including young Bernard's. The house is off South Circular Road, a 15-minute walk from St. Stephen's Green.

MORE MUSEUMS

See also "Art Galleries & Art Museums," above. The National Gallery, the National Museum, the Dublin Writers Museum, and Kilmainham Gaol Historical Museum are all listed in section 1 of this chapter, "The Top Attractions."

Dublin Civic Museum. 58 S. William St., Dublin 2. ☎ **01/679-4260.** Free admission. Tues–Sat 10am–6pm; Sun 11am–2pm. Bus: 10, 11, or 13.

In the old City Assembly House, a fine 18th-century Georgian structure next to the Powerscourt Townhouse Centre, this museum focuses on the history of the Dublin area from medieval to modern times. In addition to old street signs, maps, and prints, you can see Viking artifacts, wooden water mains, coal covers—and even the head from the statue of Lord Nelson, which stood in O'Connell Street until it was blown up in 1965. Exhibits change three or four times a year.

GAA Museum. Croke Park, Dublin 3. ☎ **01/836-3222.** Admission £3 ($4.20) adults, £2 ($2.80) students, £1.50 ($2.10) children, £6 ($8.40) families. May–Sept daily 9:30am–5pm; Oct–Apr Tues–Sat 10am–5pm, Sun 12–5pm. Bus: 3, 11, 11A, 16, 16A, 51A, or 123.

On the grounds of Croke Park, principal stadium of the Gaelic Athletic Association, this museum dramatically presents the athletic heritage of Ireland. The Gaelic Games (Gaelic football, hurling, handball, and camogie) have long been contested on an annual basis between teams representing the various regions of Ireland. Test your skills with interactive exhibits, and peruse the extensive video archive of football finals dating back to 1931. The 12-minute film *A Sunday in September* captures admirably the hysteria of the final match. Note that the museum is open only to new stand ticket holders on match days.

✪ **Heraldic Museum/Genealogical Office.** 2 Kildare St., Dublin 2. ☎ **01/603-0200.** Fax 01/662-1062. Free admission. Mon–Wed 10am–8:30pm; Thurs–Fri 10am–4:30pm; Sat 10am–12:30pm. DART: Pearse. Bus: 5, 7A, 8, 9, 10, 14, or 15.

The only one of its kind in the world, this museum focuses on the uses of heraldry. Exhibits include shields, banners, coins, paintings, porcelain, and stamps depicting coats of arms. In-house searches by the office researcher are billed at the rate of £35 ($49) per hour. This is the ideal place to start researching your roots.

Natural History Museum. Merrion St., Dublin 2. ☎ **01/677-7444.** Free admission. Tues–Sat 10am–5pm; Sun 2–5pm. DART: Pearse. Bus: 7, 7A, 8, or 13A.

A division of the National Museum of Ireland, the recently renovated Natural History Museum is considered one of the finest traditional museums in the world. In addition to presenting the zoological history of Ireland, it contains examples of major animal groups from around the world, including many that are rare or extinct. The Blaschka glass models of marine animals are a big attraction.

Number Twenty Nine. 29 Lower Fitzwilliam St., Dublin 2. ☎ **01/ 702-6165.** Admission £2.50 ($3.50) adults, £1 ($1.40) seniors and students, free for children under 16. MC, V. Tues–Sat 10am–5pm; Sun 2–5pm. Closed 2 weeks before Christmas. DART: Pearse. Bus: 7, 8, 10, or 45.

This unique museum is in the heart of one of Dublin's fashionable Georgian streets. The restored four-story town house is designed to reflect the lifestyle of a middle-class family during the period from 1790 to 1820. The exhibition ranges from artifacts and artworks of the time to carpets, curtains, decorations, plasterwork, and bell pulls. The nursery holds dolls and toys of the era.

Waterways Visitor Centre. Grand Canal Quay, Ringsend Rd., Dublin 2. ☎ **01/677-7510.** Admission £2 ($2.80) adults, £1.50 ($2.10) seniors, £1 ($1.40) children or students, £5 ($7) families. June–Sept daily 9:30am–5:30pm; Oct–May Wed–Sun 12:30–5pm. Last admission 45 min. prior to closing. DART: Pearse (5-min. walk). Bus: 1 or 3.

Heading south from Dublin on the DART, you may have noticed the tiny Waterways Visitor Centre, a brilliant white cube floating on the Grand Canal Basin amidst massive derelict brick warehouses. This intriguing modern building is home to a fascinating exhibit describing the history of Ireland's inland waterways, a network of canals connecting Dublin westward and northward to the Shannon watershed. The center's shiny white exterior gives way inside to the subdued tones of Irish oak wall panels and a hardwood ship's floor—a series of exhibits describe aspects of canal design, and several interactive models attempt to demonstrate dynamically the daily operations of the canals. No longer used for transporting goods, the canals of Ireland are now popular with boaters and hikers, and there's some information here for those interested in these activities.

A SIGHT & SOUND SHOW

Dublin Experience. Trinity College, Davis Theatre, Dublin 2. ☎ **01/ 608-1688.** Admission £3 ($4.20) adults, £2.50 ($3.50) seniors, students, and children. Daily late May to early Oct, hourly shows 10am–5pm. DART: Tara St. Bus: 5, 7A, 8, 15A, 15B, 15C, 46, 55, 62, 63, 83, or 84.

An ideal orientation for first-time visitors to the Irish capital, this 45-minute multimedia sight-and-sound show traces the history of Dublin from the earliest times to the present.

It takes place in the Davis Theater of Trinity College, on Nassau Street.

3 Especially For Kids

Dublin's parks give families on the go a respite from the city's ruckus. In **Merrion Square** and **St. Stephen's Green** you will find lawns for picnicking, ducks for feeding, play-grounds for swinging, and gardens for viewing. Horse-loving youngsters will especially enjoy taking a family carriage tour around the parks (see section 4 of this chapter, "Organized Tours").

West of Dublin's city center, the vast **Phoenix Park** entices visitors and locals alike (see "The Top Attractions," earlier in this section). Phoenix Park is home to the **Dublin Zoo** (see below), myriad trails, amazing trees, sports fields, play-grounds, and herds of lovely free-roaming deer. You will dis-cover mansions, castles, and many secret gardens. Ice-cream vendors and teahouses spring up in all the right places to keep you going. Those weary of walking can take a trail ride through the park thanks to the nearby **Ashtown Riding Sta-bles** (see section 6, "The Great Outdoors").

If a day with Vikings appeals to your family, don't miss **Dublin's Viking Adventure** (see below) or the lively **Viking Splash Tour** in a reconditioned World War II amphibious "Duck" vehicle. You'll see Dublin from land and water with a Viking tour guide who will keep the whole family dry and well entertained (see section 4 of this chapter, "Organized Tours").

Interactive creative activities for families can be found in the **Temple Bar** area. **The Ark** (see below) offers unique arts classes and experiences for children. The entire family will enjoy the popular **ESB Sunday Circus** held in Meeting House Square directly behind The Ark in Temple Bar. These captivating theater, puppet, dance, music, and circus events are all free but do require that you pick up tickets for the show from 2pm on the show day at the Essex Street entrance to Meeting House Square. Performance times vary from 2 to 4pm on Sundays from May to August, and the schedule of events can be found through Temple Bar Properties, 18 Eustace St., Temple Bar, Dublin 2 (☎ **01/677-2255**), or the Cultureline (☎ **01/671-5717**).

✪ **The Ark: A Cultural Centre for Children.** Eustace St., Temple Bar, Dublin 2. ☎ **01/670-7788.** Fax 01/670-7758. www.ark.ie. Individual activities £2–£4 ($2.80–$5.60). Daily 10am–4pm. Closed mid-Aug to mid-Sept. DART: Tara St. Bus: 51, 51B, 37, or 39.

The Ark is a unique new cultural center where an experienced staff teaches children with respect and sensitivity. The handsomely renovated building has three modern main floors that house a theater, a gallery, and a workshop for hands-on learning sessions. The wonderful semicircular theater can be configured to open onto either of the other spaces, or outdoors onto Meeting House Square. This exciting center offers organized mini-course experiences (1 to 2 hours long) designed around themes in music, visual arts, and theater. In its debut year, the Ark offered numerous activities in photography, the concept of an Ark and animal making, music and instrument making, and the art of architecture. The workshops, performances, tours, and artist- and musician-in-residence programs are geared toward specific age groups, and the associated activities are kept small. Check the current themes and schedule, and book accordingly. The Ark enjoys huge popularity with children, families, and teachers.

✪ **Dublin Zoo.** The Phoenix Park, Dublin 8. ☎ **01/677-1425.** www.dublinzoo.ie. Admission £6.30 ($8.80) adults, £3.70 ($5.20) seniors and children 3–16, free for children under 3; £18.50–£23.50 ($25.90–$32.90) family, depending on number of children. V. Summer Mon–Sat 9:30am–6pm, Sun 10:30am–6pm. Bus: 10, 25, or 26.

Established in 1830, this is the third-oldest zoo in the world (after those in London and Paris), nestled in the city's largest playground, the Phoenix Park, about 2 miles (3.2km) west of the city center. The 30-acre zoo provides a naturally landscaped habitat for more than 235 species of wild animals and tropical birds. Highlights for youngsters include the Children's Pets' Corner and a train ride around the zoo. New additions to the zoo, part of a $24 million redevelopment, are the "Fringes of the Arctic" exhibition, the "World of Primates," the "World of Cats," and the "City Farm and Pets Corner." Current plans to double the size of the zoo focus on the creation of an "African Plains" area. The zoo also has a restaurant, coffee shop, and gift shop.

✪ **Dublin's Viking Adventure.** Temple Bar (enter from Essex St.), Dublin 8. ☎ **01/679-6040.** Fax 01/679-6033. Admission £4.95 ($6.95) adults, £3.95

($5.55) seniors and students, £2.95 ($4.15) children, £13.50 ($18.90) family.
AE, MC, V. Mar–Oct Tues–Sat 10am–4:30pm; Nov–Feb Tues–Sat 10am–1pm
and 2–4:30pm. DART: Tara St., then no. 90 bus. Bus: 51, 51B, 79, or 90.

This popular new attraction brings you on an imaginative
journey through time to an era when Dublin was a bustling
Norse town. The "Vikings" who populate the village create
a lively, authentic atmosphere in their period houses and
detailed costumes. The townspeople engage in the activities of
daily life in the Wood Quay area along the Liffey, while you
watch and interact with them.

Lambert Puppet Theatre and Museum. 5 Clifden Lane, Monkstown,
County Dublin. ☎ **01/280-0974.** www.lambertpuppettheatre.com. No box
office; call for same-day reservations. Admission £5 ($7). Shows Sat–Sun
3:30pm. DART: Salthill. Bus: 7, 7A, or 8.

Founded by master ventriloquist Eugene Lambert, this
300-seat suburban theater presents puppet shows designed to
delight audiences both young and young at heart. During
intermission, you can browse in the puppet museum or look
for a take-home puppet in the gift shop.

4 Organized Tours

BUS TOURS
Dublin Bus. 59 Upper O'Connell St., Dublin 1. ☎ **01/873-4222.**

This company operates several different tours. Seats can be
booked in advance at the office or at the ticket desk, Dublin
Tourism, Suffolk Street. All tours depart from the office, but
free pickup from many hotels is available for morning tours.
Tours include the nearly 3-hour **Grand Dublin Tour** on a
double-decker bus, with either an open-air or glass-enclosed
upper level. It's a great vantage point for picture taking. The
cost is £10 ($14) adults, £5 ($7) children under 14. It operates year-round at 10:15am and 2:15pm.

For more flexible touring, there is a guided **Dublin City
Tour.** The continuous service connects 10 major points of
interest, including museums, art galleries, churches and cathedrals, libraries, and historic sites. For the flat fare of £7 ($9.80)
adults, £3.50 ($4.90) children under 14, £12 ($16.80) for a
family of four, you can ride the bus for a full day, getting off
and on as often as you wish. It operates daily from 9:30am
to 6:30pm.

Dublin Bus also offers a 3-hour **(North) Coast and Castle Tour,** departing daily at 10am, and a nearly 4-hour South Coast Tour, departing daily at 11am and 2pm. The cost of each tour is £12 ($16.80) adults, £6 ($8.40) children under 14.

Gray Line Tours—Ireland. Gray Line Desk, Dublin Tourism Centre, Suffolk St., Dublin 2. ☎ **01/605-7705.** E-mail: grayline@tlp.ie.

A branch of the world's largest sightseeing organization, this company offers a fully guided panoramic hop-on, hop-off city tour of Dublin from late March to the end of November. You can join the tour at any of a number of pickup points along the route. Tours leave daily at 10am from 14 Upper O'Connell St., and at 10am from the Dublin Tourism Center on Suffolk Street, and every 20 minutes thereafter. The last departures are 4pm from Suffolk Street, 4:30pm from O'Connell Street. Gray Line also offers a range of full-day excursions from Dublin to such nearby sights as Glendalough, Newgrange, and Powerscourt. Grayline's Dublin city tour costs £8.50 ($11.90) adults, £7.50 ($10.50) seniors and students, £3 ($4.20) children, £20 ($28) family. Adult fares for their other tours range from $18 to $37.

VIKING SPLASH TOURS

New to the Dublin scene in the summer of 2000, this is a different way to see the town, especially its Viking-related sights. Aboard a reconditioned World War II amphibious landing craft, or "duck," this tour starts on land (from Bull Alley Street beside St. Patrick's Cathedral) and eventually splashes into the Grand Canal. Tours depart roughly every half hour Monday to Saturday 9am to 6:30pm and Sunday 11am to 6:30pm and last an hour and 15 minutes. It costs £9 ($12.60) for adults and £5 ($7) for children under 12. To contact the tour operators, call ☎ **01/296-6047** or point your browser to **www. vikingsplashtours.com**.

WALKING TOURS

The **Dublin Tourism Office,** St. Andrew's Church, Suffolk Street, Dublin 2, has been a pioneer in the development of self-guided walking tours around Dublin. To date, four tourist trails have been mapped out and signposted throughout the city: Old City, Georgian Heritage, Cultural Heritage, and Rock 'n Stroll/Music Theme. For each trail, the tourist office has produced a handy booklet that maps out the route and provides commentary about each place along the trail.

Historical Walking Tours of Dublin. From Trinity College. ☎ **01/ 878-0227.** Tickets £5 ($7) adults, £4 ($5.60) seniors and students. May–Sept Mon–Fri 11am and 3pm, Sun 11am, noon, 3pm; Oct–April Fri–Sun noon.

This basic 2-hour sightseeing walk takes in Dublin's historic landmarks, from medieval walls and Viking remains around Wood Quay to Christ Church, Dublin Castle, City Hall, and Trinity College. All guides are history graduates of Trinity College, and participants are encouraged to ask questions. Tours assemble at the front gate of Trinity College; no reservations are needed. Walking tours of Trinity College are offered at Trinity's Front Square, just inside the front gate.

Jameson Literary Pub Crawl. 37 Exchequer St., Dublin 2. ☎ **01/ 670-5602.** Tickets £6 ($8.40) per person. Year-round. Times vary.

Walking in the footsteps of Joyce, Behan, Beckett, Shaw, Kavanagh, and other Irish literary greats, this guided tour, winner of the "Living Dublin Award," visits a number of Dublin's most famous pubs with literary connections. Actors provide appropriate performances and commentary between stops. The tour assembles at the Duke Pub on Duke Street (off Grafton Street).

Traditional Irish Musical Pub Crawl. Leaves from Oliver St. John Gogarty pub and restaurant, 57/58 Fleet St. (at Anglesea St.), Temple Bar. ☎ **01/ 478-0193.** Tickets £6 ($8.40) adults, £5 ($7) students and seniors. Mid-May to Oct daily 7:30pm; Nov and Feb to mid-May Fri–Sat 7:30pm. Tickets on sale at 7pm or in advance from Dublin Tourist Office.

To explore and sample the traditional music scene, meet at the Oliver St. John Gogarty pub and restaurant. The price includes a songbook. Two professional musicians, who sing as you make your way from one famous pub to another in Temple Bar, lead the tour. It lasts 2½ hours. The "crawl" better describes the way back to your hotel.

Walk Macabre. Dublin Tourism, Suffolk St., Dublin 2. ☎ **01/605-7769.** Tickets £6 ($8.40) per person. Daily 7:30pm.

The Trapeze Theatre Company offers this 90-minute walk through Dublin's Twilight Zone, revisiting local scenes of murder and intrigue. The tour includes readings and reenactments from some of the darker pages of W. B. Yeats, James Joyce, Bram Stoker, Oscar Wilde, and Sheridan LeFanu.

Rated "R" for violent content, this is not for weak stomachs or light sleepers. Advance booking is essential. Tours leave from the main gates of St. Stephen's Green, opposite Planet Hollywood.

The Zosimus Experience. 28 Fitzwilliam Lane, Dublin 2. ☎ **01/661-8646.** www.zosimus.com. £6 ($8.40) per person. Daily at nightfall, by appointment.

This is the latest rage on the walking tour circuit. Its creators call it a "cocktail mix" of ghosts, murderous tales, horror stories, humor, circus, history, street theater, and whatever's left, all within the precincts of medieval Dublin. You've guessed by now that it's indescribable, and also great fun. It's essential to book in advance, when you'll receive all the specifics you need to be in the right place (outside the main gate of Dublin Castle) at the right time. Because the hour of nightfall varies, you'll learn the exact meeting time when you reserve a place. The experience lasts approximately 1½ hours.

HORSE-DRAWN CARRIAGE TOURS

Tour Dublin in style in a handsomely outfitted horse-drawn carriage with a driver who will comment on the sights as you travel the city's streets and squares. To arrange a ride, consult one of the drivers stationed with carriages at the Grafton Street side of St. Stephen's Green. Rides range from a short swing around the Green to an extensive half-hour Georgian tour or an hour-long Old City tour. Rides are available on a first-come, first-served basis from approximately April to October (weather permitting), and will run you between £10 and £40 ($14 to $56) for one to four passengers, depending on duration of ride.

BICYCLE TOURS

Dublin Bike Tours. 3 Mornington Rd., Ranelagh, Dublin 6. Bookings at Dublin Tourism Centre, Suffolk St., Dublin 2. ☎ **01/679-0899** or 087/ 284-0799 (mobile). E-mail: DublinBikeTours@connect.ie. £15–£30 ($21–$42) per person, depending on tour. Daily 10am, 2pm, 6pm. "Dublin at Dawn" Sat 6am.

Riding a bike in Dublin isn't recommended. Traffic is very heavy, the streets are narrow, and pedestrians crowd every corner. For those determined to take to the streets on wheels, Dublin Bike Tours is a very good option for tours of the city and environs along mostly quieter back streets and roads at a relaxed pace. The 3-hour standard Dublin bike tour is broken by frequent stops, including one for refreshments. A range of other enticing Dublin-area tours is on offer. Or, if you want to set out on your own, you can rent bikes and all the gear, from helmets to baby seats, here as well.

5 Tracing Your Irish Roots

Whether your name is Kelly or Klein, you might have some ancestral ties with Ireland—about 40 million Americans do. If you are planning to visit Ireland to trace your roots, you'll enjoy the greatest success if you do some planning. The more information you can gather about your family before your visit, the easier it will be to find your ancestral home or even a distant cousin once you arrive.

For the personal pursuit of Irish kin, *Tracing Your Ancestors in Ireland,* published by the Irish Tourist Board, provides many points of departure. It outlines the range of resources for genealogical research in Dublin, as well as throughout the island, and helps you get started. It's free of charge at any Irish Tourist Board office.

In Ireland, you can do the research and footwork yourself, or you can use the services of a commercial agency. One of the best firms is **Hibernian Research Co.,** P.O. Box 2097, Dublin 6 (☎ **01/496-6522;** fax 01/497-3011). The researchers, all trained by the Chief Herald of Ireland, have a combined total of more than 100 years' professional experience in working on all aspects of family histories. Among the cases that Hibernian Research handled were U.S. President Ronald Reagan, Canadian Prime Minister Brian Mulrooney, and Ireland's own President Mary Robinson.

You may also wish to consult **ENECLANN,** a Trinity College Dublin Campus Company, at the Innovation Centre, O'Reilly Institute, Trinity College, Dublin 2 (☎ **01/608-2391;** fax 01/671-0281; www.eneclann.tcd.ie). A full description of their highly qualified and touted genealogical services and their fees are available on their Web site.

If you prefer to do the digging yourself, Dublin City is the location for all the Republic of Ireland's centralized genealogical records. Here are the major sources of information.

The National Library, Kildare Street, Dublin 2 (☎ **01/603-0200**), has resources that include an extensive collection of pre-1880 Catholic records of baptisms, births, and marriages.

Its other genealogical material includes trade directories, journals of historical and archaeological societies, local histories, and most newspapers. In addition, the library has a comprehensive indexing system that enables you to identify the material you need to consult.

The Genealogical Office, 2 Kildare St., Dublin (☎ **01/ 661-8811;** fax 01/662-1062), attached to the National Library, incorporates the office of the Chief Herald and operates a specialist consultation service on how to trace your ancestry. In-house searches by the office researcher are billed at the rate of £35 ($49) per hour.

The Office of the Registrar General, Joyce House, 8/11 Lombard St. E., Dublin 2 (☎ **01/671-1000**), is the central repository for records relating to births, deaths, and marriages in the Republic (Catholic marriages from Jan 1, 1864; all other marriages from Apr 1, 1845). This office does not engage in genealogical research. Full birth, death, or marriage certificates each cost £5.50 ($7.70). General searches cost £12 ($16.80). The office is open weekdays from 9:30am to 12:30pm and 2:15 to 4:30pm.

The National Archives, Bishop Street, Dublin 8 (☎ **01/ 407-2300;** fax 01/407-2333; www.nationalarchives.ie), was previously known as the Public Record Office. A fire severely damaged this facility in the early 1920s, and many valuable source documents were lost. However, numerous records rich in genealogical interest are still available. They include *Griffith's Primary Valuation of Ireland, 1848–63,* which records the names of all those owning or occupying land or property in Ireland at the time; the complete national census of 1901 to 1911; and tithe listings, indexes to wills, administrations, licenses, and marriage bonds. In addition, there is also an ever-expanding collection of Church of Ireland Parish Registers on microfilm. You'll also find partial surviving census returns for the 19th century, reports and records relating to the period of the 1798 rebellion, crime and convict records, and details of those sentenced to transportation to Australia. There is no fee for conducting personal searches for family history and genealogy in the archives, and an instruction booklet is provided to get you started. There is a fee for photocopies. The National Archives reading room is open Monday to Friday, 10am to 5pm.

The Registry of Deeds, Kings Inns, Henrietta Street, Dublin 1 (☎ **01/670-7500;** fax 01/804-8406; www.irlgov.ie/landreg), has records that date from 1708 and relate to all the usual transactions affecting property—notably leases, mortgages, and settlements—and some wills. The fee of £10 ($14) per day includes instructions on how to handle the indexes.

If you know the county or town that your ancestors came from, you can also consult the local genealogical centers, parish records, and libraries throughout Ireland and Northern Ireland. Or you can begin your search by visiting a couple of especially helpful sites on the Web: **www.genealogy.ie** and **www.familysearch.com**.

6 The Great Outdoors

BEACHES   The following beaches on the outskirts of Dublin offer safe swimming and sandy strands. All can be reached by city bus: **Dollymount,** 3.5 miles (5.6km) away; **Sutton,** 7 miles (11km) away; **Howth,** 9 miles (15km) away; and **Portmarnock** and **Malahide,** each 10 miles (16km) away. In addition, the southern suburb of **Dun Laoghaire,** 7 miles (11km) away, offers a beach (at Sandycove) and a long bayfront promenade that's ideal for strolling in the sea air. For more details, inquire at the Dublin Tourism Office.

FISHING   The greater Dublin area offers a wide range of opportunities for freshwater angling on local rivers, reservoirs, and fisheries. A day's catch might include perch, rudd, pike, salmon, sea trout, brown trout, or freshwater eel. The **Dublin Angling Initiative,** Balnagowan, Mobhi Boreen, Glasnevin, Dublin 9 (☎ 01/837-9209), offers a guide—the *Dublin Freshwater Angling Guide,* available for £1 ($1.40)—to tell you everything you'll need to know about local fishing.

GOLF   Dublin is one of the world's great golfing capitals. A quarter of Ireland's courses—including 5 of the top 10—lie within an hour's drive of the city. Visitors are welcome, but be sure to phone ahead and make a reservation. The following four are among the leading 18-hole courses in the Dublin area.

The **Elm Park Golf Club,** Nutley Lane, Dublin 4 (☎ 01/269-3438), is on the south side of Dublin. The inland par-69 course is very popular with visitors because it is within

3.5 miles (5.6km) of the city center and close to the Jurys, Berkeley Court, and Burlington hotels. Greens fees are £40 ($56) on weekdays, £50 ($70) on weekends.

✪ **Portmarnock Golf Club,** Portmarnock, County Dublin (☎ **01/846-2968**), is 10 miles (16km) from the city center on Dublin's north side, on a spit of land between the Irish Sea and a tidal inlet. Opened in 1894, the par-72 championship course has been the scene of leading tournaments, including the Dunlop Masters (1959, 1965), Canada Cup (1960), Alcan (1970), St. Andrews Trophy (1968), and many an Irish Open. Many experts consider Portmarnock the benchmark of Irish golf. Greens fees are £75 ($105) on weekdays, £95 ($133) on weekends.

✪ **Royal Dublin Golf Club,** Bull Island, Dollymount, Dublin 3 (☎ **01/833-6346**), is often compared to St. Andrews. The century-old par-73 championship seaside links is on an island in Dublin Bay, 3 miles (4.8km) northeast of the city center. Like Portmarnock, it has been rated among the world's top courses and has played host to several Irish Opens. The home base of Ireland's legendary champion Christy O'Connor, Sr., the Royal Dublin is well known for its fine bunkers, close lies, and subtle trappings. Greens fees are £65 ($91) on weekdays, £80 ($112) on weekends.

St. Margaret's Golf Club, Skephubble, St. Margaret's, County Dublin (☎ **01/864-0400**), one of Dublin's newest championship golf venues, is a par-72 parkland course 3 miles (4.8km) west of Dublin Airport. In 1995, St. Margaret's was host to the Irish Open. Greens fees are £40 ($56) on weekdays, £50 ($70) on weekends.

HORSEBACK RIDING   For equestrian enthusiasts of any experience level, almost a dozen riding stables are within easy reach. Prices average about £15 ($21) an hour, with or without instruction. Many stables offer guided trail riding, as well as courses in show jumping, dressage, prehunting, eventing, and cross-country riding. For trail riding through the Phoenix Park, **Ashtown Riding Stables** (☎ **01/838-3807**) are ideal. They're located in the village of Ashtown, adjoining the park and only 10 minutes by car or bus (nos. 37, 38, 39, or 70) from the city center. Among the other riding centers close to the downtown are **Calliaghstown Riding Centre,** Calliaghstown, Rathcoole, County Dublin (☎ **01/458-9236**);

and **Carrickmines Equestrian Centre,** Glenamuck Road, Foxrock, Dublin 18 (☎ **01/295-5990**).

WALKING   The walk from Bray to Greystones along the rocky promontory of **Bray Head** is a great excursion, with beautiful views back toward Killiney Bay, Dalkey Island, and Bray, the southern terminus of the DART line. It's readily accessible from Dublin. Follow the beachside promenade south through town; at the outskirts of town the promenade turns left and up, beginning the ascent of Bray Head. Shortly after the ascent begins, a trail branches to the left—this is the cliffside walk, which continues another 3½ miles (5.6km) along the coast to Greystones. From the center of Greystones, a train will take you back to Bray. This is an easy walk, about 2 hours one way.

Dalkey Hill and **Killiney Hill** drop steeply into the sea, and command great views of Killiney Bay, Bray Head, and Sugarloaf Mountain. To get there, go south on Dalkey Avenue from the center of Dalkey (in front of the post office), a short distance from the Dalkey DART station. About half a mile from the post office, you'll pass a road ascending through fields on your left—this is the entrance to the Dalkey Hill Park. From the parking lot, climb a series of steps to the top of Dalkey Hill; from here you can see the expanse of the bay, the Wicklow Hills in the distance, and the obelisk topping nearby Killiney Hill. If you continue on to the obelisk, there is a trail leading from there down on the seaward side to Vico Road, another lovely place for a seaside walk. It's about half a mile from the parking lot to Killiney Hill.

6

Shopping

*K*nown the world over for its handmade products and fine craftsmanship, Ireland offers many unique shopping opportunities. Dublin, as Ireland's commercial center, is a one-stop source for the country's best wares. Also, due to Ireland's wholehearted membership in the European Union, Irish shops are brimming with imported goods from the Continent.

Grafton Street, although only several blocks long, is Dublin's answer to Chicago's "Magnificent Mile," with a parade of fine boutiques, fashionable department stores, and specialty shops. Because it's limited to pedestrian traffic, Grafton Street often attracts street performers and sidewalk artists, giving it a festive atmosphere. The smaller streets radiating out from Grafton—Duke, Dawson, Nassau, and Wicklow—are also lined with fine small book, handcraft, and souvenir shops.

Nearby is **Temple Bar,** the hub of Dublin's Left Bank artsy district and the setting for art and music shops, secondhand clothing stores, and a host of other increasingly fine and interesting boutiques.

On the north side of the Liffey, the **O'Connell Street** area is the main inner-city shopping nucleus, along with its nearby offshoots—Abbey Street for crafts, Moore Street for its open-air market, and Henry Street, a pedestrian-only strip of department stores and indoor malls. Close at hand, west of O'Connell, are both the ILAC Centre and the new Jervis Shopping Centre.

Generally, Dublin shops are open from 9am to 5:30 or 6pm Monday to Saturday, Thursday until 8pm. There are exceptions, particularly during tourist season (May to September or October), when many shops also have Sunday hours, usually midmorning to 4pm or 5pm. Throughout the year, many bookshops are open on Sundays.

Major department stores include **Arnotts,** 12 Henry St., Dublin 1, and 112 Grafton St., Dublin 2 (☎ **01/872-1111**);

Brown Thomas, 15–20 Grafton St., Dublin 2 (☎ **01/ 679-5666**); and **Clerys,** Lower O'Connell Street, Dublin 1 (☎ **01/878-6000**).

Dublin also has several clusters of shops in **multistory malls** or ground-level arcades, ideal for indoor shopping on rainy days. These include the **ILAC Centre,** Henry Street, Dublin 1; the **Jervis Shopping Centre,** Mary Street, Dublin 1; **Royal Hibernian Way,** 49/50 Dawson St., Dublin 2; and **St. Stephen's Green Shopping Complex,** St. Stephen's Green, Dublin 2.

1 Getting Your VAT Refund

When shopping in the Republic of Ireland and Northern Ireland, bear in mind that the price of most goods, excluding books and children's clothing and footwear, already includes valued-added tax (VAT), a government tax of 17.36%. VAT is a hidden tax—it is already included on the price tags and in prices quoted to you.

As a visitor, you can avoid paying this tax, *if* you follow a few simple procedures. *Note:* EU residents are not entitled to a VAT refund on goods purchased. As of July 1, 1999, EU residents are not entitled to duty-free shopping in airports and other transit terminals.

The easiest way to make a VAT-free purchase is to arrange for a store to ship the goods directly abroad to your home; such a shipment is not subject to VAT. However, you do have to pay for shipping, so you might not save that much in the end.

If you want to take your goods with you, you must pay the full amount for each item, including all VAT charges (unless you are shopping at a store that offers tax-free purchases to non-EU visitors). However, you can have that tax refunded to you in a number of ways. Here are the main choices.

For a store refund, get a full receipt at the time of purchase that shows the name, address, and VAT paid. (Customs does not accept cash-register tally slips.) Save your receipts until you're ready to depart Ireland; go to the Customs Office at the airport or ferry port to have your receipts stamped and your goods inspected. A passport and other forms of identification (a driver's license, for example) may be required. Stamped receipts should then be sent to the store where you made the purchase, which will then issue a VAT refund check to you by mail to your home address. Most stores deduct a small handling fee for this service.

Global Refund (☎ **800/566-9828**) is one of several private companies offering a cash refund on purchases made at thousands of shops that display a variety of stickers, such as "Tax Back," "Cash Refund," and "Tax Saver." Refunds can be collected in the currency of your choice as you depart from Dublin or Shannon Airport. The nominal fee for this service is calculated on the amount of money you spend in each store. These booths are open year-round (except Dec 25 and 26) in the arrivals halls of Dublin Airport and Shannon Airport.

To get a refund, do the following:

1. Make purchases from stores displaying an appropriate sticker, and be sure to get VAT-refund vouchers from these participating shops each time you make a purchase.
2. Fill out each form with your name, address, passport number, and other required details.
3. When departing Ireland, have any vouchers with a value of over £200 ($280) stamped and validated by a Customs official.
4. Go to the VAT-refund booth corresponding to your vouchers at Dublin Airport (Departures Hall) or Shannon Airport (Arrivals Hall), turn in your stamped forms, and receive cash payments in U.S. or Canadian dollars, British pounds sterling, or Irish punts.

If you are departing from Ireland through a ferry port, or if you don't have time to get to the ETS booth before you leave, you can send your stamped vouchers to the appropriate VAT refund company and receive a refund by mail, or have your refund applied to your credit-card account.

2 Shopping A to Z

ART

Combridge Fine Arts. 17 S. William St., Dublin 2. ☎ **01/677-4652.** DART: Pearse. Bus: 15A, 15B, 15C, 55, or 83.

In business for more than 100 years, this shop features works by modern Irish artists as well as quality reproductions of classic Irish art.

Davis Gallery. 11 Capel St., Dublin 1. ☎ **01/872-6969.** Bus: 34, 70, or 80.

One block north of the Liffey, this shop offers a wide selection of Irish watercolors and oil paintings, with emphasis on Dublin scenes, wildlife, and flora.

M. Kennedy and Sons Ltd. 12 Harcourt St., Dublin 2. ☎ **01/475-1749.** Bus: 62.

If you are looking for a souvenir that reflects Irish art, try this interesting shop, established more than 100 years ago. It's a treasure trove of books on Irish artists and works, and it stocks a lovely selection of fine-art greeting cards, postcards, and bookmarks. There are all types of artists' supplies as well, and an excellent art gallery on the upstairs level.

BOOKS

✪ **Eason and Son Ltd.** 40–42 Lower O'Connell St., Dublin 1. ☎ **01/ 873-3811.** www.eason.ie/. DART: Connolly. Bus: 25, 34, 37, 38A, 39A, 39B, 66A, or 67A.

For more than a century, Eason's—at this central location and at many branches throughout Ireland—has been synonymous with books. This branch offers a comprehensive selection of books and maps about Dublin and Ireland. Open Monday, Tuesday, Wednesday, and Saturday 8:30am to 6:45pm, Thursday until 8:45pm, Friday until 7:45pm, Sunday 1 to 5:45pm.

Eason/Hanna's Bookshop. 1 Dawson St., Dublin 2. ☎ **01/677-1255.** www.hannas.ie. DART: Pearse. Bus: 5, 7A, 8, or 62.

Located across from Trinity College, the newly merged Hanna's Eason or Eason Hanna's bookshop combines the scholarly bent of the old Fred Hanna's bookshop with the lighter, more populist appeal of Eason's, where you can expect to find everything from pulp fiction to paperclips.

✪ **Greene's Bookshop Ltd.** 16 Clare St., Dublin 2. ☎ **01/676-2554.** DART: Pearse. Bus: 5, 7A, 8, or 62.

Established in 1843, this shop near Trinity College is one of Dublin's treasures for bibliophiles. It's chock-full of new and secondhand books on every topic from religion to the modern novel. The catalog of Irish-interest books is issued five to six times a year. Open weekdays 9am to 5:30pm, Saturday 9am to 5pm.

⚫ **Hodges Figgis.** 57 Dawson St., Dublin 2. ☎ **01/677-4754.** www. hodgesfiggis.ie. DART: Pearse. Bus: 10, 11A, 11B, 13, or 20B.

This three-story landmark store has great charm and browse appeal. Although it has everything, the sections on Irish literature, Celtic studies, folklore, and maps of Ireland are particularly good. The recently opened Hodges Figgis Cafe on the first floor seats 60 and serves wine and light meals. Open weekdays 9am to 7pm, Saturday until 6pm, Sunday noon to 6pm.

Waterstone's. 7 Dawson St., Dublin 2. ☎ **01/679-1415.** DART: Pearse. Bus: 10, 11A, 11B, 13, or 20B.

Less than a block south of Trinity College, this literary emporium has extensive sections on Irish interests, as well as crime, gay literature, health, New Age, sports, women's studies, the arts, and wine.

CERAMICS

Louis Mulcahey. 51c Dawson St., Dublin 2. ☎ **01/670-9311.** DART: Pearse. Bus: 10, 11A, 11B, 13, or 20B.

The ceramic creations of Louis Mulcahey are internationally renowned. For years he has been exporting his work throughout Ireland and the rest of the world from his studio on the Dingle Peninsula. This modest new shop across from the Shelbourne Hotel gives him a base in Dublin. In addition to pottery, he designs furniture, lighting, and hand-painted silk and cotton lampshades.

CHINA & CRYSTAL

The China Showrooms. 32/33 Abbey St., Dublin 1. ☎ **01/878-6211.** www.chinashowrooms.ie. DART: Connolly. Bus: 27B or 53A.

Established in 1939, this is Ireland's oldest china and crystal shop in continuous operation. It's a one-stop source for fine china such as Belleek, Aynsley, Royal Doulton, and Rosenthal; hand-cut crystal from Waterford, Tipperary, and Tyrone; and handmade Irish pottery. Worldwide shipping is available.

⚫ **Dublin Crystal Glass Company.** Brookfield Terrace, Carysfort Ave., Blackrock, County Dublin. ☎ **01/288-7932.** www.dublincrystal.ie. DART: Blackrock. Bus: 114.

This is Dublin's own distinctive hand-cut crystal business, founded in 1764 and revived in 1968. Visitors are welcome to browse in the factory shop and see the glass being made and engraved.

CRAFT COMPLEXES

✪ **DESIGNyard.** 12 E. Essex St., Temple Bar, Dublin 2. ☎ **01/677-8453.** DART: Tara St. Bus: 21A, 46A, 46B, 51B, 51C, 68, 69, or 86.

The first thing you'll notice about DESIGNyard is its design. The Victorian warehouse, gorgeously converted into a chic contemporary applied-arts center, has a commissioned set of four wrought-iron gates—abstracts of the city plans of Dublin, Madrid, New York, and Vienna. The ground-floor Jewellery Gallery exhibits and sells contemporary Irish and European jewelry. The first-floor Crafts Council Gallery displays and sells Irish contemporary crafts, including furniture, ceramics, glass, lighting, and textiles. All exhibited pieces are for sale. You may also make an appointment to commission an original work of Irish applied art and design. Whether you see it as a shop or a museum, DESIGNyard is well worth a visit. Open Monday and Wednesday to Saturday 10:30am to 5:30pm, Tuesday 11am to 5:30pm.

Powerscourt Townhouse Centre. 59 S. William St., Dublin 2. ☎ **01/679-4144.** Bus: 10, 11A, 11B, 13, 16A, 19A, 20B, 22A, 55, or 83.

Housed in a restored 1774 town house, this four-story complex consists of a central skylit courtyard and more than 60 boutiques, craft shops, art galleries, snack bars, wine bars, and restaurants. The wares include all kinds of crafts, antiques, paintings, prints, ceramics, leather work, jewelry, clothing, hand-dipped chocolates, and farmhouse cheeses.

Tower Design Centre. Pearse St. (off Grand Canal Quay), Dublin 2. ☎ **01/677-5655.** Limited free parking. DART: Pearse. Bus: 2 or 3.

Along the banks of the Grand Canal, this 1862 sugar refinery was beautifully restored in 1983. In the nest of craft workshops, you can watch the artisans at work. The merchandise ranges from fine-art greeting cards and hand-marbled stationery to pewter, ceramics, pottery, knitwear, hand-painted silks, copperplate etchings, all-wool wall hangings, silver and gold Celtic jewelry, and heraldic gifts. Open Monday to Friday from 9am to 5:30pm.

FASHION

See also "Knitwear," below.

MEN'S

F.X. Kelly. 48 Grafton St., Dublin 2. ☎ **01/677-8142.** DART: Pearse. Bus: 10, 11A, 11B, 13, or 20B.

A long-established ready-to-wear shop, this place blends old-fashioned charm with modern design. It offers a handsome selection of styles, with emphasis on conventional clothing as well as items such as creased linen suits, painted ties, and designer sportswear. Closed Tuesday.

✪ **Kevin & Howlin.** 31 Nassau St., Dublin 2. ☎ **01/677-0257.** DART: Pearse. Bus: 7, 8, 10, 11, or 46A.

Opposite Trinity College, this shop has specialized in men's tweed garments for more than 50 years. The selection includes hand-woven Donegal tweed suits, overcoats, and jackets. In addition, there is a wide selection of scarves, vests, Patch caps, and Gatsby, Sherlock Holmes, and Paddy hats.

Louis Copeland and Sons. 39–41 Capel St., Dublin 1. ☎ **01/872-1600.** Bus: 34, 70, or 80.

With a distinctive old-world shop front, this store stands out on the north side of the River Liffey. It is known for high-quality work in made-to-measure and ready-to-wear men's suits, coats, and shirts. There are branches at 30 Pembroke St., Dublin 2 (☎ **01/661-0110**), and 18 Wicklow St., Dublin 2 (☎ **01/677-7038**).

WOMEN'S

✪ **Cleo.** 18 Kildare St., Dublin 2. ☎ **01/676-1421.** www.netsolutions.ie/cleo. DART: Pearse. Bus: 10, 11A, 11B, 13, or 20B.

For more than 50 years, the Joyce family has created designer ready-to-wear clothing in a rainbow of vibrant tweed colors—elegant ponchos, capes, peasant skirts, coat-sweaters, decorative crios belts, and brimmed hats. A new line of hand-knit sweaters incorporates 4,000- to 5,000-year-old designs from carved cairn stones found at Newgrange.

Pat Crowley. 3 Molesworth Place, Dublin 2. ☎ **01/661-5580.** Fax 01/661-2476. DART: Pearse. Bus: 10, 11A, 11B, 13, or 20B.

This designer emphasizes individuality in her exclusive line of tweeds and couture eveningwear.

Sybil Connolly. 71 Merrion Sq., Dublin 2. ☎ **01/676-7281.** DART: Pearse. Bus: 5, 7A, or 8.

Irish high fashion is synonymous with this world-renowned made-to-measure designer. Eveningwear and Irish linen creations are her specialties.

GIFTS & KNICKKNACKS

House of Ireland. 37–38 Nassau St., Dublin 2. ☎ **01/677-7473.** www.hoi.ie. DART: Pearse. Bus: 5, 7A, 15A, 15B, 46, 55, 62, 63, 83, or 84.

This shop opposite Trinity College is a happy blend of European and Irish products, from Waterford and Belleek to Wedgwood and Lladró. It also carries tweeds, linens, knitwear, Celtic jewelry, mohair capes, shawls, kilts, blankets, and dolls. Ask about the 10% gift offer for mentioning this guide!

The Kilkenny Shop. 6–10 Nassau St., Dublin 2. ☎ **01/677-7066.** DART: Pearse. Bus: 5, 7A, 15A, 15B, 46, 55, 62, 63, 83, or 84.

A sister operation of the Blarney Woollen Mills (see below), this modern multilevel shop is a showplace for original Irish designs and quality products, including pottery, glass, candles, woolens, pipes, knitwear, jewelry, books, and prints. The pleasant cafe is ideal for coffee and pastries or a light lunch.

Weir and Sons. 96 Grafton St., Dublin 2. ☎ **01/677-9678.** DART: Pearse. Bus: 10, 11A, 11B, 13, or 20B.

Established in 1869, this is the granddaddy of Dublin's fine jewelry shops. It sells new and antique jewelry as well as silver, china, and glass items. There is a second branch at the ILAC Centre, Henry Street (☎ **01/872-9588**).

HERALDRY

Heraldic Artists. 3 Nassau St., Dublin 2. ☎ **01/679-7020.** www.roots.ie. DART: Pearse. Bus: 5, 7A, 8, 15A, 15B, 46, 55, 62, 63, 83, or 84.

For more than 20 years, this shop has been known for helping visitors locate their family roots. In addition to tracing surnames, it sells all the usual heraldic items, from family crest parchments, scrolls, and mahogany wall plaques to books on researching ancestry.

House of Names. 26 Nassau St., Dublin 2. ☎ **01/679-7287.** DART: Pearse. Bus: 5, 7A, 8, 15A, 15B, 46, 55, 62, 63, 83, or 84.

As its name implies, this company offers a wide selection of Irish, British, and European family names affixed—along with their attendant crests and mottoes—to plaques, shields, parchments, jewelry, glassware, and sweaters.

JEWELRY

The Steensons. 16 S. Frederick St., Dublin 2. ☎ and fax **01/672-7007.** DART: Pearse. Bus: 5, 7A, 15A, 15B, 46, 55, 62, 63, 83, or 84.

Bill and Christina Steenson, based in the North, have long been two of the most celebrated goldsmiths in Ireland. This, their first shop in the Republic, opened in November 1999 and was an immediate success. No wonder, as their workmanship and design are exquisite. The focus here is on contemporary Irish design, though roughly 20% of their inventory comes from other European sources, especially Germany.

KNITWEAR

Blarney Woollen Mills. 21–23 Nassau St., Dublin 2. ☎ **01/671-0068.** DART: Pearse. Bus: 5, 7A, 8, 15A, 15B, 46, 55, 62, 63, 83, or 84.

A branch of the highly successful Cork-based enterprise of the same name, this shop is opposite the south side of Trinity College. Known for its competitive prices, it stocks a wide range of woolen knitwear made at the home base in Blarney, as well as crystal, china, pottery, and souvenirs.

Dublin Woollen Mills. 41–42 Lower Ormond Quay, Dublin 1. ☎ **01/677-0301.** Bus: 70 or 80.

Since 1888, this shop has been a leading source of Aran handknit sweaters, vests, hats, jackets, and scarves, as well as lambswool sweaters, kilts, ponchos, and tweeds at competitive prices. It's on the north side of the River Liffey next to the Halfpenny Bridge. The shop offers a 5% discount for those with current international student cards.

✪ **Monaghan's.** 15/17 Grafton Arcade, Grafton St., Dublin 2. ☎ **01/677-0823.** DART: Pearse. Bus: 10, 11A, 11B, 13, or 20B.

Established in 1960 and operated by two generations of the Monaghan family, this store is a prime source of cashmere sweaters for men and women. It boasts the best selection of colors, sizes, and styles anywhere in Ireland. Other items include traditional Aran knits, lambswool, crochet, and Shetland wool products. There's another store at 4/5 Royal Hibernian Way, off Dawson Street (☎ **01/679-4451**).

MARKETS

Blackrock Market. 19a Main St., Blackrock. ☎ **01/283-3522.** DART: Blackrock. Bus: 5, 7, 7A, 8, 17, 45, or 114.

More than 60 vendors run stalls that offer everything from gourmet cheese to vintage clothing at great prices in an indoor/outdoor setting. Open Saturday 11am to 5:30pm, Sunday noon to 5:30pm, including public holidays.

Moore Street Market. Moore St., Dublin 1. No phone. DART: Connolly. Bus: 25, 34, 37, 38A, 66A, or 67A.

For a walk into the past, don't miss the Moore Street Market, full of streetside barrow vendors plus plenty of local color and chatter. It's the city's principal open-air fruit, flower, fish, and vegetable market.

✪ **Mother Red Caps Market.** Back Lane (off High St.), Dublin 8. ☎ **01/453-8306.** Bus: 21A, 78A, or 78B.

In the heart of Old Dublin, this enclosed market, which calls itself the "mother of all markets," is surely one of Dublin's best. The stalls offer a trove of hidden treasures (some more in hiding than others), including antiques, used books and coins, silver, handcrafts, leather products, knitwear, music tapes, and furniture. There's even a fortune-teller! It's worth a trip here just to sample the wares at the Ryefield Foods stall (farm-made cheeses, baked goods, marmalades, and jams). Open Friday to Sunday 10am to 5:30pm.

MUSIC

The Celtic Note. 14–15 Nassau St., Dublin 2. ☎ **01/670-4157.** www.celticnote.ie. DART: Pearse. Bus: 5, 7A, 15A, 15B, 46, 55, 62, 63, 83, or 84.

Despite its modest size, this is perhaps the finest single source of recorded Irish music in Dublin. At the least, it's a fine place to start your search for the Irish artist or tune you can't do without. The staff is experienced and helpful, and you can listen to a CD before purchasing it. You'll pay full price here, but you're likely to find what you're looking for.

7

Dublin After Dark

A more appropriate title for this section might be "Dublin Almost Dark," because during high season, Dublin's nightlife takes place mostly in daylight. Situated roughly 53° north of the equator, Dublin in June gets really dark only as the pubs are closing. Night, then, is just a state of mind.

One general fact to keep in mind concerning Dublin's nightlife is that there are very few fixed points. Apart from a handful of established institutions, venues come and go, change character, open their doors to ballet one night and cabaret the next. *In Dublin* and *The Event Guide* offer the most thorough and up-to-date listings. They can be found on almost any magazine stand.

The award-winning Web site of the *Irish Times* (**www. ireland.com**) offers a "what's on" daily guide to cinema, theater, music, and whatever else you're up for. *Time Out* now covers Dublin as well; check their Web site at **www.timeout. com/Dublin**.

Advance bookings for most large concerts, plays, and so forth can be made through **Ticketmaster Ireland** (☎ **01/ 677-9409;** www.ticketmaster.ie), with ticket centers in most HMV stores, as well as at the Dublin Tourism Centre, Suffolk Street, Dublin 2.

1 The Pub Scene

The mainstay of Dublin social life, by night and by day, is unquestionably the pub. More than 1,000 specimens are spread throughout the city, on every street, at every turn. In *Ulysses,* James Joyce referred to the puzzle of trying to cross Dublin without passing a pub; his characters quickly abandoned the quest as fruitless, preferring to sample a few in their path. Most visitors should follow in their footsteps and drop in on a few pubs.

The origin of pubs reaches back several centuries to a time when, for lack of trendy coffee bars or health clubs, neighbors would gather in a kitchen to talk and maybe sample some home brew. As a certain spot grew popular, word spread and people came from all directions, always assured of a warm welcome. Such places gradually became known as public houses—"pubs," for short. In time, the name of the person who tended a public house was mounted over the doorway, and many pubs still bear a family or proprietor's name, such as Davy Byrnes, Doheny and Nesbitt, or W. Ryan. Many, in fact, have been in the same family for generations. Although they might have added televisions, pool tables, and dartboards, their primary purpose is still to be a stage for conversation and a warm spot to down a pint or pack in an inexpensive lunch of pub grub. Pub grub is often a lot better than its name suggests; in recent years, many pubs have converted or expanded into restaurants, serving excellent unpretentious meals at prices to which you can lift a pint.

Hours in May to September are 10:30am to 11:30pm Monday to Saturday. October to April hours are 10:30am to 11pm. On Sunday year-round, bars are open from 12:30 to 2pm and from 4 to 11pm. Nightclubs and discos close at 2am. If the pub does not appear to be closing when the appointed hour arrives, it's because the official closing times are often not the actual closing times. Some laws, it seems, are made to be broken.

You will need no assistance finding a pub, but here are a few suggestions of some of the city's most distinctive.

PUBS FOR CONVERSATION & ATMOSPHERE

✪ **Brazen Head.** 20 Lower Bridge St., Dublin 8. ☎ **01/679-5186.**

This brass-filled, lantern-lit pub claims to be the city's oldest, and it might very well be, considering that it was licensed in 1661 and occupies the site of an even earlier tavern dating from 1198. Nestled on the south bank of the River Liffey, it is at the end of a cobblestone courtyard and was once the meeting place of Irish freedom fighters such as Robert Emmet and Wolfe Tone. A full à la carte menu is offered.

The Castle Inn. Christ Church Place, Dublin 8. ☎ **01/475-1122.**

Situated between Dublin Castle and Christ Church Cathedral, this recently rejuvenated bilevel pub exudes an "old city" atmosphere. It has stone walls, flagstone steps, suits of armor, big stone fireplaces, beamed ceilings, and lots of early Dublin memorabilia. From May to September, it is also the setting for an Irish Ceili (traditional music and dance session) and Banquet.

Davy Byrnes. 21 Duke St. (off Grafton St.), Dublin 2. ☎ **01/677-5217.**

Referred to as a "moral pub" by James Joyce in *Ulysses,* this imbibers' landmark has drawn poets, writers, and literature lovers ever since. It dates from 1873, when Davy Byrnes first opened the doors. He presided for more than 50 years, and visitors can still see his likeness on one of the turn-of-the-century murals hanging over the bar.

Doheny and Nesbitt. 5 Lower Baggot St., Dublin 2. ☎ **01/676-2945.**

The locals call this Victorian-style pub simply "Nesbitt's." The place houses two fine old "snugs"—small rooms with trap doors where women were served drinks in days of old—and a restaurant.

Flannery's Temple Bar. 47/48 Temple Bar. ☎ **01/497-4766.**

In the heart of the trendy Temple Bar district on the corner of Temple Lane, this small three-room pub was established in 1840. The decor is an interesting mix of crackling fireplaces, globe ceiling lights, old pictures on the walls, and shelves filled with local memorabilia. There's live Irish music daily.

J. W. Ryan. 28 Parkgate St., Dublin 7. ☎ **01/677-6097.**

A Victorian gem with a fine gourmet restaurant. You'll see some of Dublin's best traditional pub features, including a metal ceiling, a domed skylight, beveled mirrors, etched glass, brass lamp holders, a mahogany bar, and four old-style snugs. It's on the north side of the Liffey, near the Phoenix Park.

The Long Hall. 51 S. Great George's St., Dublin 2. ☎ **01/475-1590.**

Tucked into a busy commercial street, this is one of the city's most photographed pubs, with a beautiful Victorian decor of filigree-edged mirrors, polished dark woods, and traditional snugs. The hand-carved bar is said to be the longest counter in the city.

Neary's. 1 Chatham St., Dublin 2. ☎ **01/677-7371.**

Adjacent to the back door of the Gaiety Theatre, this celebrated enclave is a favorite with stage folk and theatergoers. Its trademarks are the pink-and-gray marble bar and the brass hands that support the globe lanterns adorning the entrance.

Palace Bar. 21 Fleet St., Dublin 2. ☎ **01/677-9290.**

This old charmer is decorated with local memorabilia, cartoons, and paintings that tell the story of Dublin through the years.

✪ **Stag's Head.** 1 Dame Court (off Dame St.), Dublin 2. ☎ **01/679-3701.**

Mounted stags' heads and eight stag-themed stained-glass windows dominate the decor, and there are wrought-iron chandeliers, polished Aberdeen granite, old barrels, skylights, and ceiling-high mirrors. Look for the stag sign inlaid into the sidewalk. This place is a classic.

PUBS WITH TRADITIONAL & FOLK MUSIC

✪ **Kitty O'Shea's.** 23–25 Upper Grand Canal St., Dublin 4. ☎ **01/660-9965.** No cover.

Just south of the Grand Canal, this popular pub is named after the sweetheart of 19th-century Irish statesman Charles Stewart Parnell. The decor reflects the Parnell era, with ornate oak paneling, stained-glass windows, old political posters, cozy alcoves, and brass railings. Traditional Irish music is on tap most every night.

Mother Red Caps Tavern. Back Lane, Dublin 8. ☎ **01/454-4655.** No cover except for concerts.

A former shoe factory in the heart of the Liberties section of the city, this large two-story pub exudes Old Dublin atmosphere. It has eclectic mahogany and stripped-pine furnishings, antiques and curios on the shelves, and walls lined with old paintings and 19th-century newspaper clippings. On Sundays, there is usually a midday session of traditional Irish music; everyone is invited to bring an instrument and join in. On many nights, there is traditional music on an informal basis or in a concert setting upstairs.

O'Donoghue's. 15 Merrion Row, Dublin 2. ☎ **01/661-4303.** No cover for music.

Tucked between St. Stephen's Green and Merrion Street, this smoke-filled enclave is widely heralded as the granddaddy of traditional music pubs. A spontaneous session is likely to erupt at almost any time of the day or night.

Oliver St. John Gogarty. 57/58 Fleet St. ☎ **01/671-1822.**

Situated in the heart of Temple Bar and named for one of Ireland's literary greats, this pub has an inviting old-world
atmosphere, with shelves of empty bottles, stacks of dusty
books, a horseshoe-shaped bar, and old barrels for seats. There
are traditional music sessions almost every night from 9 to
11pm, as well as Saturday at 4:30pm, and Sunday from noon
to 2pm.

LATE-NIGHT PUBS

If you're still going strong when the pubs shut down (11pm in
winter, 11:30pm in summer), you might want to crawl to a
"late-night pub"—one with a loophole allowing it to remain
open after hours. Late-nighters for the 18-to-25 set include
Hogans, 35 S. Great George's St., Dublin 2 (☎ **01/
677-5904**), and the **Club mono** (see "More Music," below).
After-hours pubs that attract the young and hip but are still
congenial for those over 25 include **Whelans,** 25 Wexford St.,
Dublin 2 (☎ **01/478-0766**), and the second-oldest pub in
Dublin, the **Bleeding Horse,** 24–25 Camden St., Dublin 2
(☎ **01/475-2705**). For the over-30 late crowd, these will fill
the bill and the glass: **Break for the Border,** Lower Steven's
Street, Dublin 2 (☎ **01/478-0300**); **Bad Bob's Backstage
Bar,** East Essex Street, Dublin 2 (☎ **01/677-5482**); **Major
Tom's,** South King Street, Dublin 2 (☎ **01/478-3266**); and
Sinnotts, South King Street, Dublin 2 (☎ **01/478-4698**).

2 The Club & Music Scene

Dublin's club and music scene is confoundingly complex and
volatile. Jazz, blues, folk, country, traditional, rock, and comedy move from venue to venue, night by night. The same club
could be a gay fetish scene one night and a traditional music
hotspot the next, so you have to stay on your toes to find what
you want. The first rule is to get the very latest listings and see
what's on and where (see the introduction to this chapter for
a couple of suggested resources). Keeping all this in mind, a
few low-risk generalizations might prove helpful to give you a
sense of what to expect.

One fact unlikely to change is that the night scene in
Dublin is definitively young, with a retirement age of about
25. The only exceptions are some hotel venues that are outside

the city center, very costly, or both. If you're over 25, your club choices are limited unless you happen to be a recognizable celebrity. In fact, even if you are or can pass for under 25, you may find yourself excluded unless you can present just the right image—a composite of outfit, hair, attitude, and natural endowment. Many of the most sizzling spots in Dublin (we'll call them trendy from here on) have a "strict" or "unfriendly" door policy, admitting only those who look and feel right for the scene within. The sought-after "look" might be unkindly described as "geek-chic" or, more neutrally, "retro."

Most trendy clubs have DJs and live music, and the genre of current choice is something called "rave," which I won't try to put into words. Another occasional ingredient of the trendy club scene in Dublin is "E" or "Ecstasy," the drug of choice among even the youngest clubgoers. Clubbers on "E" don't drink anything but water, which they must consume in great quantities. Though it may seem commonplace in this milieu, Ecstasy is both illegal and potentially lethal, and definitely not a wise vacation experience.

Cover charges tend to fluctuate not only from place to place, but from night to night and from person to person (some people can't buy their way in, while others glide in gratis). Average cover charges range from nominal to £10 ($14).

HIPPER THAN THOU

If you think you might pass muster, several of the more established cutting-edge clubs (with reputedly strict door policies) are the following:

The Kitchen. 6/8 Wellington Quay, Dublin 2. ☎ **01/677-6635.** Wed–Sun 11pm–2am.

In the basement of the Clarence Hotel in the heart of the Temple Bar district, this is one of Dublin's hottest, hippest nightclubs, partly owned by the rock group U2.

Lillie's Bordello. 45 Nassau St., Dublin 2. ☎ **01/679-9204.** Daily 10pm–1am or later.

This private three-story nightclub with two bars is open to members and nonmembers every night. The place has a stylish, self-consciously decadent ambience, with a mix of music every night.

Late-Night Bites

Although Dublin is keeping later and later hours, it is still nearly impossible to find anything approaching 24-hour dining. One place that comes close is the **Coffee Dock at Jurys Hotel,** Ballsbridge, Dublin 4 (☎ **01/660-5000**). It is open Monday 7am to 4:30am, Tuesday to Saturday 6am to 4:30am, Sunday 6am to 10:30pm. **Bewley's,** 78/79 Grafton St., Dublin 2 (☎ **01/ 677-6761**), is open until 1am on Friday and Saturday. **Juice,** 73–83 S. Great George's St., Dublin 2 (☎ **01/475-7856**), serves a limited menu Friday and Saturday until 4am.

POD. 35 Harcourt St., Dublin 2. ☎ **01/478-0166.** www.pod.ie. Wed–Sat 11pm–2am or later.

POD stands for "Place of Dance." Operated by John Reynolds (nephew of the former prime minister of Ireland, Albert Reynolds) the POD—a "European nightclub of the year"—has also won a European design award for its colorful Barcelona-inspired decor. It's as loud as it is dazzling to behold.

Republica. Earl of Kildare Hotel, Kildare St., Dublin 2. ☎ **01/679-4388.**

This is a new club to keep your eye on. When it opened in 1998, it was touted as the new benchmark in hip, with a really young scene. The fire didn't catch, however, and it changed management within a couple of months. Since then it has been widening its scene and finding its way.

Rí-Rá. 1 Exchequer St., Dublin 2. ☎ **01/677-4835.** Nightly 11:30pm–4am or later.

Though trendy, Rí-Rá has a friendlier door policy than most of its competition, so this may be the place to try first.

KINDER & GENTLER CLUBS

These established clubs, while they attract young singles and couples, have friendly door policies and are places where people of almost any age and ilk are likely to feel comfortable.

Annabel's. Burlington hotel, Upper Leeson St., Dublin 4. ☎ **01/660-5222.** Tues–Sat 10pm–2am.

Just south of the Lower Leeson Street nightclub strip, this club is one of the longest lasting in town. It welcomes a mix of tourists and locals of all ages with a disco party atmosphere.

Club M. Anglesea St., Dublin 2. ☎ **01/671-5622.** Tues–Sun 11pm–2am. Admission £5 ($7) Sun–Thurs, £7 ($9.80) Fri, £8 ($11.20) Sat.

In the basement of Blooms hotel, in the trendy Temple Bar district close to Trinity College, this club boasts Ireland's largest laser lighting system. It offers DJ-driven dance or live music for the over-23 age bracket.

YET MORE CLUBS

A few more places to try include: **Court,** in the Harcourt Hotel, Harcourt Street, Dublin 2 (☎ **01/478-3677**); **Rumours,** in the Gresham Hotel, O'Connell Street, Dublin 1 (☎ **01/872-2850**); the **Vatican,** Harcourt Street, Dublin 2 (no phone—did you really expect to ring the Vatican?); and **Zanzibar,** Lower Ormond Quay, Dublin 1 (on the north side of the Liffey near Halfpenny Bridge; ☎ **01/878-7212**).

MORE MUSIC

For live music, there are several top choices. On a given night, you can find almost anything—jazz, blues, rock, traditional Irish, country, or folk. Rock was dominant in the 1980s—in the wake of U2's success—when Dublin spawned new bands weekly, but it is no longer in the front seat. Instead, there's a real mix, so again, check the listings. The principal live music venues include **Whelans,** 25 Wexford St., Dublin 2 (☎ **01/478-0766**); **Eamon Doran's** (mostly an under-25 crowd), 3A Crown Alley, Temple Bar, Dublin 2 (☎ **01/679-9114**); the **Club mono,** 26 Wexford St., Dublin 2 (☎ **01/475-8555**); and a real favorite, **Midnight at the Olympia,** 74 Dame St., Dublin 2 (☎ **01/677-7744**).

3 Comedy & Cabaret

COMEDY CLUBS

The Irish comedy circuit is relatively new and quite popular. The timing, wit, and twist of mind required for comedy seems to me so native to the Irish that I find it difficult to draw a sharp line between those who practice comedy for a living and those who practice it as a way of life. You'll find both in the flourishing Dublin comedy clubs. Here are some of our favorites. Again, this is a mobile scene, so check the latest listing for details. Admission prices range from £4 ($5.60) to £15 ($21) depending on the night and the performer.

Comedy Improv/Comedy Cellar. International Bar, 23 Wicklow St., Dublin 2. ☎ **01/677-9250.**

A very small, packed venue, full of enthusiastic exchange. This is up-close, in-your-face improv, with nowhere to hide, so stake out your turf early.

Ha'Penny Bridge Inn. Beside Merchant's Arch, Wellington Quay, Dublin 2. ☎ **01/677-0616.**

Home to the Ha'Penny Laugh Improv Comedy Club and the Battle of the Axe. The former plays host to some of Ireland's funniest people, many of whom are on stage. The latter is a weekly show in which comedians, singers, songwriters, musicians, actors, and whoever storm the open mike in pursuit of the Lucky Duck Award.

Murphy's Laughter Lounge. O'Connell Bridge, Dublin 1. ☎ **1-800-COMEDY.**

This new 400-seat comedy venue is the current prime-time king of the Irish comedy circuit. It attracts the most popular stand-ups on the Irish scene—the O'Seinfelds, as it were—as well as international acts.

DINNER SHOWS & TRADITIONAL IRISH ENTERTAINMENT

Most of these shows are aimed at tourists, although locals also attend and enjoy them.

✪ **Abbey Tavern.** Abbey Rd., Howth, County Dublin. ☎ **01/839-0307.** Box office Mon–Sat 9am–5pm. Dinner 7pm, show 9pm; nightly in the summer months and 3 or 4 nights a week during the off-season, depending on demand. From Nov to Feb it's best to call ahead to find out on which nights shows will be offered.

After you've ordered an à la carte dinner, the show—authentic Irish ballad music, with its blend of fiddles, pipes, tin whistles, and spoons—costs an extra £3.50 ($4.90). The price of a full dinner and show averages £30 to £35 ($42–$49).

✪ **Culturlann Na hÉireann.** 32 Belgrave Sq., Monkstown, County Dublin. ☎ **01/280-0295.** www.comhaltas.com. Ceili dances Fri 9pm–midnight; informal music Fri–Sat 9:30–11:30pm; stage show mid-June to early Sept Mon–Thurs 9–10:30pm. Tickets for ceilis £5 ($7); informal music £1.50 ($2.10); stage show £6 ($8.40). DART: Monkstown. Bus: 7, 7A, or 8.

This is the home of Comhaltas Ceoltoiri Éireann, an Irish cultural organization that has been the prime mover in encouraging a renewed appreciation of and interest in Irish traditional music. The year-round entertainment programs include old-fashioned ceili dances and informal music sessions. In the summer, there's an authentic fully costumed show featuring traditional music, song, and dance. No reservations are necessary for any of the events.

Jurys Irish Cabaret. In Jurys Hotel and Towers, Pembroke Rd., Ballsbridge, Dublin 4. ☎ **01/660-5000.** May–Oct Tues–Sun dinner 7:15pm, show 8pm. Tickets £39 ($54.60). AE, DC, MC, V. Free parking. DART: Lansdowne Rd. Bus: 5, 7, 7A, or 8.

Ireland's longest-running show (more than 30 years) offers a unique mix. You'll see and hear traditional Irish and international music, rousing ballads and Broadway classics, toe-tapping set dancing and graceful ballet, humorous monologues and telling recitations, plus audience participation.

4 The Gay & Lesbian Scene

New gay and lesbian bars, clubs, and venues appear monthly, it seems, and many clubs and organizations, such as the Irish Film Centre, have special gay events or evenings once a week to once a month. The social scene ranges from quiet pub conversation and dancing to fetish nights and hilarious contests. Cover charges range from £3 to £10 ($4.20 to $14), depending on the club or venue, with discounts for students and seniors.

Check the *Gay Community News, In Dublin, The Event Guide,* or **"Dublin's Pink Pages"** (http://indigo.ie/~outhouse/) for the latest listings. Folks on the help lines, **Lesbians Organizing Together** (☎ 01/872-7770) and **Gay Switchboard Dublin** (☎ 01/872-1055), are also extremely helpful in directing you to activities of particular interest. (See "Tips for Travelers with Special Needs," in chapter 1, for details on many of these resources.)

The George Bar and Night Club. 89 S. Great George's St., Dublin 2. ☎ 01/478-2983. Admission £3–£7 ($4.20–$9.80). Daily 12:30–11pm; Wed–Sun 12:30pm–2:30am. DART: Tara St. Bus: 22A.

The George was the first gay bar in Dublin. It now houses two bars—one quiet and the other trendy, with dance music—and an after-hours nightclub, the Block, upstairs. It is a comfortable mixed-age venue. The nightclub hours are daily (except Tues and Wed) 9:30pm to 2am. Theme nights include "Carwash," a

1970s disco night every Thursday, and bingo in the bar Sundays at 5pm.

Out on the Liffey. 27 Upper Ormond Quay, Dublin 1. ☎ **01/872-2480.**
DART: Tara St. Walk up the Liffey and cross at Parliament Bridge. Bus: 34, 70,
or 80.

A 1996 addition to the gay and lesbian scene, this relaxed,
friendly pub caters to a balance of men and women and serves
up pub food with good conversation. In 1998, "Out" expanded to include a happening late-night venue, Oscar's, where
you can dance (or drink) until you drop.

Stonewallz. Molloy's Bar, High Street (beside Christchurch), Dublin 8.
☎ **01/872-7770.** Admission £4 ($5.60). No credit cards. Fri 10:30pm–2am.
Bus: 21A, 50, 50A, 78, 78A, or 78B.

Stonewallz, one of Dublin's most popular women-only clubs,
has moved to a new, more central, and expanded venue, offering three floors of music, each with its own style.

5 The Performing Arts

THEATER

Dublin has a venerable and vital theatrical tradition, in which
imagination and talent have consistently outstripped funding.
Apart from some mammoth shows at the Point, production
budgets and ticket prices remain modest, even minuscule,
compared with those in New York or any other major U.S.
city. With the exception of a handful of houses that offer a
more or less uninterrupted flow of productions, most theaters
mount shows only as they find the funds and opportunity to
do so. A few venerable (or at least well-established) theaters
offer serious drama more or less regularly.

In addition to the major theaters listed below, other venues
present fewer, although on occasion quite impressive, productions. They also book music and dance performances. They
include the **Focus Theatre,** 6 Pembroke Place, off Pembroke
Street, Dublin 2 (☎ **01/676-3071**); the **Gaiety Theatre,**
South King Street, Dublin 2 (☎ **01/677-1717**); the
Olympia, 72 Dame St., Dublin 2 (☎ **01/677-7744**); the
Players, Trinity College, Dublin 2 (☎ **01/677-3370,** ext.
1239); the **Project@The Mint,** Henry Place, off Henry
Street, Dublin 1 (☎ **1850-260027**); and the **Tivoli,**
135–138 Francis St., opposite Iveagh Market, Dublin 8
(☎ **01/454-4472**).

⭐ **Abbey Theatre.** Lower Abbey St., Dublin 1. ☎ **01/878-7222.** www. abbeytheatre.ie. Box office Mon–Sat 10:30am–7pm; shows Mon–Sat 8pm, Sat 2:30pm. Tickets £8–£16 ($11.20–$22.40). Senior, student, and children's discounts available Mon–Thurs evening and Sat matinee.

For more than 90 years, the Abbey has been the national theater of Ireland. The original theater, destroyed by fire in 1951, was replaced in 1966 by the current functional, although uninspired, 600-seat house. The Abbey's artistic reputation in Ireland has risen and fallen many times and is at present reasonably strong.

Andrews Lane Theatre. 9–17 St. Andrews Lane, Dublin 2. ☎ **01/679-5720.** Box office Mon–Sat 10:30am–7pm; shows Mon–Sat 8pm in theater, 8:15pm in studio. Tickets £8–£12 ($11.20–$16.80).

This relatively new venue has an ascending reputation for fine theater. It consists of a 220-seat main theater where contemporary work from home and abroad is presented, and a 76-seat studio geared for experimental productions.

The City Arts Centre. 23–25 Moss St., at City Quay. ☎ **01/677-0643.**

The City Arts Centre is an affiliate of Trans Europe Halles, the European network of independent arts centers. It presents a varied program, from dramatic productions, theatrical discussions, and readings by local writers to shows by touring companies from abroad. In May 2000, it was home to the World Stories Festival. Average ticket prices range from £5 to £7 ($7 to $9.80).

The Gate. 1 Cavendish Row, Dublin 1. ☎ **01/874-4368.** Box office Mon–Sat 10am–7pm; shows Mon–Sat 8pm. Tickets £13–£15 ($18.20–$21) or £10 ($14) for previews. AE, DC, MC, V.

Just north of O'Connell Street off Parnell Square, this recently restored 370-seat theater was founded in 1928 by Hilton Edwards and Michael MacLiammoir to provide a venue for a broad range of plays. That policy prevails today, with a program that includes a blend of modern works and the classics. Although less known by visitors, the Gate is easily as distinguished as the Abbey.

The Peacock. Lower Abbey St., Dublin 1. ☎ **01/878-7222.** www.abbeytheatre. ie. Box office Mon–Sat 10:30am–7pm; shows Mon–Sat 8:15pm, Sat 2:45pm. Tickets £5–£12 ($7–$16.80).

In the same building as the Abbey, this 150-seat theater features contemporary plays and experimental works. It books poetry readings and one-person shows, as well as plays in the Irish language.

CONCERTS

Music and dance concerts take place in a range of Dublin venues—theaters, churches, clubs, museums, sports stadiums, castles, parks, and universities—all of which can be found in local listings. The three institutions listed below stand out as venues where most world-class performances take place.

National Concert Hall. Earlsfort Terrace, Dublin 2. ☎ **01/475-1572.** www. nch.ie. Box office Mon–Sat 11am–7pm, Sun (on performance days) from 7pm. Tickets £8–£25 ($11.20–$35). Lunchtime concerts £4 ($5.60). DC, MC, V.

This magnificent 1,200-seat hall is home to the National Symphony Orchestra and Concert Orchestra, and host to an array of international orchestras and performing artists. In addition to classical music, there are evenings of Gilbert and Sullivan, opera, jazz, and recitals. The box office is open Monday to Friday from 10am to 3pm and from 6pm to close of concert. Open weekends 1 hour before concerts. Parking is available on the street.

The Point. East Link Bridge, North Wall Quay. ☎ **01/836-3633.** Tickets £10–£50 ($14–$70). AE, DC, MC, V.

With a seating capacity of 3,000, The Point is Ireland's newest large theater/concert venue, attracting top Broadway-caliber shows and international stars. The box office is open Monday to Saturday 10am to 6pm. Parking is £3 ($4.20) per car.

Royal Dublin Society (RDS). Merrion Rd., Ballsbridge, Dublin 2. ☎ **01/668-0645.** www.rds.ie. Box office hours vary according to events; shows 8pm. Most tickets £10–£30 ($14–$42).

Although best known as the venue for the Dublin Horse Show, this huge show-jumping arena is also the setting for major music concerts. It holds seating and standing room for more than 6,000 people.

8

Side Trips from Dublin

*F*anning out a little over 12 miles (19km) in each direction, Dublin's southern and northern suburbs offer a variety of interesting sights and experiences. All are easy to reach by public transportation or rental car.

1 Dublin's Southern Suburbs

Stretching southward from Ballsbridge, Dublin's prime southern suburbs, **Dun Laoghaire,** ✪ **Dalkey,** and **Killiney,** are on the edge of Dublin Bay. They all offer lovely seaside views and walks. Dun Laoghaire has a long promenade and a bucolic park, Killiney has a stunning expanse of beach, and Dalkey has something for just about everyone.

Thanks to DART service, these towns are easily accessible from downtown Dublin. They offer a good selection of restaurants and fine places to stay. A hillside overlooking Dublin Bay outside the village of Killiney is the setting for the Dublin area's only authentic deluxe castle hotel, Fitzpatrick Castle (see "Accommodations," below).

If you're traveling to Ireland by ferry from Holyhead, Wales, your first glimpse of Ireland will be the port of Dun Laoghaire. Many people decide to base themselves here and commute into downtown Dublin each day. As a base, it is less expensive than Dalkey, but less attractive too.

ATTRACTIONS

Dalkey Castle and Heritage Centre. Castle St., Dalkey, County Dublin. ☎ **01/285-8366.** Admission £2.50 ($3.50) adults, £2 ($2.80) seniors and students, £1.50 ($2.10) children, £8 ($11.20) family. Apr–Oct Mon–Fri 9:30am–5pm, Sat–Sun 11am–5pm; Nov–Mar Sat–Sun 11am–5pm DART: Dalkey. Bus: 8.

The lovely seaside village of Dalkey, on the southern edge of the ancient Pale, makes a memorable outing, whether for several hours or for an entire day. However long your stay,

Dalkey's Heritage Centre, housed in a 16th-century tower house, is the place to begin. Its fascinating exhibitions unfold this venerable town's remarkable history. Then, from the center's battlements, you can put it all in place as well as enjoy vistas of the Dublin area coastline. Adjoining the center is a medieval graveyard and the Church of St. Begnet, Dalkey's patron saint, whose foundations may be traced to Ireland's Early Christian period. Booklets sketching the history of the town, the church, and the graveyard are available at the Heritage Centre. You'll see and appreciate more of this landmark town if you purchase these and take them next door to the Queens Bar for a pint and quick scan. "Those who are patient," wrote the playwright Hugh Leonard, "and will sit, wait and listen or will linger along the tree-shaded roads running down to the sea, can hear the centuries pass."

The Ferryman. Coliemore Rd. (at stone wharf, adjacent to a seaside apartment complex). ☎ **01/283-4298.** Island ferry round-trip £5 ($7) adults, £3 ($4.20) children; rowboat rental £8 ($11.20)/hr. June–Aug, weather permitting.

Young Aidan Fennel heads the third generation of Fennels to ferry visitors to nearby Dalkey Island, whose only current inhabitants are a small herd of wild goats and the occasional seal. Aidan is a boat builder, and his brightly painted fleet is mostly from his own hand. The island, settled about 6000 B.C., offers three modest ruins: a church that's over 1,000 years old, ramparts dating from the 15th century, and a martello tower constructed in 1804 to make Napoleon think twice. Now the island is little more than a lovely picnic spot. If you want to build up an appetite and delight your children or sweetheart, row out in one of Aidan's handmade boats.

James Joyce Museum. Sandycove, County Dublin. ☎ **01/280-9265.** Admission £2.70 ($3.80) adults, £2.20 ($3.10) seniors and students, £1.40 ($1.95) children, £7.95 ($11.15) family. Apr–Oct Mon–Sat 10am–1pm and 2–5pm; Sun 2–6pm. Closed Nov–Mar. DART: Sandycove. Bus: 8.

Sitting on the edge of Dublin Bay about 6 miles (9.7km) south of the city center, this 40-foot granite monument is one of a series of martello towers built in 1804 to withstand an invasion threatened by Napoleon. The tower's great claim to fame is that James Joyce lived here in 1904. He was the guest of Oliver Gogarty, who had rented the tower from the Army for an annual fee of £8 ($11.20). Joyce, in turn, made the tower the setting for the first chapter of *Ulysses,* and it has been

Side Trips from Dublin

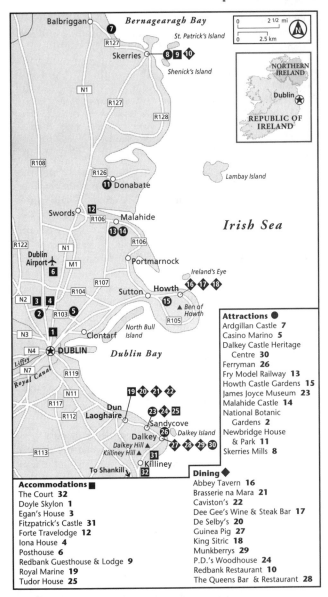

Balbriggan

Bernagearagh Bay

St. Patrick's Island

R127

Skerries

Shenick's Island

N1

R127

R128

R126

Donabate

Lambay Island

Swords

R106

Malahide

R106

Irish Sea

R122

N1

Dublin Airport ✈

M1

Portmarnock

Ireland's Eye

R107

R104

Sutton

Howth

N2

R103

North Bull Island

Ben of Howth

R105

DUBLIN

Clontarf

Dublin Bay

Liffey

N3

N4

N7

Royal Canal

R119

N11

R117

Dun Laoghaire

R112

Sandycove

Dalkey

Dalkey Island

Dalkey Hill ▲
Killiney Hill ▲

Killiney

R113

To Shankill ↓

0   2 1/2 mi
0   2.5 km

N

NORTHERN IRELAND

Dublin ⊛

REPUBLIC OF IRELAND

Attractions ●
Ardgillan Castle **7**
Casino Marino **5**
Dalkey Castle Heritage Centre **30**
Ferryman **26**
Fry Model Railway **13**
Howth Castle Gardens **15**
James Joyce Museum **23**
Malahide Castle **14**
National Botanic Gardens **2**
Newbridge House & Park **11**
Skerries Mills **8**

Accommodations ■
The Court **32**
Doyle Skylon **1**
Egan's House **3**
Fitzpatrick's Castle **31**
Forte Travelodge **12**
Iona House **4**
Posthouse **6**
Redbank Guesthouse & Lodge **9**
Royal Marine **19**
Tudor House **25**

Dining ◆
Abbey Tavern **16**
Brasserie na Mara **21**
Caviston's **22**
Dee Gee's Wine & Steak Bar **17**
De Selby's **20**
Guinea Pig **27**
King Sitric **18**
Munkberrys **29**
P.D.'s Woodhouse **24**
Redbank Restaurant **10**
The Queens Bar & Restaurant **28**

known as Joyce's Tower ever since. Its collection of Joycean memorabilia includes letters, documents, first and rare editions, personal possessions, and photographs.

ACCOMMODATIONS
Expensive

✪ **Fitzpatrick Castle Hotel.** Killiney Hill Rd., Killiney, County Dublin. ☎ **01/284-0700.** Fax 01/285-0207. www.fitzpatrickhotels.com. 113 units. TV TEL. £149–£178 ($208.60–$249.20) double. No service charge. Breakfast £10.50 ($14.70). AE, DC, MC, V. DART: Dalkey. Bus: 59.

With a fanciful Victorian facade of turrets, towers, and battlements, this restored 1741 gem is an ideal choice for those who want to live like royalty. A 15-minute drive from the center of the city, it is between the villages of Dalkey and Killiney, on 9 acres of gardens and hilltop grounds with romantic vistas of Dublin Bay. Two generations of the Fitzpatrick family pamper guests with 20th-century comforts in a regal setting of medieval suits of armor, Louis XIV–style furnishings, Irish antiques, original oil paintings, and specially woven shamrock-pattern green carpets. Most of the guest rooms have four-poster or canopy not-so-firm beds, and many have balconies with sweeping views of Dublin and the surrounding countryside. Nonsmoking rooms are available. In spite of its size and exacting standards, the castle never fails to exude a friendly, family-run atmosphere.

Dining/Diversions: Choices include a Victorian-style French and Irish restaurant, Truffles; the Castle Grill for informal meals; the posh Cocktail Bar; and the Dungeon, a pub and nightclub.

Amenities: 24-hour room service, concierge, laundry service, courtesy minibus service to downtown and the airport, indoor swimming pool, gym, saunas, squash and tennis courts, hairdressing salon, guest privileges at nearby 18-hole golf course.

Royal Marine. Marine Rd., Dun Laoghaire, County Dublin. ☎ **800/44-UTELL** from the U.S., or 01/280-1911. Fax 01/280-1089. www.ryan-hotels.com. 103 units. TV TEL. £90–£220 ($126–$308) double. Rates include full breakfast and service charge. AE, DC, MC, V. DART: Dun Laoghaire. Bus: 7, 7A, or 8.

A tradition along the seafront since 1870, this four- and five-story landmark sits on a hill overlooking the harbor, 7 miles (11km) south of Dublin City. It's a good place to stay for ready access to the ferry across the Irish Sea to and from Wales. Basically a Georgian building with a wing of modern rooms, the Royal Marine has public areas that have been beautifully restored and recently refurbished, with original molded ceilings and elaborate cornices, crystal chandeliers, marble-mantled fireplaces, and antique furnishings. The rooms, many of which offer wide-windowed views of the bay, carry through the Georgian theme, with dark woods, traditional floral fabrics, and four-poster or canopy beds. Some newer rooms have light woods and pastel tones. All units have up-to-date facilities, including hair dryers and garment presses.

Dining/Diversions: The dining room has a panoramic view of the bay, and there's a lounge bar.

Amenities: 24-hour room service, concierge, laundry service.

MODERATE

The Court Hotel. Killiney Bay Rd., Killiney, County Dublin. ☎ **800/ 221-2222** from the U.S. Fax 01/285-2085. www.killineycourt.ie. 86 units. TV TEL. £89–£134 ($124.60–$187.60) double. Rates include full Irish breakfast and service charge. AE, DC, MC, V. DART: Killiney. Bus: 59.

Situated on 4 acres of gardens and lawns, this three-story Victorian hotel enjoys a splendid location overlooking Killiney Bay and convenient access to Dublin (the DART station is nearby). The hotel's multiple lounges and popular restaurants were recently refurbished and are bright and welcoming. The guest rooms, many of which have views of the bay, are adequate but unremarkable. There's a concierge, and room service and laundry service are available. The real draw of this hotel is its lovely setting, which is convenient for excursions to Dublin as well as evening strolls on one of the most beautiful beaches on Ireland's east coast.

Note: The Court will give up to a 20% discount to guests carrying this guide.

Tudor House. Dalkey (off Castle St. between the church and Archbolds Castle), County Dublin. ☎ **01/285-1528.** Fax 01/284-8133. www.iol.ie/tudor. 6 units (all with shower only). TV TEL. £70–£90 ($98–$126) double. Rates include full breakfast and service charge. MC, V. DART: Dalkey, then 7-min. walk.

This handsome Gothic Revival Victorian manor house, built in 1848, has been lovingly restored to its original elegance by Katie and Peter Haydon. Set back from the town center, nestled behind a church, Tudor House rises to give all the guest rooms a pleasing view of Dublin Bay over the roof and treetops of Dalkey. The decor is tasteful and serene, enhanced by antiques and fresh flowers. The blue Wedgwood Room is particularly spacious and offers a firm double bed beneath a glittering chandelier; down the hall, the cozy corner room is bright and comfortable, with twin beds. The nearby DART commuter rail cannot be seen but may be heard by a light sleeper; the Dun Laoghaire ferry port is 1¾ miles (2.8km) away. Business and touring guests alike appreciate the splendid breakfast and helpful attention of the knowledgeable hosts. The Haydons can arrange baby-sitting, laundry, dry cleaning, fax, and Internet services.

DINING
EXPENSIVE

Brasserie na Mara. Harbour, Dun Laoghaire, County Dublin. ☎ **01/ 280-6767.** Reservations required. 4-course table d'hôte lunch £12.95 ($18.15); 4-course fixed-price dinner £20.95 ($29.35); main courses £10–£16 ($14–$22.40). Mon–Fri 12:30–2:30pm; Mon–Sat 6:30–10pm. DART: Dun Laoghaire. Bus: 7, 7A, 8, or 46A. SEAFOOD/CONTEMPORARY IRISH.

Award-winning chef Adrian Spelman keeps this fine seafood restaurant high on the charts, even in ever-steepening competition. Set squarely in the bustle of Dun Laoghaire's busy seafront, this elegant restaurant has been a benchmark for South Dublin cuisine since 1971. In addition to the house specialty, seafood, you can count on an array of poultry and meat dishes, from guinea fowl to Irish beef, as well as vegetarian options. Flaming desserts—another specialty—provide both high drama and suitable closure.

Guinea Pig. 17 Railway Rd., Dalkey, County Dublin. ☎ **01/285-9055.** Reservations required. 5-course table d'hôte £28.50 ($39.90). Special-value menu Sun–Fri 6–8pm, Sat 6–7pm £14.50 ($20.20). AE, DC, MC, V. Sun 5–9:30pm; Mon–Sat 5:30–11:30pm. DART: Dalkey. Bus: 8. SEAFOOD/FRENCH.

The Guinea Pig, like its namesake, is small and easily overlooked, but to do so would be a loss—it's a fine restaurant with a well-deserved following. The menu emphasizes whatever is freshest and in season. It often includes a signature dish called *symphony de la mer* (a potpourri of fish and crustaceans), wild salmon with coriander sauce, fillets of lemon sole with cockle and mussel sauce, and rack of lamb. While offering a worthy wine list, the Guinea Pig also offers a surprisingly adequate house white and red for a fraction of the price of their rack-mates. The culinary domain of chef-owner Mervyn Stewart, a former mayor of Dalkey, the restaurant is decorated in Irish country style with Victorian touches.

MODERATE

Caviston's Seafood Restaurant. 59 Glasthule Rd., Dun Laoghaire, County Dublin. ☎ **01/280-2715.** Reservations recommended. Main courses £7.50–£15 ($10.50–$21). DC, MC, V. Tues–Sat 3 sittings: noon, 1:30pm, 3pm.

Fresh, fresh fish is the hallmark of this tiny restaurant in Dun Laoghaire. It's run by the Caviston family, whose neighboring delicatessen and fish shop is legendary. There's no doubt that such expertise in scales and fins transfers to the preparation of fish in the restaurant itself: fish dishes are simply prepared, depending on one or two well-chosen ingredients to enhance delicate flavors. Unfortunately, the pleasure of lunch here dissipates quickly under the impatient influence of a waitstaff who rush diners in order to accommodate three lunchtime sittings.

De Selby's. 17/18 Patrick St. (off George's St.), Dun Laoghaire, County Dublin. ☎ **01/284-1761.** Reservations recommended. Dinner main courses £6.95–£13.95 ($9.75–$19.55). AE, CB, DC, MC, V. Mon–Thurs noon–2:30pm and 5–10pm; Fri–Sat noon–2:30pm and 5–11pm; Sun noon–10pm. DART: Dun Laoghaire. Bus: 7, 7A, 8, or 46A. INTERNATIONAL.

Named after a self-styled Dun Laoghaire philosopher in a Flann O'Brien book, this restaurant is in the center of the town. Its partially restored brick walls and fresh decor are accompanied by a new menu, which features more fresh fish entrees. There's also an outdoor eating area. The menu includes traditional Irish stew, Dublin Bay scampi, salmon en croûte, grilled lamb cutlets, steaks, and burgers. It's a busy spot, especially on weekends, patronized by those enjoying a day's outing at the seaport.

Munkberrys. Castle St., Dalkey, County Dublin. ☎ **01/284-7185.** Reservations recommended. 4-course fixed-price dinner £21.95 ($30.75). Main courses £8.50–£15.50 ($11.90–$21.70). Early-bird fixed-price dinner (Mon–Sat 5:30–7pm) £14.95 ($20.95). AE, DC, MC, V. Mon–Fri noon–2:30pm; Mon–Fri 5:30–10pm; Sat 5:30–10:30pm; Sun noon–6pm. DART: Dalkey. CONTINENTAL.

Crisp linens, candlelit glass, and tasteful contemporary art lend an immediate calm to this intimate street-front restaurant. The excitement here lies in the food, provoking at once both the eye and the palate. The crostini of goats cheese with fresh figs and spicy tomato chutney arrives on a swirl of delicious and mysterious sauces. The spinach ricotta tortelloni with a stilton, pistachio, and cognac sauce and the roast fillet of salmon with a saffron vermouth sauce are perfectly prepared and elegant to behold. It is a struggle to decide between the lemon crème brûlée with hazelnut biscuit, the steamed date pudding with butterscotch, and the Italian ice cream. While the service is especially attentive, there is no appreciable separation of smokers and nonsmokers, who are potentially at arm's length from each other. Nonsmokers may want to arrive early and ask for whatever isolation is possible.

✪ **P.D.'s Woodhouse.** 1 Coliemore Rd., Dalkey center, County Dublin. ☎ **01/284-9399.** Reservations recommended. Main courses £7.95–£15.95 ($11.15–$23.35). Service charge 10%. AE, CB, DC, MC, V. Mon–Sat 6–11pm; Sun 4–9:30pm. DART: Dalkey. IRISH/MEDITERRANEAN.

This restaurant is brought to you by Hurricane Charlie, the worst tropical storm to hit Ireland in recent memory. The first and only oak-wood barbecue bistro in Ireland, P.D.'s Woodhouse depends on oaks ripped up by Charlie and stored in Wicklow. Like Charlie, the wild Irish salmon in caper and herb butter is devastating, as is the white sole. But whatever you do, don't miss the Halumi cheese kebabs—conversation-stopping grilled Greek goat cheese. On the other hand, the nut kebabs, one of several vegetarian entrees, are unnecessarily austere.

✪ **The Queens Bar and Restaurant.** 12 Castle St., Dalkey, County Dublin. ☎ **01/285-4569.** Reservations not accepted. Dinner main courses £7.85–£13.95 ($11–$19.55); bar menu £1.90–£7.25 ($2.65–$10.15). AE, DC, MC, V. Bar daily noon–midnight; bar food Mon–Sat noon–5pm, Sun 12:30–5pm. Restaurant Mon–Sat 6–11pm, Sun 6–10pm. DART: Dalkey. Bus: 8. INTERNATIONAL.

One of Ireland's oldest inns, this historic establishment has won a pocketful of awards, including Dublin's best pub in 1992. It has great atmosphere and food to match. In the center of town, the informal trattoria has an open kitchen—a contrast to the usual pub grub. The low end of the menu leans toward pastas and pizzas, while the high end includes spicy Jamaican jerk chicken, T-bone steak, half a roast crispy duck, and the catch of the day. In addition, there are daily specials and an interesting selection of antipasti. Upstairs, a recent development, the Vico Restaurant and Piano Bar, adds new flavors and style to this revered and flourishing establishment.

PUBS

P. McCormack and Sons. 67 Lower Mounttown Rd. (off York Rd.), Dun Laoghaire, County Dublin. ☎ **01/284-2634.**

If you rent a car and head toward the city's southern seaside suburbs, this is a great place to stop for refreshment. Park in the lot and step into the atmosphere of your choice. The main section has an old-world feel, with globe lamps, stained-glass windows, books and jugs on the shelves, and lots of nooks and crannies for a quiet drink. In the skylit, plant-filled conservatory area, classical music fills the air, and outdoors you'll find a festive courtyard beer garden. The pub grub here is top-notch, with a varied buffet table of lunchtime salads and meats.

The Purty Kitchen. Old Dunleary Rd., Dun Laoghaire, County Dublin. ☎ **01/284-3576.** No cover for traditional music; cover £5–£6 ($7–$8.40) for blues and rock in the Loft.

Housed in a building that dates from 1728, this old pub has a homey atmosphere, with an open brick fireplace, cozy alcoves, a large fish mural, and pub poster art on the walls. There's often free Irish traditional music in the main bar area (the schedule varies, so call ahead). Blues and rock musicians play upstairs in the Loft on Thursday and Sunday at 9pm, and there's dance music with a DJ on Friday and Saturday at 9pm.

2 Dublin's Northern Suburbs

Dublin's northern suburbs are best known as the home of **Dublin International Airport,** but they're also home to a delightful assortment of castles, historic buildings, gardens, and other attractions. In addition, the residential suburbs of **Drumcondra** and **Glasnevin** offer many good lodgings.

Just north of Dublin, the picturesque suburb of **Howth** offers panoramic views of Dublin Bay, beautiful hillside gardens, and many fine seafood restaurants. Best of all, it is easily reached on the DART. Farther north along the coast, but only 20 minutes from Dublin Airport, lies the bustling and attractive seaside town of **Skerries.** Skerries is a convenient and appealing spot to spend your first or last night in Ireland; or stay longer and explore all this area has to offer, including a resident colony of grey seals and the lowest annual rainfall in Ireland.

ATTRACTIONS

Ardgillan Castle and Park. Balbriggan, County Dublin. ☎ **01/849-2212.** Admission to house £3 ($4.20) adults, £2 ($2.80) seniors and students, £6.50 ($9.10) family. Castle open Oct–Dec and Feb–Mar Tues–Sun 11am–4:30pm; Apr–June Tues–Sun 11am–6pm; July–Aug daily 11am–6pm; Sept Tues–Sun 11am–6pm. Park open daily dawn to dusk. Closed Jan. Free parking year-round. Signposted off N1. Bus: 33.

Between Balbriggan and Skerries, north of Malahide, this recently restored 18th-century castellated country house sits right on the coastline. The house, home of the Taylour family until 1962, was built in 1738. It contains some fine period furnishings and antiques, as well as a public tearoom. But the real draw is the setting, right on the edge of the Irish Sea, with miles of walking paths and coastal views as well as a rose garden and an herb garden.

Casino Marino. Malahide Rd., Marino, Dublin 3. ☎ **01/833-1618.** Admission £2 ($2.80) adults, £1.50 ($2.10) seniors and group members, £1 ($1.40) students and children, £5 ($7) family. Feb–Apr and Nov Sun and Thurs noon–4pm; May and Oct daily 10am–5pm; June–Sept daily 9:30am–6:30pm. Closed Dec–Jan. Bus: 20A, 20B, 27, 27A, 27B, 42, 42B, or 42C.

Standing on a gentle rise 3 miles (4.8km) north of the city center, this 18th-century building is considered one of the finest garden temples in Europe. Designed in the Franco-Roman neoclassical style by Scottish architect Sir William Chambers, it was constructed in the garden of Lord Charlemont's house by the English sculptor Simon Vierpyl. Work commenced in 1762 and was completed 15 years later. It is particularly noteworthy for its elaborate stone carvings and compact structure, which make it appear to be a single story (it is actually two stories tall).

The Fry Model Railway. Malahide, County Dublin. ☎ **01/846-3779.** Admission £2.90 ($4.05) adults, £2.20 ($3.10) seniors and students, £1.70 ($2.40) children, £7.95 ($11.15) family. Apr–Oct Mon–Sat 10am–5pm, Sun 2–6pm; Nov–Mar Sun 2–5pm. Closed for tours 1–2pm year-round. Suburban Rail to Malahide. Bus: 42.

On the grounds of Malahide Castle (see listing below), this is an exhibit of rare handmade models of more than 300 Irish trains, from the introduction of rail to the present. The trains were built in the 1920s and 1930s by Cyril Fry, a railway engineer and draftsman. The complex includes items of Irish railway history dating from 1834, and models of stations, bridges, trams, buses, barges, boats, the River Liffey, and the Hill of Howth.

Howth Castle Rhododendron Gardens. Howth, County Dublin. ☎ **01/ 832-2624.** Free admission. Apr–June daily 8am–sunset. DART: Howth. Bus: 31.

On a steep slope about 8 miles (13km) north of downtown, this 30-acre garden was first planted in 1875 and is best known for its 2,000 varieties of rhododendrons. Peak bloom time is in May and June. *Note:* The castle and its private gardens are not open to the public.

✪ **Malahide Castle.** Malahide, County Dublin. ☎ **01/846-2184.** E-mail: malahidecastle@dublintourism.ie. Admission £3.15 ($4.40) adults, £2.65 ($3.70) students and seniors, £1.75 ($2.45) children under 12, £8.75 ($12.90) family; gardens free. AE, MC, V. Combination tickets with Fry Model Railway and Newbridge House available. Apr–Oct Mon–Sat 10am–5pm, Sun 11am– 6pm; Nov–Mar Mon–Fri 10am–5pm, Sat–Sun 2–5pm; gardens May–Sept daily 2–5pm. Closed for tours 12:45–2pm (restaurant remains open). Suburban Rail to Malahide. Bus: 42.

About 8 miles (13km) north of Dublin, Malahide is one of Ireland's most historic castles. Founded in the 12th century by Richard Talbot, it was occupied by his descendants until 1973. The fully restored interior is the setting for a comprehensive collection of Irish furniture, dating from the 17th to the 19th centuries. One-of-a-kind Irish historical portraits and tableaux on loan from the National Gallery line the walls. The furnishings and art reflect life in and near the house over the past 8 centuries.

After touring the house, you can explore the 250-acre estate, which includes 20 acres of prized **gardens** with more than 5,000 species of plants and flowers. The Malahide grounds also contain the **Fry Model Railway** museum (see above) and **Tara's Palace,** an antique dollhouse and toy collection.

✪ **National Botanic Gardens.** Botanic Rd., Glasnevin, Dublin 9. ☎ **01/ 837-7596.** Free admission. Guided tour £1.50 ($2.25). Apr–Oct Mon–Sat 9am–6pm and Sun 11am–6pm; Nov–Mar Mon–Sat 10am–4:30pm and Sun 11am–4:30pm. Bus: 13, 19, or 134.

Established by the Royal Dublin Society in 1795 on a rolling 50-acre expanse of land north of the city center, this is

Dublin's horticultural showcase. The attractions include more than 20,000 different plants and cultivars, a Great Yew Walk, a bog garden, a water garden, a rose garden, and an herb garden. A variety of Victorian-style glass houses are filled with tropical plants and exotic species. Remember this spot when you suddenly crave refuge from the bustle of the city. It's a quiet, lovely haven, within a short walk of Glasnevin Cemetery. All but the rose garden is wheelchair accessible. Parking is free for now, but a fee is being considered for later in 2000 or 2001.

Newbridge House and Park. Donabate, County Dublin. ☎ **01/843-6534.** Admission £3 ($4.20) adults, £2.60 ($3.65) seniors and students, £1.65 ($2.30) children, £8.25 ($11.55) family. Apr–Sept Tues–Sat 10am–1pm and 2–5pm, Sun 2–6pm; Oct–Mar Sat–Sun 2–5pm. Suburban rail to Donabate. Bus: 33B.

This country mansion 12 miles (19km) north of Dublin dates from 1740 and was once the home of Dr. Charles Cobbe, an archbishop of Dublin. Occupied by the Cobbe family until 1984, the house is a showcase of family memorabilia such as hand-carved furniture, portraits, daybooks, and dolls, as well as a museum of objects collected on world travels. The Great Drawing Room, in its original state, is reputed to be one of the finest Georgian interiors in Ireland. The house sits on 350 acres, laid out with picnic areas and walking trails. The grounds also include a 20-acre working Victorian farm stocked with animals, as well as a craft shop and a coffee shop. The coffee shop remains open during the lunch hour (1 to 2pm).

Skerries Mills. Skerries, County Dublin. ☎ **01/849-5208.** http://indigo.ie/~skerries. Admission £3 ($4.20) adults; £2.25 (3.15) seniors, students, and children; £7.50 ($10.50) family. Apr–Sept daily 10:30am–6pm; Oct–Mar daily 10:30am–4:30pm. Closed Dec 20–Jan 1. Suburban Rail. Bus: 33. Skerries town and the Mills signposted North of Dublin off the N1.

This fascinating new 45-acre historical complex has been open for only a year and is already becoming a major attraction. Why? Well, for one thing, what's more basic than bread? And this site has provided it on and off since the 12th century. Originally part of an Augustinian Priory, the mill has had many lives (and deaths). Last known as the Old Mill Bakery, providing loaves to the local north coast, it suffered a devastating fire in 1986 and lay in ruins until it was reborn as Skerries

Mills in 1999. An ambitious restoration project has brought two restored windmills and a watermill, complete with grinding, winnowing, and threshing wheels, back into operation. And there's even an adjoining field of grains—barley, oats, and wheat, all that's needed for the traditional brown loaf—sown, harvested, and threshed using traditional implements and machinery. The result is not only the sweet smell of fresh bread but an intriguing glimpse into the past, brought to life not only by guided tours but also by the opportunity to put your own hand to the stone and to grind your own flour on rotary or saddle querns. Then, if you've worked up an appetite, there's a lovely tearoom, often hosting live music, Irish dancing, and other events. Besides all this, there are rotating special exhibits and a fine gift shop of Irish crafts.

ACCOMMODATIONS

MODERATE

Doyle Skylon. Upper Drumcondra Rd., Dublin 9. ☎ **800/42-DOYLE** from the U.S., or 01/837-9121. Fax 01/837-2778. www.doylehotels.com. 88 units. TV TEL. £94–£128 ($131.60–$179.20) double. Rates include full Irish breakfast and service charge. AE, DC, MC, V. Bus: 3, 11, 16, 41, 41A, or 41B.

With a modern five-story facade of glass and concrete, this hotel stands out on the city's north side, situated midway between downtown and the airport. Set on its own grounds in a residential neighborhood next to a college, it is just 10 minutes from the heart of the city. Several major bus routes stop outside the door. Guest rooms contain all the latest amenities and colorful, Irish-made furnishings. For full-service dining, the Rendezvous Room is a modern, plant-filled restaurant with an Irish and Continental menu. For drinks, try the Joycean pub. The hotel has a concierge, room service, laundry service, and a gift shop.

Posthouse. Dublin Airport, County Dublin. ☎ **800/225-5843** from U.S., or 01/808-0500. Fax 01/844-6002. 249 units. TV TEL. £90–£180 ($126–$252) double. Rates include service charge and full breakfast. AE, DC, MC, V. Bus: 41 or 41C.

This is the only hotel on the airport grounds, 7 miles (11km) north of the city center. Behind a modern three-story brick facade, it has a sunken skylit lobby with a central courtyard surrounded by guest rooms. The rooms are contemporary and functional, with windows looking out into the courtyard or toward distant mountain vistas. Each room is equipped with standard furnishings plus a full-length mirror, a hair dryer, tea/coffee-making facilities, and a trouser press. Nonsmoking rooms and rooms for travelers with disabilities may be requested. The hotel has a concierge, 24-hour room service, valet laundry service, and a courtesy coach to and from the airport. There's a gift shop on the premises. Dining choices include the Garden Room restaurant for Irish cuisine, and Sampans for Chinese food (at dinner only). The Bodhrán Bar is a traditional Irish bar with live music on weekends.

INEXPENSIVE

Egan's House. 7/9 Iona Park (between Botanic and Lower Drumcondra Rds.), Glasnevin, Dublin 9. ☎ **800/937-9767** from the U.S., or 01/830-3611. Fax 01/830-3312. www.holiday/ireland.com. 23 units. TV TEL. £56–£62 ($78.40–$86.80) double. Continental breakfast £4.20 ($5.90); full Irish breakfast £6 ($8.40). Children under 12 stay for 50% off in parents' room. MC, V. Limited free parking available. Bus: 3, 11, 13, 13A, 16, 19, 19A, 41, 41A, or 41B.

This two-story red-brick Victorian guest house is in the center of a pleasant residential neighborhood. It's within walking distance of the Botanic Gardens and a variety of sports facilities, including tennis, swimming, and a gym. Operated by John and Betty Egan, it offers newly redecorated rooms in a variety of sizes and styles, including ground-floor rooms. All offer such conveniences as hair dryers and tea/coffeemakers. Rooms for smokers and nonsmokers are available. The comfortable public rooms have an assortment of traditional dark woods, brass fixtures, and antiques.

Forte Travelodge. N1 Dublin-Belfast road, Swords, County Dublin. ☎ **800/CALL-THF** from the U.S., or 1800/709-709 in Ireland. Fax 01/840-9235. 100 units. TV. £49.95–£59.95 ($69.95–$83.95) double. No service charge. AE, DC, MC, V. Bus: 41 or 43.

About 8 miles (13km) north of downtown and 1½ miles (2.4km) north of Dublin airport, this recently expanded two-story motel offers large no-frills accommodations at reasonable prices. Each of the basic rooms, with a double bed and sofa bed, can sleep up to four people. The red-brick exterior blends nicely with the countryside, and the interior is clean and modern. Public areas are limited to a modest reception area, public pay phone, and adjacent budget-priced Little Chef chain restaurant and lounge.

Iona House. 5 Iona Park, Glasnevin, Dublin 9. ☎ **01/830-6217.** Fax 01/830-6732. 10 units. TV TEL. £68 ($95.20) double. No service charge. Rates include full breakfast. MC, V. Closed Dec–Jan. Parking available on street. Bus: 19 or 19A.

A sitting room with a glowing open fireplace, chiming clocks, brass fixtures, and dark wood furnishings sets a welcoming tone for guests at this two-story red-brick Victorian home. Built around the turn of the century, it has been operated as a guesthouse by John and Karen Shouldice since 1963. Iona House is in a residential neighborhood 15 minutes from the city center, between Lower Drumcondra and Botanic Roads, within walking distance of the Botanic Gardens. The newly refurbished rooms offer modern hotel-style appointments, orthopedic beds, and contemporary Irish-made furnishings. There are a lounge and a small patio. Seven nonsmoking rooms are available.

Redbank Guesthouse and Lodge. 7 Church St. and Convent Lane, Skerries, County Dublin. ☎ **01/849-1005** or 01/849-0439. Fax 01/849-1598. www.guesthouseireland.com. 12 units (several with shower only). TV TEL. Guesthouse £70 ($98) double. Lodge £54 ($75.60) double. Rates include service and full Irish breakfast. Guesthouse B&B and dinner for 2 £120 ($168). Lodge B&B and dinner for 2 £110 ($154). AE, DC, MC, V. Parking on street and lane. Suburban rail. Bus: 33.

Within a leap of each other, these two comfortable nooks in the heart of Skerries town are only 20 to 30 minutes by car from Dublin Airport, and so provide a convenient first or last night's lodging for your Ireland holiday. Better yet, they virtually abut the deservedly touted Redbank Restaurant (see under "Dining" below), so you can be guaranteed a memorable introductory or farewell meal in the country. The seven rooms in the guesthouse are generally a bit more spacious than the five in the lodge. Beige or yellow walls, dark wood furnishings, blue carpets, traditional white bedspreads, and floral drapes compose the unassuming and inviting country style of the rooms, all of which have hair dryers and tea/coffeemakers. The showers are excellent, just what you need after or before a long journey! And whatever you do, if you spend the night at the Redbank, be sure to dine here as well.

DINING
EXPENSIVE

✪ **King Sitric.** East Pier, Howth, County Dublin. ☎ **01/832-5235.** Reservations required. Dinner main courses £16–£25 ($22.40–$35); fixed-price dinner £32 ($44.80). AE, DC, MC, V. May–Sept Mon–Sat noon–3pm; year-round Mon–Sat 6:30–10:30pm. DART: Howth. Bus: 31 or 31A. SEAFOOD.

Right on the bay, 9 miles (15km) north of Dublin, this long-established restaurant is in a 150-year-old former harbormaster's building. On a fine summer evening, it is well worth a trip out here to savor the finest of local fish and crustaceans, creatively prepared and presented. Entrees include poached ray with capers and black butter, fillet of sole with lobster mousse, roast pheasant, grilled monkfish, sirloin steak with red wine sauce, and Howth fish ragout, a signature combination of the best of the day's catch. King Sitric also offers an award-winning wine list.

✪ **Redbank Restaurant.** 7 Church St., Skerries, County Dublin. ☎ **01/849-1005.** Reservations recommended. Dinner main courses £11–£19 ($15.40–$26.60); fixed-price dinners £28–£30 ($39.20–$42). AE, DC, MC, V. Mon–Sat 7–9:45pm; Sun 12:30–2:15pm. Suburban rail. Bus: 33. SEAFOOD/CONTEMPORARY IRISH.

Founded in 1983 by Terry and Margaret McCoy, the Redbank has been winning friends, influencing people, and garnering awards for nearly 20 years. The Redbank was literally a bank (The Munster & Leinster Ltd.) before it was a restaurant and uses the old vault as its wine cellar (that is, for its liquid assets). The lounge/bar where you order and await your meal as it is being cooked to order is particularly appealing, with a sure touch of elegance, and the larger of the two dining rooms is entirely nonsmoking.

Terry McCoy is an exuberant and inspired chef, who draws his inspiration first from the waters off Skerries harbor. The seafood selection *Paddy Attley* offers a platter of three fish of the day landed in the Skerries Harbor, each served in a uniquely enhancing sauce. Equally indescribable is the mound of char-grilled Dublin Bay prawns which arrive with a flattering red bib to protect and adorn the diner. The truth is that a dinner here is a both a spectacle and feast, and not to be missed. And, if full bliss has somehow eluded you by the time the dessert trolley is wheeled in, utter your last words of the night and succumb to the chocolate mocha. Just remember this—while restaurants are taken over by banks on a regular basis, it is the rare restaurant that takes over a bank. And this is just such a rare restaurant.

MODERATE

✪ **Abbey Tavern.** Abbey St., Howth, County Dublin. ☎ **01/839-0307.** Reservations recommended. Main courses £11–£22 ($15.40–$30.80). MC, V. Mon–Sat 7–11pm. DART: Howth. Bus: 31. SEAFOOD/INTERNATIONAL.

Well known for its nightly traditional music ballad sessions, this 16th-century tavern also has a full-service restaurant upstairs. Although the menu changes by season, entrees often include such dishes as scallops *Ty Ar Mor* (with mushrooms, prawns, and cream sauce), crêpes fruits de mer, poached salmon, duck with orange and Curaçao sauce, and veal à la crème. After a meal, you might want to join the audience downstairs for some lively Irish music.

Dee Gee's Wine and Steak Bar. Harbour Rd., Howth, County Dublin. ☎ **01/839-2641.** Reservations recommended on weekends. Dinner main courses £7–£13 ($9.80–$18.20). MC, V. Oct–Apr daily 7am–7pm; May–Sept daily 7am–9pm. DART: Howth. Bus: 31. IRISH.

If you plan a day's outing to Howth, don't miss this place. Facing Howth Harbour and Dublin Bay, this informal seaside spot opposite the DART station is ideal for a cup of coffee, a snack, or a full meal. A self-service snackery by day and a more formal, table-service restaurant at night, it offers indoor and outdoor seating. Dinner entrees range from steaks and burgers to shrimp scampi and vegetable lasagna. At lunchtime, soups, salads, and sandwiches are featured. Sit, relax, and watch all the activities of Howth from a front-row seat.

3 Farther Afield to County Wicklow, the Garden of Ireland

The borders of County Wicklow start just a dozen or so miles south of downtown Dublin, and within this county you'll find some of Ireland's best rural scenery. If you're based in Dublin, you can easily spend a day or afternoon in Wicklow and return to the city for dinner and the theater. But you'll probably want to linger overnight at one of the many fine country inns.

One accessible, charming gateway to County Wicklow is the small harbor town of **Greystones,** which I hesitate to mention for fear of spoiling the secret. It is hands-down one of the most unspoiled and attractive harbor towns on Ireland's east coast. It has no special attractions except itself, and that's enough.

Wicklow's most stunning scenery and most interesting towns and attractions are inland, between Enniskerry and Glendalough. The best way to see the **Wicklow Hills** is on foot, following the **Wicklow Way** past mountain tarns and secluded glens. In this region, don't miss the picturesque villages of **Roundwood, Laragh,** and **Aughrim.**

In the southernmost corner of Wicklow, the mountains become hills and share with the villages they shelter an unassuming beauty, a sleepy tranquillity that can be a welcome respite from the bustle of Wicklow's main tourist attractions. Near **Shillelagh** village are lovely forests, great hill walking, and the curious edifice of **Huntington Castle.**

ESSENTIALS

GETTING THERE   Irish Rail (☎ **01/836-6222**) provides daily train service between Dublin and Bray and Wicklow.

Bus Eireann (☎ **01/836-6111**) operates daily express bus service to Arklow, Bray, and Wicklow towns. Both Bus Eireann and **Gray Line Tours** (☎ **01/605-7705**) offer seasonal sightseeing tours to Glendalough, Wicklow, and Powerscourt Gardens.

If you're driving, take N11 south from Dublin City and follow turnoff signs for major attractions.

VISITOR INFORMATION   Contact the **Wicklow Tourist Office,** Fitzwilliam Square, Wicklow Town, County Wicklow (☎ **0404/69117;** www.wicklow.ie). It's open Monday to Friday year-round, Saturday during peak season.

SEEING THE SIGHTS

County Wicklow offers a wide array of wonderful craft centers and workshops. ✪ **Avoca Handweavers,** in the town of Avoca (☎ **0402/35105;** www.avoca.ie), is the oldest surviving hand-weaving company in Ireland, producing a wide range of tweed clothing, knitwear, and accessories in tones of mauve, aqua, teal, and heather that reflect the local landscape. You're welcome to watch as craftspeople weave strands of yarn spun from the wool of local sheep.

The Woolen Mills Glendalough, in Laragh (☎ **0404/ 45156**), offers handcrafts from all over Ireland, such as Bantry Pottery and Penrose Glass from Waterford. Books, jewelry, and a large selection of hand-knits from the area are also sold.

Altamount Gardens. Tullow, County Carlow. ☎ **0503/59444.** Admission £2 adults ($2.80), £1.50 ($2.10) seniors and students, £1 ($1.40) children under 16, £5 ($7) family. Mar 17–Sept Thurs–Sun 10:30am–6:30pm.

The lush, colorful extravagance of Altamount is the result of 55 years of nurturing by the late Corona North. A shadowy avenue of venerable beech trees leads to bright lawns and the splash of flowers growing beneath ancient yew trees. Graveled walks weave around a large lake, constructed as a famine relief project, and the delights of this garden lie not only in its aesthetic and botanical diversity but also in the many birds that find sanctuary here. In early June, spectacular drifts of bluebells fill the forest floor on slopes overlooking the River Slaney. The moss-green depths of the Ice Age Glen, a rockstrewn cleft leading to the river, are currently closed to the public, but the walk through the Glen can sometimes be made with a guide, by request—and it's a beautiful walk, concluding with an ascent up 100 hand-cut granite steps through the bluebell wood, and past a small temple with fine views of the southern Wicklow Hills.

Avondale House & Forest Park. Rathdrum, County Wicklow. ☎ **0404/46111.** Admission £3.50 ($4.90) adults, £3 ($4.20) seniors and children under 16, £9 ($12.60) family. Daily mid-March to end Oct 11am–5pm. Parking £3 ($4.20). Entrance to park and house signposted off R752.

In a fertile valley between Glendalough and the Vale of Avoca, this is the former home of Charles Stewart Parnell (1846–91), one of Ireland's great political leaders. Built in 1779, the house is now a museum dedicated to his memory. Set in the surrounding 523-acre estate and boasting signposted nature trails alongside the Avondale River, Avondale Forest Park is considered the cradle of modern Irish forestry. A new exhibition area commemorates the American side of the Parnell family, most notably Admiral Charles Stewart of U.S.S. *Constitution.*

✪ **Glendalough.** County Wicklow. ☎ **0404/45325** or 0404/45352. Admission free to site; £2 ($2.80) adults, £1.50 ($2.10) seniors, £1 ($1.40) children and students under 16, £5 ($7) family for exhibits and audiovisual presentation. Daily mid-Oct to mid-Mar 9:30am–5pm; mid-Mar to May and Sept to mid-Oct 9:30am–6pm; June–Aug 9am–6:30pm. Head 7 miles (11km) east of Wicklow on T7 via Rathdrum.

In the 6th century, St. Kevin chose this idyllically secluded setting for a monastery. Over the centuries, it became a leading center of learning, with thousands of students from Ireland, Britain, and all over Europe. In the 12th century, St. Lawrence O'Toole was among the many abbots who followed St. Kevin and spread the influence of Glendalough. But like so many early Irish religious sites, Glendalough fell into the hands of plundering Anglo-Norman invaders, and its glories came to an end by the 15th century.

Today, visitors can stroll from the upper lake to the lower lake and walk through the remains of the monastery complex, long since converted to a burial place. Although much of the monastic city is in ruins, the remains do include a nearly perfect round tower, 103 feet high and 52 feet around the base, as well as hundreds of timeworn Celtic crosses and a variety of churches. One of these is St. Kevin's chapel, often called St. Kevin's Kitchen, a fine specimen of an early Irish barrel-vaulted oratory with a miniature round belfry rising from a stone roof. A striking new visitor center at the entrance to the site provides helpful orientation, with exhibits on the archaeology, history, folklore, and wildlife of the area.

The main entrance to the monastic complex has been spoiled by a sprawling hotel and hawkers of various sorts, so you may want to cross the river at the visitor center and walk along the banks. You can cross back again at the monastic site, bypassing the trappings of commerce that St. Kevin once fled.

Huntington Castle. Clonegal, County Carlow (off N80, 4 miles/6.5km from Bunclody). ☎ **054/77552.** Guided tour £3.50 ($4.90) adults, £1.50 ($2.10) children. Jun–Aug daily 2–6pm; May and Sept Sun 2–6pm; other times by appointment.

At the confluence of the rivers Derry and Slaney, this castle was of great strategic importance from the time it was built, in the early 17th century. It was at the center of conflicts in the area until the early 20th century, when the IRA briefly used it as a headquarters. The castle is unlike many others you'll visit, since it has a lived-in feel. The magnificent decrepitude derives in part from the sometimes-overwhelming assortment of debris left by previous generations. The house has many stories to tell, and young Alexander Durdin-Robertson, whose ancestors built the place, seems to know them all; he gives a great tour. Don't forget to visit the garden, where waist-high weeds hide a lovely yew walk and one of the first hydroelectric facilities in Ireland. The castle's basement is home to a temple of the Fellowship of Isis, a religion founded here in 1976.

Killruddery House & Gardens. Off the main Dublin–Wicklow road (N11), Killruddery, Bray, County Wicklow. ☎ **01/286-2777.** House and garden tour £4.50 ($6.30) adults, £3 ($4.20) seniors and students over 12, £1 ($1.40) children; gardens only £3 ($4.20) adults, £2 ($2.80) seniors and students over 12, 50p (70¢) children. House May–June and Sept daily 1–5pm; gardens Apr–Sept daily 1–5pm.

This estate has been the seat of the earl of Meath since 1618. The original part of its mansion, dating from 1820, features a Victorian conservatory modeled on the Crystal Palace in London. The gardens are a highlight, with a lime avenue, a sylvan theater, foreign trees, exotic shrubs, twin canals, and a round pond with fountains that's edged with beech hedges. They are the only surviving 17th-century French-style gardens in Ireland.

Mount Usher Gardens. On the main Dublin–Wicklow road (N11), Ashford, County Wicklow. ☎ **0404/40116.** Admission £4 ($5.60) adults; £3 ($4.20) seniors, students, and children 5–12. Guided tours £20 ($28); call for reservation. Mar 17–Oct 31 daily 10:30am–6pm.

Encompassing 20 acres along the River Vartry, this sylvan site was once home to an ancient lake and more recently laid out in the informal, free-range "Robinsonian" style. It contains more than 5,000 tree and plant species from all parts of the world, including spindle trees from China, North American swamp cypress, and Burmese juniper trees. Fiery rhododendrons, fragrant eucalyptus trees, giant Tibetan lilies, and snowy camellias also compete for your eye. Informal and responsive to their natural setting, these gardens have an almost untended feel—a floral woodland, without pretense yet with considerable charm. A spacious tearoom overlooks the river and gardens. The courtyard at the entrance to the gardens contains an interesting assortment of shops, which are open year-round.

National Sea Life Centre. Strand Rd., Bray, County Wicklow. ☎ **01/286-6939.** www.sealife.ie. Admission £5.50 ($7.70) adults, £4.50 ($6.30) seniors, £4 ($5.60) students, £3.95 ($5.53) children, £17 ($23.80) family. Open year-round daily 10am–5pm.

When seen and enjoyed for what it is, Sea Life is surely worth a visit. The hyperbole of its title, however, reflects more closely the enthusiasm of its staff than the scale of the edifice. And more power to them, as Sea Life offers good family fun, even if it's a tad overpriced. Situated at water's edge, the center provides a family-focused introduction to the denizens of the nearby deep.

The labyrinthine path through the aquarium begins with a rock tunnel carved by a winding freshwater stream; from there, you follow the water's course toward the open sea, from freshwater river to tidal estuary to storm-pounded harbor and finally to the briny deep. Along the way, kids are quizzed on what they're learning, as they use "magic" glasses to read coded questions and find the answers on special scratch pads they've been given. One remarkable feature here is the close access visitors have to the sea life. It's possible (though not encouraged) to reach down and put your hand into many of the tanks; and, when you bend over and eyeball the fish, they as often as not return the favor, surfacing and staring back only inches from your face. Such keen alertness and interpersonal rapport coming from a ray or plaice was a surprise. Once you reach "the Deep" the emphasis is on scary critters, the ones with the sharpest teeth or the deadliest venom, like sharks (of course) and the dreaded blue-ringed octopus, whose bite carries enough poison to kill 10 people. The terror is sweeter than chocolate to children. You won't spend all day here, more like an hour or less; but you may come away on first-name terms with a Goby and that's more than okay.

✪ **Powerscourt Gardens, House Exhibition, and Waterfall.** Off the main Dublin–Wicklow road (N11), Enniskerry, County Wicklow. ☎ **01/ 204-6000.** Gardens and house exhibition £5 ($7) adults, £4.50 ($6.30) seniors and students, £3 ($4.20) children 5–16, free for children under 5; gardens only £4 ($5.60) adults, £3.50 ($4.90) seniors and students, £2 ($2.80) children 5–16, free for children under 5; waterfall £2 ($2.80) adults, £1.50 ($2.10) seniors and students, £1 ($1.40) children 5–16, free for children under 5. AE, MC, V. Gardens and house exhibition daily Mar–Oct 9:30am–5:30pm, Nov–Feb 9:30am–dusk; waterfall daily Mar–Oct 9:30am–7pm, Nov–Feb 10:30am–dusk.

On a 1,000-acre estate less than a dozen miles south of Dublin city sits one of the finest gardens in Europe, designed and laid out by Daniel Robertson between 1745 and 1767. This property is filled with splendid Greek- and Italian-inspired statuary, decorative ironwork, a petrified-moss grotto, lovely herbaceous borders, a Japanese garden, a circular pond and fountain with statues of winged horses, and the occasional herd of deer. Stories have it that Robertson, afflicted with gout, was pushed around the grounds in a wheelbarrow to oversee the work. This service is no longer offered, but I doubt you'll mind the walk.

An 18th-century manor house designed by Richard Cassels, the architect of Russborough House (see below) and the man credited with the design of Dublin's Parliament house, stood proudly on the site until it was gutted by fire in 1974. The partially restored house contains a variety of high-quality gift shops and an exhibition, complete with video presentation, on the history of Powerscourt. The additional entrance fee to "the house" is actually for entrance to this exhibition, primarily the video, which is mediocre.

The pleasant cafeteria serves delicious, reasonably priced lunches with a view that's not to be believed. The adjacent garden center and pavilion is staffed with highly knowledgeable green thumbs who can answer questions. In my opinion, the waterfall is too little too far away at too high a price. After all, if you want to see water pouring down in Ireland, most days you can just look up.

Russborough House. Off N81, Blessington, County Wicklow. ☎ **045/ 865239.** Admission to main rooms £4 ($5.60) adults, £3 ($4.20) seniors and students, £2 ($2.80) children under 12. May–Sept daily 10:30am–5:30pm; Oct Sun 10:30am–5:30pm. Closed Nov–Apr.

Ensconced in this 18th-century Palladian house is the world-famous Beit Art Collection, with paintings by Vernet, Guardi, Bellotto, Gainsborough, Rubens, and Reynolds. The house is furnished with European pieces and decorated with bronzes, tapestries, and some fine Francini plasterwork. To visit the maze and rhododendron garden, call for an appointment. On the premises are a restaurant, shop, and playground.

St. Mullin's Monastery. On the scenic Barrow Dr., 7½ miles (12km) north of New Ross, St. Mullins, County Carlow. Admission free at any time to site; Heritage Centre open at the discretion of Seamus Fitzgerald.

This little gem is a well-kept secret. On a sunny day its idyllic setting—in a sleepy hamlet beside the River Barrow, ringed by soft carpeted hills—is cause enough for a visit. Besides that, this is a fascinating spot, an outdoor minimuseum of sorts, spanning Irish history from the early Christian period to the present, all in no more than several acres. There are the ruins of a monastery founded here at Ross-Broc (Badger Wood) by St. Moling (Mullin) in roughly A.D. 614. Plundered again and again by the Vikings in the 9th and 10 centuries, it was annexed in the 12th century by a nearby Augustinian abbey.

Here, too, is a steep grassy motte and the outline of its accompanying bailey constructed by the Normans in the 12th century. In the Middle Ages, the monastery ruins were a popular destination, especially in the grip of the Black Death in 1348, when pilgrims would cross the river barefoot, circle the burial spot of St. Mullin nine times in prayer, adding small stones to the cairn marking the spot, and drink from the healing waters of the saint's well. The truth is that these ruins and waters are still the site of an annual "pattern" or pilgrimage near or on July 25.

Adjoining the monastery buildings is an ancient "working" cemetery still in use, where, contrary to common practice, Protestants and Catholics have long lain side by side. You'll also find the graves of 20 heroes from the 1798 Rebellion, including that of General Thomas Cloney. Be sure to find among the graveyard's stones the clandestine "penal altar" with a peephole from which the priest could see the top of the earthen motte or mound where a sentry stood lookout for British troops enforcing the ban on Catholic worship. If it's open at the time of your visit, the modest Heritage Centre in the adjoining 19th-century church contains some informative exhibitions and booklets and the ever-helpful local docent Seamus Fitzgerald. Even if the Heritage Centre is closed, there's a helpful site map and history mounted at the entrance to the cemetery.

✪ **Wicklow Mountains National Park.** Glendalough, County Wicklow. ☎ **0404/45425.** Visitor Centre May–Aug daily 10am–6pm; Apr and Sept Sat–Sun 10am–6pm; closed other months.

Nearly 50,000 acres of County Wicklow make up this new national park. The core area surrounds Glendalough, including the Glendalough Valley and Glendalough Wood Nature Reserves. You'll find an information station at the Upper Lake at Glendalough. Information is available here on hiking in the Glendalough Valley and surrounding hills, including maps and descriptions of routes. (See "Sports & Outdoor Pursuits," below, for suggestions.) Free guided nature walks begin from the center on Tuesdays (departing 11am and returning 1:30pm) and Thursdays (departing 3pm and returning 4pm). The closest parking is at Upper Lake, where you'll pay £1.50 ($2.10) per car; my advice is to walk up from the Glendalough Visitor Centre, where the parking is free.

Wicklow's Historic Gaol. Kilmantin Hill, Wicklow Town, County Wicklow.
☎ **0404/61599.** www.wicklow.ie/gaol. Tour £4.20 ($5.90) adults; £3.30
($4.60) senior and students, £2.60 ($3.65) children, £12 ($16.80) family with
up to 3 children. Apr 17–Sept daily 10am–6pm (last admission at 4:50pm).

Once you learn what took place within these walls, you'll find
it hard to believe that Wicklow Gaol closed its doors only as
recently as 1924, after more than 2 centuries of terror. After
passing under the hanging beam, visitors are lined up against
the wall of the "day room" and confronted with some dark
facts of prison life in 1799, when more than 400 prisoners,
most of them rebels, occupied the gaol's 42 cells. Fed once
every 4 days and allowed to walk in the prison yard for 15
minutes every four weeks, they must have found the hanging
rope looking less and less hideous. Within the main cellblock,
visitors are allowed to roam the gaol's individual cells and to
discover their stories through a series of exhibitions and audiovisual presentations. The impact of these stories is immediate
and powerful, for children as well as for adults, because this
gaol once held both. And, as many prisoners were sent off to
penal colonies in Australia and Tasmania, that story, too, is
told here, with the help of a stage-set wharf and prison ship.
There's an in-house cafe when you're all done, but its appeal is
likely to be undercut by the less-than-appetizing experience
you've just been through. Who can recommend jail, and yet I
left informed and moved.

SPORTS & OUTDOOR PURSUITS

GOLF   County Wicklow's verdant hills and dales offer
numerous opportunities for golfing. The new **Rathsallagh
Golf Club** (☎ **045/403316**) is an 18-hole, par-72 championship course at Dunlavin. Greens fees are £40 ($56) week-
days and £50 ($70) weekends. The seaside **European Club,**
Brittas Bay (☎ **0404/47415**), is a championship links with
greens fees of £45 ($63) year-round. At the parkland **Glen-
malure Golf Club,** Greenane, Rathdrum (☎ **0404/46679**),
greens fees start at £15 ($21) weekdays and £20 ($28) weekends. The **Arklow Golf Club** (☎ **0402/32492**), a seaside
par-68 course, charges greens fees of £18 ($25.20).

HORSEBACK RIDING   With its valleys, glens, secluded
paths, and nature trails, County Wicklow is perfect for horseback riding. More than a dozen stables and equestrian centers

offer horses for hire and instructional programs. Rates for horse hire average £10 to £20 ($14 to $28) per hour. Among the leading venues are **Broomfield Riding School,** Broomfield, Tinahely (☎ **0402/38117**), and **Brennanstown Riding School,** Hollybrook, Kilmacanogue (☎ **01/286-3778**). At the **Paulbeg Riding School,** Shillelagh (☎ **055/29100**), experienced riders can explore the beautiful surrounding hills, and beginners can receive expert instruction from Sally Duffy, a friendly woman who gives an enthusiastic introduction to the sport.

Devil's Glen Holiday and Equestrian Village, Ashford (☎ **0404/40013** or 0404/40637; www.devilsglen.ie), splendidly situated at the edge of Devil's Glen, offers a full range of equestrian opportunities, as well as spotless, spacious, fully-equipped self-catering apartments, cottages, and bungalows, each with two or three bedrooms. The accommodations make a great base from which to explore the Wicklow Mountains and coastline, whether or not you ever climb into a saddle. Weekly rates run from £260 to £585 ($364 to $819), depending on season and size of unit. Weekend (Fri to Sun) and midweek (Mon to Thurs) rates are also available. Most lessons and rides cost £15 ($21) per hour for adults and £12 ($16.80) per hour for children under 12. Both the equestrian center and the self-catering village are open year-round.

WALKING   The **Wicklow Way** is a signposted walking path that follows forest trails, sheep paths, and country roads from the hills south of Dublin to the trail's terminus in Clonegal. It takes about 5 to 7 days to walk its entirety, with overnight stops at B&Bs and hostels along the route. Most people choose to walk sections as day trips; I've highlighted some of my favorites below.

You can pick up information and maps at the Wicklow National Park center in Glendalough or at any local tourist office. Information on less strenuous walks can be found in a number of local publications. Check out the ***Wicklow Trail Sheets*** available at tourist offices. They provide a map and route description for several short walks.

The most spectacular walks in Wicklow are in the north and central parts of the county, an area traversed by the Wicklow Way and numerous short trails. One lovely walk on the Way begins at the **Deerpark parking lot** near the Dargle

River and continues to Luggala, passing Djouce Mountain; the next section, between Luggala and Laragh, traverses some wild country around Lough Dan.

You won't want to miss the **southern section of the Wicklow Way,** through Tinahely, Shillelagh, and Clonegal. Although not as rugged as the terrain in central Wicklow, the hills here are voluptuously round, with delightful woods and glens hidden in their folds. Through much of this section, the path follows quiet country roads. Consider treating yourself to a night at **Park Lodge B&B,** Clonegal, Shillelagh (☎ **055/ 29140**), near the trail's terminus; double rooms run £72 to £80 ($100.80 to $112).

ACCOMMODATIONS
VERY EXPENSIVE

✪ **Tinakilly House Hotel.** On R750, off the Dublin–Wexford road (N11), Rathnew, County Wicklow. ☎ **800/525-4800** from the U.S., or 0404/69274. Fax 0404/67806. www.tinakilly.ie. 53 units. TV TEL. £130–£190 ($182–$266) double; £190 ($266) junior suite; £240 ($336) captain's suite with sea view. No service charge. Rates include full breakfast. AE, DC, MC, V.

Dating from the 1870s, this was the home of Capt. Robert Charles Halpin, commander of the *Great Eastern,* who laid the first successful cable connecting Europe with America. With a sweeping central staircase said to be the twin of the one on the ship, Tinakilly is full of seafaring memorabilia, paintings, and Victorian antiques. Many of the individually furnished rooms have views of the Irish Sea. Opened as a hotel by the Power family in 1983, it is adjacent to the Broadlough Bird Sanctuary and a 7-acre garden of beech, evergreen, eucalyptus, palm, and American redwood trees. Most of the rooms recently underwent a full renovation very much in keeping with the Victorian style. Don't be daunted by the wide selection of rooms here, because you really can't go wrong. While the Captain's Suites and the full suites are quite grand, even the standard attic rooms are cozy and truly charming.

In the mere 17 years since opening, Tinakilly House has garnered a wall of well-deserved prestigious awards, including recently being ranked no. 75 in the "Top 100 Hotels of the World" by the London *Times.*

Dining: The Brunel Restaurant, in the new east wing, is well known for fresh fish and local game. The kitchen blends country-house cooking with a nouvelle cuisine influence.

Vegetables, fruits, and herbs come from the house gardens, and all breads are baked fresh daily on the premises (see listing below under "Dining").

Amenities: For rainy days or simply to regain your waist after you've succumbed to a feast, there's a small yet useful fitness suite with a treadmill and several other exercise machines.

EXPENSIVE

✪ **Rathsallagh House.** Dunlavin, County Wicklow. ☎ **800/323-5463** from the U.S., or 045/403112. Fax 045/403343. www.rathsallagh.com. 29 units. TV TEL. £110–£210 ($154–$294) double. No service charge. Rates include full breakfast. AE, DC, MC, V. Closed Dec 23–31. No children under 12 accepted.

On the western edge of County Wicklow, this rambling, ivy-covered country house sits amid 530 acres of parks, woods, and farmland. The original house on the property was built between 1702 and 1704 and owned by a horse-breeding family named Moody. It was burned down in the 1798 Rebellion, and the Moodys moved into the Queen Anne–style stables, which were converted into a residence and served as a private home until the 1950s. Joe and Kay O'Flynn bought the property in 1978 and opened it as a country-house hotel 10 years later. Each room is individually decorated and named accordingly. Most rooms have a sitting area, a huge walk-in closet, and window seats, and some have Jacuzzis. All have hair dryer, tea/coffeemaker, vanity desk, good reading lamps over the bed, and antique furnishings. A recent recipient of the American Express Best-Loved Hotels of the World award, this much-touted guesthouse has a particularly warm, welcoming, unpretentious feel to it, a splendid home away from home.

Dining: The dining room, under the personal supervision of Kay O'Flynn, is widely noted for its excellent food, using local ingredients and vegetables and herbs from the garden.

Amenities: 18-hole championship golf course, modest-sized indoor heated swimming pool, sauna, hard tennis court, archery, croquet, and billiards.

INEXPENSIVE

Derrybawn Mountain Lodge. Laragh, County Wicklow. ☎ **0404/45644.** Fax 0404/45645. E-mail: derrybawnlodge@eircom.net. 8 units. £50–£60 ($70–$84) double. No service charge. Rates include full breakfast. MC, V.

This elegant, comfortable fieldstone manor house in an idyllic parkland setting looks out over the surrounding hills. The rooms (all no-smoking) are spacious, bright, tastefully furnished, and outfitted with orthopedic beds. Public areas include a sitting room, dining room, and rec room with snooker table and facilities for making tea and coffee. Located just outside Laragh village, the place is convenient to fishing streams and hiking trails (including the Wicklow Way), and a great place from which to explore Wicklow's natural wonders.

Slievemore. The Harbour, Greystones (signposted on N11), County Wicklow. ☎ **01/287-4724.** 8 units (all with shower only). TV. £45 ($63) double. No service charge. Rates include full Irish breakfast. No credit cards. Free parking. Bus: 84.

This mid–19th-century harbor house offers white-glove cleanliness, spacious comfort, and (if you book early and request a seafront room) a commanding view of Greystones Harbor, Bray Head, and the Irish Sea. Proprietor Pippins Parkinson says that "people stumble on Greystones, find it by accident." Whether you're accident-prone or not, stay here, reserve a table for dinner at nearby Coopers (see "Dining," below), and you won't forget the day you stumbled on Greystones.

Tudor Lodge. Laragh, County Wicklow. ☎ and fax **0404/45554.** 6 units, all with private bathroom (shower only). TV. June–Sept £50 ($70) double; Sept–May £27 ($37.80) single, £45 ($63) double. MC, V.

The whitewashed walls of Tudor Lodge are fresh and inviting, recalling the rusticity of a country cottage. Bedrooms are spacious, and each has a small desk as well as both double and twin beds, tea/coffeemaker, and hair dryer. The dining room and living room are equally hospitable: large windows open to views of green meadows and the slopes of the Wicklow mountains. A brick fireplace and beamed ceilings make the living room a cozy retreat, and in 2000, a sunroom was added. A generous stone terrace lies just outside, and a riverside patio overlooks the Avonmore River at the end of the garden. Hosts Des and Liz Kennedy offer guests an appetizing array of breakfast choices, and will also prepare dinner for larger groups. Otherwise, the restaurants and pubs of Laragh are a short and scenic walk away. No smoking.

SELF-CATERING

Fortgranite Estate. Baltinglass, County Wicklow. ☎ **0508/81396.** Fax 0508/73510. 3 cottages. TV TEL. £150–£395 ($210–$553) per week. No credit cards, but personal checks are accepted. From Baltinglass, drive 3 miles (4.8km) southeast on R747.

Fortgranite is—and has been for centuries—a working farm in the rolling foothills of the Wicklow Mountains. Its meadows and stately trees create a sublime retreat. Its unique stone cottages, formerly occupied by the estate's workers, are being restored and refurbished with appreciable care and charm by M. P. Dennis. Three are available to rent for a week or longer. The gate lodges—Doyle's and Lennon's—each have one double bedroom, sleeping two and fully equipped with all essentials. The third, Stewards's Cottage, sleeps four and is furnished with lovely antiques. All have open fireplaces, and each has its own grounds and garden. Tranquillity, charm, and warmth are the operative concepts at Fortgranite, so those in search of something grand and luxurious will be disappointed. Think "cottage" and "character," and you will be delighted. Plan ahead, because word is out and availability is at a premium. Golf, fishing, hill walking, horse racing and riding, and clay-pigeon shooting can all be found nearby. Smoking is discouraged.

Manor Kilbride. N. Blessington, County Wicklow. ☎ **01/458-2105.** Fax 01/458-2607. 4 cottages. Cottages £280–£500($392–$700) per week year-round. AE, MC, V. 18 miles (29km) from Dublin. On N81, take Kilbride/Sally Gap turn 4 miles (6.5km) north of Blessington; after 1 mile (1.6km), left at sign for Sally Gap. Entrance gates 50 yd. (46m) ahead on right.

Gracefully situated amid 40 acres of mature gardens and wooded walks in the Wicklow Mountain foothills, Charles and Margaret Cully's Manor is a haven of charm and cordiality.

The grounds of the Manor include two small lakes and a stretch of the River Brittas. Four lovely stone self-catering cottages are available. The two courtyard cottages and the river lodge sleep four; the gate lodge is better suited to a couple. These are four-star cottages, with original beams and exposed stone walls and every amenity. The Cullys are rather lavish in their welcome baskets, so there's no need for an immediate trip to the market.

Tynte House. Dunlavin center, County Wicklow. ☎ **045/401561.** Fax 045/401586. www.iol.ie/~jclawler. 7 units, 4 homes, 4 apts, 4 cottages. TV TEL. £37 ($51.80) double. Self-catering units £140–£310 ($196–$434) per week. Dinner £12.50 ($17.50). AE, MC, V.

Dunlavin is a drowsy three-pub town in western Wicklow, 30 miles (48km) southwest of Dublin. It's as convenient as it is peaceful. Tynte House, a lovingly preserved 19th-century family farm complex with new apartment units and holiday cottages, offers an attractive array of options for overnight and longer-term guests. The driving force is Mrs. Caroline Lawler, "brought up in the business" of divining visitors' needs and surpassing their expectations. In 2000, she was named one of the top 20 "landladies" in the U.K. and Ireland.

The guest rooms are warm and comfortable. The self-catering mews (renovated stables) houses have one to three bedrooms; the apartments hold one or two bedrooms; and the four new cottages range from two to four bedrooms and have working fireplaces. All are brilliantly designed and furnished with one eye on casual efficiency and the other on good taste. They have bold, bright color schemes, light pine furniture, spacious tiled bathrooms, cable TV, and open kitchens fully equipped with microwave, dishwasher, washer, and dryer. The no. 3 mews house and the open-plan apartment are our favorites, but none will disappoint. All mattresses are new, but some are firmer than others. This is a great anchorage for families, with a grassy play area and treehouse, an outdoor barbecue and picnic tables, a tennis court, and a game room with Ping-Pong and pool. Exact prices depend on the season and the size of the unit. Shorter stays and weekend discounts may be negotiated in the off-season.

DINING
EXPENSIVE

✪ **Brunel Restaurant.** In the Tinakilly House Hotel. On R750, off the Dublin–Wexford road (N11), Rathnew, County Wicklow. ☎ **0404/69274.** Fixed-price dinner £36 ($50.40). AE, DC, MC, V. Open year-round 12:30–2pm and 7:30–9pm. IRISH/FRENCH.

This extraordinary restaurant, which *Bon Appétit* magazine has called "a beacon to restore hope to the traveller's heart," has won as many accolades as the hotel to which it belongs (see above). The table d'hôte menu changes daily, which leaves us mostly with adjectives rather than nouns for its description. The cuisine is confidently balanced—sophisticated without being fussy; elegant without acrobatics. After all, chefs too are bound by the Hippocratic oath and must first, do no harm, a duty taken deeply to heart in the Tinakilly kitchen. From then on, it's a matter of inspiration. The service, too, is precise and intuitive, letting the ritual follow its own course. All this makes for a meal you remember, like the char-grilled tiger prawns and lemongrass with fennel oil, the cream of roast chestnut and celery soup, the caramelized scallops on saffron potato mash, and the loin of Wicklow lamb, which I enjoyed. The wine list is vast and, while international, focuses on France. For an explosive finale, I recommend the warm fresh fruit salad served on an amaretto pâté bomb.

MODERATE

✪ **Coopers.** Above the Beach House, The Harbour, Greystones, County Wicklow. ☎ **01/287-3914.** Reservations recommended. Fixed-price early-bird 2-course dinner (Mon–Fri 5:30–7:30pm) £10 ($14). Main courses £8.95–£15.95 ($12.55–$22.35); no service charge. AE, MC, V. Mon–Sat 5:30–11pm; Sun 12:30–4pm and 5:30–10pm. INTERNATIONAL/SEAFOOD.

Coopers is the perfect reward after making the cliff walk from Bray to Greystones. This is one of the most tasteful dining environments I've found in Ireland—vaulted beamed ceilings, exposed brick and stone walls, stained glass, three fireplaces, wrought-iron fixtures, and linen table settings. It's a warm, relaxed, comfortable place for couples and families of any age. The menu is a rarity in that it understates its offerings, with ordinary descriptions like "smoked lamb" for extraordinary fare. Roast duckling and steamed sea trout are specialties, and there's a fine wine list. There are spectacular views of the open sea on two sides, and a piano player on Friday and Saturday nights. Coopers is no secret, so book well ahead.

Roundwood Inn. Main St. (R755), Roundwood, County Wicklow. ☎ **01/281-8107.** Reservations recommended for dinner. Main courses £11–£16 ($15.40–$22.40). MC, V. Wed–Sat 1–2:30pm and 7:30–9:30pm. Pub food all day every day. IRISH/CONTINENTAL.

Dating from 1750, this old coaching inn is the focal point of an out-of-the-way spot in the mountains, Roundwood, that's said to be the highest village in Ireland. It has an old-world atmosphere, with open log fireplaces and antique furnishings. Menu choices range from steaks and sandwiches to traditional Irish stew, fresh lobster, smoked salmon, and seafood pancakes. In the bar, a déjà vu house specialty is chicken in the basket.

INEXPENSIVE

Avoca Handweavers Tea Shop. Avoca, County Wicklow. ☎ **0402/35105.** Lunch £2.35–£5.95 ($3.30–$8.35). Daily 9:30am–5pm. AE, DC, MC, V. TRADITIONAL/VEGETARIAN.

This innovative cafeteria is worth a visit for lunch, even if you're not interested in woolens. The wholesome meals are surprisingly imaginative for cafeteria fare. I had a delicate pea and mint soup, prepared with vegetable stock, accompanied by a deliciously hearty spinach tart. Other dishes on the often-changing menu might include sesame glazed chicken or locally smoked Wicklow trout. The tea shop has a regular local clientele, in addition to the busloads of visitors who come to shop.

The Opera House. Market Sq., Wicklow Town, County Wicklow. ☎ **0404/66422.** Reservations recommended Fri–Sun. Main courses £6.95–£14.95 ($9.75–$20.95). No service charge. MC, V. Daily Jun–Aug 11am–11pm, Sept–May 6–11pm. Occasionally closes on Tues in the winter. ITALIAN/SEAFOOD.

This Irish trattoria is a unique find in this traditional harbor town. The faux Mediterranean decor is warm and tasteful; outside, picnic tables provide streetside dining for nonsmokers. The smoked salmon and tagliatelle flamed in a cream-and-vodka sauce is a delicious bargain, and the house French table wine (£10.50/$14.70) suits both wallet and palate. The service is enthusiastic, if stretched a bit thin on weekends. For a delightful conclusion, treat yourself to the lemon brûlée.

Poppies Country Cooking. Enniskerry, County Wicklow. ☎ **01/282-8869.** All items 60p–£5.50 (84¢–$7.70). No credit cards. Daily 9am–7pm. IRISH.

This 10-table self-service eatery opposite the main square is popular for light meals and snacks all day. The menu ranges from homemade soups and salads to hominy pie, nut roast, baked salmon, vegetarian quiche, and lasagna.

Poppies Country Cooking. Trafalgar Rd., Greystones, County Wicklow. ☎ **01/287-4228.** All items 60p–£5.50 (84¢–$7.70). No credit cards. Mon–Sat 10am–6pm, Sun 11:30am–7pm. IRISH HOMESTYLE.

Poppies of Enniskerry has done it again, this time in Greystones, a short walk from the bus or train. With the warm, familiar feel of a neighbor's kitchen—the neighbor who can really cook—this is a local hangout. From fist-sized wholegrain scones to vegetarian nut roast, the portions are generous. Seating overflows the 10 tables into a lovely flowered tea garden out back, if and when the sun appears, April to October. *A note of warning:* The desserts are diet-breakers, so try not to even look unless you are prepared to fall. Homemade jams, preserves, salad dressing, and even local artwork are on sale.

PUBS

Cartoon Inn. Main St., Rathdrum, County Wicklow. ☎ **0404/46774.**

With walls displaying the work of many famous cartoonists, this cottage-like pub claims to be the country's only cartoon-themed pub. It's the headquarters for Ireland's Cartoon Festival, held in late May or early June each year. Pub grub is available at lunchtime.

The Coach House. Main St., Roundwood, County Wicklow. ☎ **01/281-8157.**

Adorned with lots of colorful hanging flowerpots, this Tudor-style inn sits in the mountains in the heart of Ireland's highest village. Dating from 1790, it is full of local memorabilia, from old photos and agricultural posters to antique jugs and plates. It's well worth a visit, whether to learn about the area or to get some light refreshment.

The Meetings. Avoca, County Wicklow. ☎ **0402/35226.**

This Tudor-style country-cottage pub stands idyllically at the "Meeting of the Waters" associated with poet Thomas Moore. An 1889 edition of Moore's book of poems is on display. Good pub grub is served every day, with traditional Irish music April to October every Sunday afternoon (from 4 to 6pm), and weekend nights all year.

See also Accommodations and Restaurant indexes below.